Beyond 9 to 5

Your career guide for the digital age

First edition

Ade McCormack

Published by Auridian Press
www.auridian.com
Enquires: info@auridian.com

First published in Great Britain in 2015. Issue 1.0

© Ade McCormack 2015

The right of Ade McCormack to be identified as the author has been asserted in accordance with the Copyright, Design and Patents Act 1988.

ISBN 978-0954765125

British Library Cataloguing in Publication Data

A CIP catalogue record for this book can be obtained from the British Library

Auridian Press is a division of Auridian Consulting Ltd.

Dedication

This book is written primarily with my son Matthew in mind. There being a correlation between his economic wellbeing and the quality of the care home to which I will eventually be dispatched.

Contents

Preface

The world is changing.

In turn the world of work is changing.

Consequently what it means to be a worker is changing too.

Despite the rapid pace of change we are experiencing, today is the slowest pace of change you will ever experience again.

This book is your guide to both enhancing your employability and to gaining more value from this activity, typically referred to as work.

This industrial era framework, within which many of us have operated, is giving way to digital-era practices. As you will read, our post-industrial approach to work is not as new as you might expect.

New technology, whilst a critical driver to the changing nature of work, is not the primary driver. Those that fully understand this will have, by their own standards, a very successful work life (or should that be life work?).

The increased clock-speed of society makes it sometimes difficult to separate the present and the future. The near future in particular is unfolding as we speak. And unfolding rapidly. This makes career-related decision making increasingly treacherous.

But who can the next generation turn to for advice? As you will read, parents, for one, are ill-equipped to provide sage advice. Their hard-earned lessons apply to a game that is becoming defunct. Today the rules of the game, as we shall see, are quite different.

Young people, in any case, might well be suspicious of career advice dispensed from people who talk about 'mobile' phones and 'digital' business, as if people might actually buy tethered phones, and where some businesses might even be devoid of new technology.

I have been living a variant of the new approach to work, that I am advocating, for the last two decades. It doesn't require you to live a hermitic life, eschewing materialism. Though it could, if that's your thing. It doesn't require working ridiculous hours by today's standards, but it would be unwise to try to stop this next-generation worker whilst they are in mid flow. It's not a case of having to work, but more a visceral need to work. It could make you very rich, though money is not the only measure of this.

Many of us are learning that discretionary time and control over your destiny trump 'golden handcuffs'.

These changes will impact individuals, organisations, countries and trading blocs. Those individuals that fail to act will become increasingly unemployable. Similarly organisations will crumble, and societies will become economic backwaters.

It is important to point out that this book is not so much a manifesto for the way we should work, but an ordering, and framing, of what is actually happening. The nature of what I do for a living enables me to observe, test and reflect on the changing world.

My aim is to enable you to move forward in your career with the minimum of anxiety and a career roadmap that capitalises on the uncertainty that lies ahead.

The intended readership is those about to enter the world of work. But it will also serve those who are already working and who want to ensure they remain economically active in the face of fundamental economic and technology shifts in the world of work.

As I will explain in the 'How to use this book' section, this book will also be of value to talent managers and government policy makers.

Caveat: My work enables me to see the world of work from many angles, including many geographies. So I feel confident that the content of this book is highly relevant to current and future workers. But nobody can predict the impact of global finance and energy wars, pandemics or natural disasters, in what is an increasingly joined-up world.

So I have developed an approach, based on reality, to empower you to take charge of your professional journey, rather than just believing me and leaping into the chasm.

I think many of you will like the principles underlying the path I am proposing to you. So it may actually transpire that together we can bend the future to ensure it plays out as I am suggesting.

A kind of career cosmic ordering service perhaps?

Ade McCormack, spring, 2015

How to use this book

Whilst I set out to write this book for the next generation of workers, I found myself including important content that on reflection might not be considered essential reading from a young person's perspective.

In creating this non-essential content, I now realise that I was addressing the needs of people like me (already in the workplace) and people whom I work with, such as talent managers and government policy makers.

It is thus important to realise that this is a reference manual and not a story (though it contains stories). Both the sections and the chapters are fairly standalone.

In broad brush terms, I would regard the whole book as essential reading for corporations and governments. Pre-workers and workers will benefit from reading the whole book, but I have made some suggestions to reduce their time investment.

There are six sections to the book, detailed as follows:

Anthroeconomics

This section makes the case that the industrial era was a blip in mankind's evolution. Thus those working under such constraints today are in effect behaving unnaturally. When I speak on this theme at conferences, the audience finds this fascinating. However, pre-workers can consider this non-essential background reading. Existing workers are encouraged to read this to understand what they are currently experiencing.

Towards a future-proofed career

This is essential reading for all. Here we explore how work is moving from competence to mastery and from process to artistry. We look at career options and the magic formula for a rewarding career.

Career vectors

Again essential reading for all. We cover the macroeconomic drivers that are shaping the world of work. We see what happens when industry takes on nature. The major emerging career themes are also identified.

Mayday Mayday

In this section we take a look at how the education system is misaligned for a post-industrial world. I also issue some words of warning to parents, businesses and governments. This is more background reading for pre-workers and existing workers. Though pre-workers might like to share the parental guidance chapter with their co-creators.

A sign of the times

Here we see how the world of work and leadership is changing. The shifting power axis from employer to employee is covered along with major technology and business trends. This is essential reading for existing workers. Pre-workers only know 'this time' so are less likely to be aghast, awed or shocked by how times have changed.

At the very least, I would recommend that pre-workers read the Great Expectations chapter to get a heads up on how lucky they will be should they manage their career skilfully.

A new approach

This final section is essential reading because it addresses the thorny issue of work-life balance.

It provides clear advice on how to treat your career as a Silicon Valley lean start up.

Guidance is provided on how to return to our true nature and become a digital nomad. Those of us who are of pre-millennial vintage will benefit greatly from reading the Digital immigrants chapter.

ooOoo

There is a lot of content. Possibly too much. But again it is a reference book and not a novel. Hopefully my guidance above will help you optimise your use of the book. Each chapter has an overview and a summary. Most importantly each chapter has an action list so that you can turn this book into career value. There are also other actionable snippets embedded in the body of each chapter.

Some points/themes have been repeated. This is not because I cobbled the book together on various plane journeys, but because their contextual relevance justifies their repetition.

All of this content has in some way or other been pressure-tested in the market. As an advisor, speaker and writer, if I am too far off the money I get shot down.

I am a voracious reader of those that are expert in this space. Their thinking has refined mine. I have included a reference section for those interested in taking their reading further.

Again this book was written with pre-workers in mind. But through following my pen, it has ended up being relevant to policy makers, enterprises and established workers too. To those 'late additions' to the target readership community, I apologise for what might seem like a casual, perhaps even frivolous, approach to such an important topic. Given my initially-intended readership, I decided that if the book was too dry, regardless of any sound advice it may contain, it would not be read. Hence my approach.

I hope you find **Beyond 9 to 5** to be of value. My aim is to help individuals, organisations and societies make the necessary adjustments to thrive in the digital economy.

Before you take the following short career-calibration exercise, I encourage you to glance over Appendix A, where I clarify some important points on which this book hinges.

Calibration

Before we move on, answer these questions as best you can. They will provide a foundation on which you can build your career plan.

1. What does a successful career look like to you?
   a. Perhaps word this as if you are looking back on your life having enjoyed a successful career. What did you do? Why did you enjoy it? What value did you serve?
2. Beyond economic stability, to what extent will money be your primary motivation?
3. To what extent do you expect your work and personal life to overlap?
4. To what extent would your ideal job be predictable or even repetitive?
5. Does the notion of providing a service appeal to you?
6. Could you imagine feeling passionate about your chosen path?
7. Given your understanding of global trends and technology advances, what risks do you anticipate that could derail your intended career path?
8. Given your life and work experiences to date, what would be a natural path for you?
9. What further skills and experience do you need to acquire to increase your chances of converging onto your ideal path?

I would encourage you to keep an open mind in respect of how you chart the course of your career. The following chapters may well give you reason to refine, or even reject, your current perspective, though the latter is not the primary intention of this book.

In any case, an open mind is essential if you are to anticipate seismic shifts in the marketplace and adapt your path to the changing market demand.

Take action

- Recognise that career planning in the traditional sense no longer applies. What might be a highly in-demand skill/profession today may become redundant/automated tomorrow.
- Recognise that a career is not something society, commerce, your school or a medieval guild is obliged to design and provide for you. You need to take ownership of your career, and be vigilant in the manner in which you steer it through these increasingly volatile times.
- Review your answers to this calibration exercise as you read the book, and when you have finished it.
    - Perhaps even take stock, from time to time, throughout your career.
- Read Appendix A!

Anthroeconomics

1 No Ordinary Mammal

Overview

The future of work is being shaped by a variety of forces. The most critical of these forces are intrinsic to our human nature. Understanding them will provide you with insights into why the future of work will pan out as I propose in this book. This in turn will enable you to harness your true nature for maximum economic impact/fulfilment.

To understand these forces, we need to take a brief look at human evolution.

Natural forces

Approximately two hundred million years ago, mammals arrived on the scene. This was a pretty significant development. One notable characteristic of this new animal class was the brain upgrade. In fact there were two upgrades.

Mammals retained the reptilian brain of their predecessors, but early on in their evolution they received the limbic brain 'bolt on'. All of a sudden we cared about our offspring and recognised the benefits of being social. This requiring empathy and cooperation.

The second more recent upgrade is called the neocortex, which enabled mammals to think prior to taking action, rather than just acting on instinct. Up until then, smart decision making wasn't an option.

On encountering a new situation, instinct would drive animals to attempt one of the following:

- Eat it.
- Mate with it.
- Attack it.
- Ignore it.
- Escape from it.

Poor instincts were punished. Specifically species that took poor decisions were eliminated. For example, birds that had a tendency to forage for food in the mouths of carnivorous dinosaurs, or just generally behave in a reckless manner, would over time become extinct.

If a species could not eliminate its bad habits before it became extinct, it became extinct.

The neocortex allowed mammals to make decisions and solve problems in real-time, so to speak. As mentioned, the limbic brain enabled mammals to see the value in cooperating with other mammals.

This led to social behaviour and social structures. So it is fair to say that teamwork is not just some modern management fad.

Back then, mammals were second class citizens relative to the dinosaurs. This limited their access to resources and thus their rate of evolution. However about sixty five million years ago, the Cretaceous-Paleogene extinction event took place (probably a big asteroid/comet colliding with the Earth), and that wasn't good news for the dinosaurs. With a few exceptions, all the dinosaur groups were eliminated.

Once the dust had settled, it was literally party time for mammals in terms of resources, and consequently they received an evolutionary boost in respect of diversity and brain power.

Tooling up

Around 2.3 million years ago, at the clever end of the mammal spectrum, it became fashionable to balance and even move about on their hind legs. Those that did it well and consistently are now referred to as Homo habilis. They were highly mobile. Their evolved problem-solving skills led to the creation and usage of tools. These tooled-up proto-humans set out to gain some respect, and ultimately to fight their way to the top of the food chain. Two million years later, with some genetic fine-tuning along the way, this outcome was achieved.

Pack man

Fast forward to two hundred thousand years ago, where our ancestors took on an anatomical structure that represents modern man (Homo sapiens). These early ancestors were scavengers and hunter gatherers.

Such work had the following characteristics:

- It required high mobility. Hunter gatherers were always on the move looking for fresh supplies of berries or just chasing lunch across the savannah.
- It was highly social. Hunter gatherers operated as a pack. Coordination of effort was critical in order to avoid lunch eating them. Thus, being highly social was important from a trust and coordination perspective, given the life-critical nature of work.
- Work was not constrained to a fixed period (eg. 9 to 5). If you hadn't eaten for several days and lunch appeared on the horizon, at say 6pm, it is unlikely you would think in work-life balance terms and all mutually agree to ignore it until 9am the next day. For the hunter-gatherer, work and life were highly integrated.

- There was a high focus on outcomes. Hunter gatherer workers focused less on the number of hours they had been foraging and more on the number of berries picked.
- There was little strategic planning. Hunter gatherers would not embark on multi-year plans to be adhered to despite changes in the environment. Hunter gatherers were much more focused on what was happening now. If a particular type of 'easy to catch' lunch was becoming depleted, the hunter gatherers would identify another food source that could be acquired in a relatively efficient manner. Similarly, if a newly-discovered type of rock made for a better spearhead, it would be adopted. This can be considered an agile or adaptive form of existence.

So the key point here is that our ancestors were highly mobile, social, outcome oriented and agile. Plus they did not try to compartmentalise work and life.

Farmers world

The agricultural revolution, circa 12,000 years ago, saw a broad shift from nomadic to more settled behaviour. So mobility became less of a characteristic of our farming ancestors. Though it wasn't eliminated, because farmers had to:

- Take their livestock to market.
- Tend to their crops and livestock.

Back then, livestock transfer transactions did not take place using online e-payment tools. It was a highly social activity. So the commercial transactions at the market comprised a high degree of 'social content', as each trader tried to establish the trustworthiness and commercial astuteness of the other party.

To some extent the stakes were lower in the agricultural era, particularly as animals became domesticated. So the 'special ops', high-octane form of social behaviour needed by the hunter gatherers when pursuing aggressive prey ceased to be a requirement.

Because livestock did not keep office hours, the need to assist the birth of a lamb, or secure an escaped bull, overwhelmed by the beauty of the cows owned by another farmer, required the farmer to be in work mode, or at least on standby, 24 -7. Back then, the idea of work-life balance was a meaningless concept.

Good farmers were not identified by their strength or endurance (ie their labour capacity). Though in fairness, feebleness was not a sought after attribute.

Again they were judged on their outcomes. These might include number of livestock sold, or number of bales of corn yielded from the land.

Farmers needed to be more strategic than their ancestors. No longer could they use the trigger of feeling hungry to initiate the process of finding something to eat. Now humans had to think ahead. They had to plan, making decisions today that would impact their future, "Do I focus on bison, pigs, barley, wheat or some combination of produce?". But farmers needed to be flexible in their strategy, because bad weather, blight or disease may have a bearing on whether they and their families survived.

So the agricultural era was quite a leap from the hunter gatherer era in respect of the impact it had on lifestyle and food supply. Nonetheless, our farming ancestors, as our hunter gatherer ancestors, were mobile and social in nature. Their working and leisure time was, by necessity, integrated. They were also living in results-oriented societies (eg. berries picked, cattle sold).

Significantly, the transition to an agricultural approach required a slightly more strategic outlook. But what characterised both hunter gatherers and agriculturalists was the speed by which they abandoned or modified their plans. Business wise, you could say they took an agile approach.

If we consider that we have been developing as humans for over two million years, twelve thousand years ago represents only a half of a per cent of the time that has passed since we were hunter gatherers. And of course much less since we were primarily farmers. In evolutionary terms our brains are wired to be hunter gatherers. So if we are to capitalise on what nature intended, we would do well to build our lives around this reality.

But as we will see in the next chapter, this evolutionary path hit a road block some two hundred years ago, and this will explain why your parents just don't 'get you'.

Summary

Our natural desire to be social, mobile, tool-using, problem solvers is extremely significant in respect of what fulfilling work should entail.

Take action

- Consider to what extent your intended/current career path satisfies these natural human drives.

2   Enter the Industrial Era

Overview

The arrival of the industrial era marked a step change for humanity. Productivity rocketed, and this had a catalytic impact on the evolution of many societies. It has significantly shaped the way we work and the way we live.

Understanding the nature of the industrial era and its impact on work today will better equip us to decide what the benefits and trade-offs are of pursuing industrial era career models.

A revolution

The industrial era, which commenced circa two hundred years ago, saw a major transition in respect of man's evolution. The development of steam power and the use of machines to automate activities previously carried out by hand, led to a step change in productivity and eventually a step change in the economic well-being of those societies that embraced the Industrial Revolution.

As the factories transitioned from the use of steam power to biofuels, the factories migrated from the waterways to the highways. The priority now was to have good transportation links to both the buyers of the goods and the suppliers of the raw materials to make those goods.

The use of machine tools increased productivity. These triggered a mass exodus from the countryside to the factories as the need for human tool handlers grew.

This revolution in the world of work had its detractors. The textile artisans of the 19th century, who had dedicated their lives to mastering their craft, were particularly unhappy at their work becoming automated. The extent of their unhappiness was such that the British army deployed more resources to fighting these machine-breaking so called Luddites, than on fighting Napoleon. Blood was spilled. Such is the nature of revolutions that have cultural, social and economic implications.

Modern day factories

At the outset of the industrial era, factories typically comprised assembly lines with workers, probably in overalls, interacting with the product under assembly.

Latterly, the look and feel of the typical factory has changed. Today they are carpeted, and the assembly lines are replaced by desks and chairs. Traditional factories still exist today, though with a lot less people involved of course. My point being that today's modern offices are simply twenty first century representations of the traditional factories.

To drive home the point, many organisations today are running an industrial era factory model. One would be forgiven for thinking that these smartly dressed (and clean) workers, with their hi-tech workstations and smart devices, are far removed from the world of assembly line factory workers. These kempt workers spend all day producing documents, updating databases and navigating spreadsheets.

Some have labelled this modern hi-tech employee as a knowledge worker.

Typically the worker's seniority can be determined by the following factors:

- Whether they occupy a desk/cubicle or an office.
- Elevation of the office above sea level.
- Proximity of office to the structural corners of the building.

Seniority is important in the industrial era model. Without the incentive of one day becoming senior, it might be hard to accept that one is spending a significant percentage of time doing personally meaningless work.

But a corner office on the top floor is but one of the perks of seniority. Others include:

- A higher salary, which allows you to take more exotic holidays, and live in more desirable properties.
- Ownership of a prestige marque car (or two), which can be parked in a reserved and prominent spot in the office forecourt.
  - Again the idea is to inspire junior workers to aspire to becoming a senior manager.
- The ability to tell others what they must do and when they must do it.
  - And to lever their economic insecurities when their work isn't up to your (sometimes arbitrary) standards.

In general, aside from the occasional encounter with their staff and their boss, office dwelling knowledge workers spend much of their time glued to their user device.

This is a grim picture of the latter stages of the industrial era, but it is a reality. The good news is that this is not necessarily your assigned fate. This book was written to lay out your options, and soon we will come to that.

But for now let's wallow in more grimness.

Suit wearing compliant cogs

For many people working in the industrial era, their role is to be a cog in the machine. A cog that works smoothly, ie one that is compliant and reliable. A cog that works predictably, ie one that is expected to repeat the same processes without variation. In the days when the factory was indeed a factory, and the workers were simply elements of the assembly line that could not yet be automated, well behaved automatons were the next best thing.

The emerging topic of management science encouraged the few that created businesses to focus on identifying the key processes of the business (eg. find customer, build car, sack employee). From then on, to continually refine the processes to maximise operational efficiency (ie do things at least cost). The trouble with humans, what with their aspirations, hangovers and emotional needs, is that they cannot always be relied upon to be compliant automatons; not good from an efficiency perspective.

Job specs = cog specs

But even for those of us working in a furnished factory (aka an office), the focus on operational efficiency is still there for industrial model organisations. Fundamentally, if you were recruited based on a clearly defined job specification, then you have been acquired as a cog for the industrial machine.

Some other realities need to be mentioned:

- In the main, job specs imply process-oriented jobs that, as well as defining the skills required, also imply, if not define, time and behaviour constraints. Asking whether the customer needs fries with that, in a cheery voice during opening hours, is an example.

- The fact that the job can be specified implies commodity labour is required. The acquirer of talent expects to have more than one option. Workers are occasionally reminded of this.
- The fact that you 'secured' the job is down to your optimised combination of standardised capability, compliance and low cost.

Today many organisations recruit people with the same degree of 'well-being consideration' as they apply to their stationery procurement.

You never hear staplers complaining. Employers are sorely aware of that fact.

We are not beasts of burden

The industrial era saw a fundamental shift in how we were rewarded. Up until then, there was a direct correlation between results and rewards. You capture the prey, you get to eat. You successfully sow a field, you reap a crop. Now in this increasingly mechanised environment, workers were just adjuncts to the machines. Labour was the term coined for industrial workers.

Back in the agricultural era, the effectiveness of your plough was defined in horsepower. In the industrial era it is manpower. And because the workers were doing nothing more than acting as a placeholder for those parts of the machine yet to be automated, they were paid for their time as opposed to their results.

This shift in the reward system was very significant. It created two new concepts that up until then hadn't existed in any systemic form. The first was called 'laziness'. Now that people were being paid for their time and not their outcomes, they became increasingly adept at doing as little as they could get away with for a unit period of work. Why work harder than you have to if the pay you receive is unaffected. And given the work felt to a large extent meaningless, laziness didn't feel like such a moral dilemma.

This emerging art of laziness, in turn, stimulated the 'science' of management. Up until then, we had leaders who inspired their people to do what everyone fundamentally knew had to be done, eg. find food and defend the tribe. This laziness issue was impacting factory output. So a new breed of worker emerged. Their role was to encourage the labour to toil. This has evolved from a physical approach (aka a beating) to a more sophisticated psychological form of manipulation (work hard or you will lose your job, home, family, cable TV subscription, and so on). Smarter management used positive reinforcement, for example, "work hard and we'll upgrade your company car to a Porsche" or "work hard and we will give you more people to manage. Thereby giving you more power at work, and more status in society".

My first role after university was as a software engineer developing real-time software for naval ship systems. For the first six months, I had no real idea of what I was doing. I was just one of five hundred people on the project. My job was to code and test seemingly random elements of the system. There were literally thousands of modules in this IT system. Only the technical architects had a sense of how they all fitted together. Whilst my job required brainpower, it was still fundamentally an assembly line job. I was expected to churn out software with no real understanding, or even ownership, of the system as a whole.

Mind you, in the system trials, when my software was responsible for shooting a 'man overboard', I was made to feel very aware of the system as a whole. Fortunately, despite us using real fighter aircraft, they were unarmed. So nobody got wet (or dead).

Returning to the point I was making, management science emerged because workers needed to be driven to do meaningless work. Today, much of the labour intensive work has been automated, or perhaps outsourced to where it can be done cheaper.

Industrialisation is good

It is important to point out that I am not implying that industrialisation is bad. I am simply implying that it is increasingly bad for workers. Or more accurately, the value proposition of workers is eroding, given the increasingly robotic alternatives.

Fundamentally, what I am trying to communicate is that the key elements of industrial work are process and compliancy. And even if you love routine (process), and are desperate to please (compliant), your economic value is in free-fall as technology alternatives arrive in the market.

Industrialisation has enabled us to get on with our lives without having to waste time producing our own food, building our own cars and creating our own medicines. Many would rightly argue that this is evolutionary progress.

The future of industry

I believe there is still a lot of mileage in the industrial model. I think some of the big changes we will see going forward include:

Decentralised leadership. Increasingly decisions need to be made at the point of opportunity, rather than operatives (such as bank clerks) having to get approval from those further up the hierarchy. So there will be more discretion on the action workers can take in, for example, a response to a customer complaint. This will be quite data-driven, so the discretion level will be constrained by the perceived value of the customer and the extent of the organisational blunder. So one could argue that this is good old process work, but more real-time and data driven.

Swarm science. Research conducted in respect of swarm behaviour, essentially reveals that you can get sophisticated things done by encoding simple instructions and responses in the workers (eg. bees and ants). This will lead to better decision making in respect of rapidly changing market demands. But if anything, it will be unattractive to workers because being part of the swarm reduces the need to use your brain, as the requisite intelligence/smartness is built into the swarm-collaboration model. This will be a somewhat dissatisfying working framework, unless you like to waggle dance, emit pheromones under certain conditions or are comfortable performing some other swarm communication protocol.

Increased and smarter automation. Human cogs will continue to be replaced by technology. As we will see in a later chapter, low value assets such as supermarket trolleys and hospital beds, along with kettles and alarm clocks, will become smarter. Even the material passing through the factory machinery will increasingly not be the 'victim' of the machinery, but will in fact tell the equipment how it is to be manipulated.

Post-industrial industrial

My view is that we are transitioning to a post-industrial era. I will cover this in subsequent chapters. But whilst we are on the subject of the industrial era, there are a number of eminent and very engaging economists who believe that what I describe as the post-industrial era is simply an evolution of the industrial era. I will argue in due course that it is not.

In any case, these industrial-evolution perspectives are useful. So it is worth looking at a couple.

Jeremy Rifkind, an economic and social theorist, talks of the three industrial generations, which can be characterised by communication and energy themes as follows:

- 1st generation – Print and steam.
- 2nd generation – Media and fossil fuels.
- 3rd generation – Internet and renewables.

Jeremy's model serves to remind us that:
- We need to explore new energy options.
- The nature of business and society are rapidly transforming as a result of the Internet.

All very true. In Jeremy's world, we are transitioning into the 3rd industrial age. Peter Marsh, an expert in industrial matters, talks about the five generations of industry. These being:

- 1st revolution – Transition from agricultural era.
- 2nd revolution – The transportation revolution.
- 3rd revolution – The science revolution.
- 4th revolution – The arrival of computers.
- 5th revolution -   Mass customisation, ie using industrial manufacturing to produce highly tailored output as demanded by empowered consumers.

The emphasis is on manufacturing real things, and so takes a somewhat narrower view of industry than me. My view is that the emerging service economy, which doesn't necessarily deal in tangible outputs, is really just another manifestation of manufacturing (which I appreciate appears to support Peter's perspective). Peter believes we are moving into the 5th industrial generation.

Now let's briefly touch on services. Examples include:

- Replacing a tooth filling.
- Enjoying a package holiday.
- Receiving a report on your competitors' strengths and weaknesses.

All have a degree of personalisation, but all are delivered via a set of processes, albeit one's where human skill (currently) defines the quality of the experience.

In either case, I have not done these authors credit in terms of their models and would recommend you explore them further. My anthropological model acknowledges the arrival of the internet of things, renewables, 3D printing and nanotechnology. But for me they are less significant from a work perspective than the anthropological shift taking place.

That said, a better understanding of their models will add texture to your understanding of the world of work and how it is evolving.

In the next chapter we will look at some of the cracks emerging in the edifice of the industrial model.

Please hang in there. This is a story with a happy ending. But it is important that you fully understand how we got to where we are, so that you can conduct your career with your eyes wide open.

Summary

The Industrial Revolution caused a seismic economic shift for the better. Traditional factories are becoming more efficient by the day and will continue to do so as technology invariably evolves. A mutation of the traditional factory is the office. In many respects, office work, whilst being physically less demanding, is fundamentally not dissimilar behaviour wise to the traditional factory model. Thus you are warned to enter an office-based career with caution.

Take action

If you work in an office. Try the following:

- Map out the 'assembly lines' that run through your organisation.
- Where do you sit on the assembly line?
- How much of your work is felt by the consumer of your organisation's output?
- How close is your role to complete automation?
- What could you do to ensure that you deliver value over and above that of a new technology replacement?

If you do not work in an office or have yet to enter the world of work, discuss the following with someone you know who works in an office.

Look out for changes in their demeanour as it becomes apparent to them that:

- They are a hair's breadth away from being outsourced/automated.
- The fact that they may have traded their technical skills to climb the greasy management pole has now left them virtually unemployable.
- Their career to date has been largely mentally unstimulating, though because of red tape and office politics, it has nonetheless been mentally very tiring.

3　Industrial Unrest

Overview

Most of us have benefited from the Industrial Revolution. However some of the pillars on which the industrial model sits are starting to look unsteady.

In this chapter, we will explore the challenges industry is having to face and the implications for our economic well-being.

Daddy, what did you do in the industrial era?

The transition between the industrial era and the next economic era, whilst seismic, is largely invisible to those currently running flat out on the furnished-factory hamster wheel. It is only when the wheel is replaced by something more automated, does it dawn on the worker how the world outside of the cage has changed.

Nonetheless, there will be a time when we can all take a more objective view on the period known as the industrial era.

For many of your younger readers, it is important to note that the world I described in the last chapter is the world in which many parents continue to earn their living.

It is also the world that has given you the economic security you enjoy today. Some readers will have enjoyed the pleasures of a big home, exotic holidays and the nice cars.

But many readers will look at their parents, who on the face of it have acquired the 'badges' to show that they have played a good economic game, and wonder why they continually clock watch and appear to be in a constant state of distractedness. They don't appear to exhibit the passion and joy for their career in the way that a professional footballer might. Or even a charity worker who spends much of their time in inhospitable or emotionally strained environments. Something is not right.

But I am a professional!

This all makes sense for blue collar work, but can you really say that about more prestigious white collar jobs that require significant training/qualifications, eg. lawyers, accountants and doctors?

There is certainly more scope in these roles to apply one's discretion/knowledge to given situations. Much of what lawyers and doctors do though hinges on case-based reasoning. In other words, the advice they give to resolve their customer's situation is based on either related best-practice (medicine) or how this has been handled in the past (law). This type of capability lends itself to automation. Customers present the conditions, and the computer searches the database for a response.

Everyone can see how blue collar work is being increasingly automated.

However the reality is that many white collar roles are heading that way or at least being 'blue collarised' (ie dumbed down). This will have serious career/quality of life implications for those who through their training and qualifications believed they had bought themselves a 'society upgrade'.

We need to roam and be social

Let us remind ourselves that our brains are wired to be hunter gatherers After all, in evolutionary terms that is what we were doing until very recently. Thus there are some compelling reasons why being an industrial worker was never in our nature.

Firstly mobility. With the arrival of the factory, workers no longer had an economic need to roam. Day after day, turning up to the same factory. Day after day, turning up to the same desk. Perhaps that is why workers use their lunchtimes to go running. I know there is no need for me to hunt at lunchtime. I simply choose to ignore the fact that my intended quarry is already secured within the confines of the canteen lasagne.

Being social was something that was entirely discouraged on the assembly line. The idea of chatting about matters unrelated to work would have once led to a beating. Or perhaps even worse, a solemn meeting with the HR function.

Breakin bad

Smart societies retrain those that have been 'automated out of work', because it is in our nature to do work or at least do something that supports our survival/economic goals. For those automated out of the system, 'official work' often gets replaced by 'unofficial work'. Such unofficial work ranges from the handling of 'black market' goods to being the kingpin in a crystal meth supply chain.

This should be no surprise to anyone given our natural desire to work coupled with the social pressure to be successful economically. Some might say that the welfare system has removed the need to do even unofficial work. This is perhaps even more worrying, as having no purpose (need to survive and care for family/tribe) really goes against the natural wiring of our brains.

I would suggest that our industrial/work policy makers look closely at the implications of having an underclass that is not just unemployed but unemployable.

There comes a point where there are not enough economic consumers to warrant the industrial output of goods and services. Societal implosion follows soon after.

Everyone's a loser, though admittedly those that sell pitchforks and coffins will thrive.

Work-life in the balance

A feature of industrial work is its contextual meaninglessness. Some might also regard industrial work as morally unsound. "Is my life really about selling people things they don't really need?" or "Does it truly matter that I work for a company that holds back its medicinal products until the demand has become sufficiently large?" or even,

> *"How do I tell my children I am a quality assurance officer for a manufacturer of inflatable sex aids for those too idle to forge genuine human relationships?"*.

Of course not all industrial work is meaningless, or immoral. But a lot of it is, unless your sole purpose in life is to make shareholders happy. Many people reconcile any associated quandaries by partitioning their working life from their non-working life. "Those taskmasters at the mill can sweat me whilst I am at work, but I will jealously protect my time outside of my contractual commitment."

Thus for the first time in mankind's history, the industrial era has heralded the concept of work-life balance.

Similarly the concept of retirement came about. Again in the tradition of work-life balance, this defined the crossover from having to work to having a life. People generally saw retirement as a life milestone where one transitioned from a life of toil to one of leisure. Surprisingly, not all retired people feel better and in some cases die unexpectedly (US National Institute on Aging research, 2009) soon after.

A loss of purpose, a loss of prestige, or even just social isolation from people who share a common esprit de corps can have fatal consequences.

Even a hamster wheel is more palatable than daytime television! Ideally one that is shared with other like-minded hamsters.

Industrial era companies today are characterised by workers leaving as close to their official 'clocking off' time as possible. Industrial era mind-set workers today can be identified by their resolute determination not to look at their work emails whilst on holiday. As a union leader, I might say this is fair enough. But in practice, the mental anguish of not knowing whether you will be returning to a work-related sh!+storm totally offsets the rejuvenation objective of the break.

Such people are not bad, and neither are the unions in respect of the importance of workers' rights. As we will see, it is just that such industrial behaviour is increasingly outmoded, untenable and undesirable in the post-industrial world.

Think ahead

One other notable characteristic of industrial era work was the need to be strategic. Clearly if the business owners planned to build cars, there would be significant capital investment in constructing the factory.

There would be significant management investment in setting up the supplier and distribution contracts that would enable the factory to turn car components into car sales. The main underlying hypothesis being that there is a market demand (volume) for cars over a period of say ten years. Given those numbers, it makes economic sense to be in the car manufacturing business. So business leaders in the industrial era had to have multi-year strategies and plans for their businesses, whilst at the same time hoping that their underlying market assumptions were accurate.

There was a time when there was a good chance that a 10 year forecast might coincide with the subsequent reality.

However, we now live in a highly interconnected and thus volatile world. Even with the most sophisticated prediction algorithms, nobody can predict the future ten years hence.

This approach of business leaders imposing their strategic will on the natural order of things has increasingly become ridiculous and a cause for concern. The stock market machinery is increasingly the source of some of today's finest fiction writers. These being CEOs of quoted companies forecasting their quarterly and yearly financial numbers.

What is perhaps even worse, is the associated corporate behaviour. Organisations become overly focused on making these figures a reality, despite what is in the interests of the staff, customers and even long term interests of the shareholders. Each day, it is becoming increasingly apparent that any boardroom-driven strategy that extends more than a few months will be viewed as delusionary by observers and eventually as malgovernance by the regulators.

This is a large crack in the industrial edifice, and it's getting larger on a daily basis.

Dark satanic mills

I have painted a grim picture for industrial era work, or hopefully I have. This is not because the industrial era is bad. In many respects the industrial model will run and run even though there will be fewer and fewer workers involved. It will be some while before we print cars on our home printer (aka home manufacturing). But I suspect car ownership will be an outmoded concept before then.

The real message is that the industrial era model is bad for workers. Whether you are a boilersuit-wearing assembly line worker or an Excel spreadsheet jockey, the chances are that if you are doing 'process' work, you will soon be surplus to requirements.

Those dark satanic mills referred to by the English poet William Blake are thought by many to be a reference to these soul-destroying factories. The fact that the factories of yesterday and the offices of today require the suppression of our natural behaviour suggests that Blake might have been on to something. The benefits of the industrial era have come at a very high personal price for workers over the last two centuries.

People are starting to question whether the acquisition of socially-validating possessions is a fair trade for discretionary time. If we worked a little less, and so acquired a little less, we might have more time to enjoy life.

Perhaps this is the reason you never see a tow bar on a hearse?

Summary

The industrial model is under stress, but it will continue to run. However as automation increases, it is not a model workers can rely upon. This is not necessarily driven by the greed of the plutocrats, but by globalisation. If an organisation can drive out cost by automation, it will. And if competing organisations do not follow, they will be at a competitive disadvantage.

In any case, the industrial model does not, in the main, support meaningful work. And where workers have options, they will typically pursue meaningful work even if that involves a decrease in material comfort.

Take action

- Make a list of career professions that you respect or are generally respected by society. Consider to what extent they can be automated.
  - Those that lend themselves to automation can be crossed off your career options list.
- Always buy high value goods from quoted companies as their quarter-ends and year-ends approach. This is when they are looking to reconcile their 'income reality' with what they have promised the market. That puts you in a position of buying power.
  - This is not a career tip, as such. But it might help offset the price of this book.

Towards a Future-Proofed Career

9   Key Skills   103

The key skills everybody needs to acquire.

4 The Artist

Overview

We have established that the role of workers in the industrial era was to perform tasks in a robotic fashion until a robot, or some piece of technology, could do the job.

Today, the power is shifting to those who have acquired the right skills. Up until now, this power only sat with diva-complex rock stars and finely tuned, but easily startled, Olympic athletes.

In this chapter you will understand why this is happening and how you can go about joining this elite but growing band of talent.

Race to the bottom

Let's take a look at how the world of work is currently playing out. Taking the banking sector as an example: Each bank is generally trying to automate humans out of their organisation. Humans are expensive, require management, have these things call aspirations and occasionally are inefficient/economically dangerous because of their recreational (and sometimes professional) interest in mind altering substances.

So the banks are in a race to turn their businesses into high tech factories with a minimised number of humans involved. This is in effect a race to the bottom, because such ruthless efficiency will ultimately create the perfect transaction machine. And when each bank is a perfect transaction machine, the competition will be such that all players will gravitate towards almost zero profit.

At some point each bank will have to reconsider how it moves back up the value chain and out of this perilous zero margin zone. What they will soon conclude is that people are the 'secret sauce' for business success. But not the suit-wearing compliant business cogs, who are merely extensions of the machine, but 'outside the box' disruptive geniuses that can apply their unique creativity to developing innovative customer services, for which the market will pay a premium.

Such a worker is for me the true digital economy worker, and the one we must strive towards. Like Picasso, who famously on request scribbled a picture on a napkin and signed it for a fellow diner. Prior to handover, he stated the price would be 25,000 dollars. Despite the eager recipient's protest that the sketch only took two minutes to produce, Picasso pointed out that it took him 25 years to develop his craft and reputation, and that value is reflected in the price.

He may not have expressed it quite like a management consultant, but you can see the point that artists invest heavily in developing their own mastery, and that has to be factored into their fee. It has nothing to do with the industrial model of being paid on a per hourly basis.

So the digital economy favours creativity over simply being a process bolt-on.

The trend over the last half century has been to expunge blue collar workers from the factory floor. And as mentioned, modern day offices are really just furnished factories, where the factory workers are called professionals.

For the majority of these professionals, the increased capability of technology has had the effect of turning them into blue collar workers and so destined them to a similar fate.

Those of us currently in work need to assess whether we are standing in the way of the 'progress steamroller', or whether we need to attend a steam roller driving skills course, so to speak (Don't worry. I am not sure I know what I mean by this either).

Worker as artist

A large part of the pre-industrial economy was driven by artisans (also known as craftsmen) who had developed very specific skills that could be applied to making consumer goods, such as furniture or cheese (primarily functional) or creating items, such as sculptures and jewellery (less functional).

Their career paths fell into three broad categories:

- **Apprentice**, where the focus is on learning the skills associated with a given craft. As an apprentice you would be tied to a master whose payment would be in the form of lodgings and food.
- **Journeyman**, where the person has developed competency in the skills, but has not been conferred mastery status by the associated governing body, typically known as a guild. They become free of their obligation to their master and so typically set out to travel the country to gain experience from different workshops.
- **Master**, is someone who has been admitted to the relevant guild and has achieved this by presenting an example of their work, literally a masterpiece, along with a sum of money. Once admitted they could run their own workshops.

In medieval times, those that sought academic mastery and achieved the requisite standard were conferred a 'Master of Arts'.

Guilds exist today in Europe, Australia and North America.

I believe that as we migrate away from the industrial division of labour model, where essentially workers were cogs in a big machine, and towards an era where functional skill is valued, the apprentice – journeyman - mastery model will rise again. In fairness to the industrial era, the division of labour model has been in use since ancient times, but is largely associated with slave management. Building pyramids comes to mind.

By 'functional', I mean produce something that is of itself useful, for example:

- Design a car.
- Create a new customer service desk.
- Develop a series of world class PowerPoint presentations.

The industrial era turned workers into cogs that were of no use unless embedded in a factory. Such skills might include:

- Attach steering wheel.
- Wash dishes.
- Test condom.

German economist Karl Marx considered this isolated 'cog work' a cause of worker alienation. This model essentially required workers to do what appeared to be highly repetitive meaningless work even though what emerged from the production line was meaningful to the market.

Later on in the book we will explore this path to mastery. A movement from alienating and meaningless work to a model where the worker is on a fulfilling journey in pursuit of their 'art' has to be a good thing. A workforce that is competent, engaged and passionate about their work is good for the individual and the society they live in.

Developing a reputation around mastery in something that the market needs is a sure fire way to avoid the unemployment abyss. This abyss has consumed, and is consuming, a large part of the working population, who have been both educated and trained to be industrial cogs.

Again we see such mastery in sports and entertainment. We also see it in science and business leadership. Mastery doesn't necessarily mean having global recognition. But it does mean being recognised within your field.

In the digital economy, your work or art is your greatest sales instrument. So doing great work will increase your chances of being offered more great work to do. Great work builds a great reputation. Increasingly, smart workers are waking up to that.

Power shift

There is no shortage of people on the planet, at around 7 billion and rising. The unemployment figures of most countries across the globe would seem to reinforce that there is a surplus of workers. But even taking into account inefficiencies in talent acquisition, vacant jobs and people with the appropriate skills (detailed elsewhere in this book) not finding each other, the skills surplus relates to skills that whilst relevant in the industrial era are of increasingly little value in the digital economy.

This is not to say that industrial business models no longer exist or that all economies today are truly digital. But the trend is away from industrial and towards digital. The problem we have is that there is a shortage of digital talent, ie people who have the skills needed to work in a highly agile customer-centric data-driven organisation.

PLEASE NOTE: As we will see, digital skills is not a synonym for software developer or technologist. Again, it is more about the ability to deliver value in an uncertain and fast moving environment.

Think of an industrial era worker as a waiter on a giant cruise ship sailing serenely across the Mediterranean. The job is very predictable, and the worst that can happen is that a passenger's steak is sent back because it is undercooked.

Now think of the digital worker as a sailor on deck in a tempest around Cape Horn. The mainsail is torn, and the sailor needs to improvise to stop the ship being flung onto the rocks.

There is a lack of digital workers. This supply-demand inefficiency is shifting the power from the employer to the digitally-skilled worker. This shift is well underway. Flexible working and BYOD (Bring Your Own Device) are examples of worker empowerment. "I will not work for you unless I can work when I want, and I can use my own technology, because quite frankly the technology I use in my personal life is superior to the tech you provide at work."

And as we will see in a later chapter, this is just the tip of the iceberg in respect of employee empowerment. If you have hankered after living the life of a rock star – "rose petals to be sprinkled in my hotel room", "I don't do stairs", "my entourage will need somewhere to work", then you are advised to develop digital economy skills and to ensure that you deliver, no exceptions, on each gig. Be aware that whilst the trend I am describing will (perhaps reluctantly) accommodate talented prima donnas, it is unlikely to extend to those whose skillset extends no further than being an incompetent poseur.

Beyond best in class

Globalisation as mentioned is not by any means a new phenomenon. It is just that with the acceleration of technology, in respect of communications in particular, the world has become much smaller.

It is no longer the case of striving to be best in your class.

If you really are serious about securing your future in the digital economy, you need to be the best in the world.

This is not as difficult as it appears. Increasingly the value people bring to work is their unique combination of skills and experiences.

There was a time when I wanted to be the best sprinter on the planet. I was (sadly) constrained by ability and physiology. However there might well have been a short period where I was the fastest human in the world with an astrophysics degree. Though possibly not. But I was almost definitely the fastest human with an astrophysics degree and with my surname.

Fortunately I have not had to sell these three uniquely combined personal attributes to gain employment, but the point is that by smartly combining your in-demand capabilities you can significantly thin out the competition.

But do keep in mind that the starting point in terms of market demand is that you are by default the world's number one at being you. Though on further inspection that in itself may not have obvious economic value. So next you have to consider your existing positives eg.:

- Speak Portuguese.
- Have great hand-eye coordination.
- Intimate knowledge of woodland animals.

In this whacky example it may be that you are ideally equipped to work with a Brazilian woodland trust, which has discovered that a new pesticide used by local farmers is neurologically damaging fat-tailed mice such that they are falling from the trees with fatal consequences.

Such opportunities might be somewhat limited. However, as long as there is a demand, and you are the best in the world, it is likely that you will do well economically. Demand being a very important word.

Being less surreal, even the best biologists in the world have to specialise, not just as a mechanism to reduce the competition, but because that is what the market needs.

Increasingly the creation of unique skill combinations will extend beyond those you have acquired through working.

Increasingly hobbies, where you have lived, and even your online social activity will play a role, as we will see later.

So becoming the best in the world can be made easier by cultivating a cocktail of capabilities for which organisations are willing to pay. And perhaps most importantly, this unique mix reflects a skillset that you are happy to invest significant time in developing, mastering and applying to real-world situations.

Anthroeconomics

As you will discover through this book, the digital economy is in effect mankind's return to its true nature. So smart organisation will respect those characteristics of human nature in designing their operating model and strategy.

Digital economy workers will similarly be inclined to move away from the comfort of being a low profile cog in a big machine to the riskier yet fulfilling role of mobile and socially capable creative destructor.

Philosophically speaking such people reject the adage 'if it ain't broke don't fix it', and embrace 'whether it's broke or not let's improve it'. In practice, when applied to the world of work, this must not be considered as some sort of annual review of your organisation's operating model. It is a continuous quest by everyone to ensure that what you and your organisation are doing today is optimised to reflect the barrage of incoming data. Such data is collectively known as 'market reality'.

Many education systems have taught us to be compliant.

In the past this has extended to 'fixing' left handed people.

In the present 'being taught to the test' often takes priority over teaching people a love of learning. The qualifications acquired by this approach are, in effect, quality assurance certificates future employers can use in making employment decisions. This has a coldly industrial feel to it.

So we need to rise up against this compliancy/quality stamp worker production model. We need to 'pipe up' when we feel there is a better way of doing something. And schools need to focus more on education and less on sheep dipping.

Digital workers take ownership of their learning. They see this as a necessary discipline to ensure they do not skid off the path as they progress their journey to mastery.

Super brain

From an evolutionary perspective, cells have mutually agreed that collaborating is more beneficial than fighting. Hence the world is largely made up of multicellular organisms, of which we are but one example.

The first signs of single cell life date back to around 4 billion years ago. Around 3.5 billion years ago we saw the arrival of multi-cellular organisms. Primates arrived circa 85 million years ago, and Homo sapiens evolved about half a million years ago. Ants, who happen to be highly collaborative, have been around 130 million years.

Taking these random 'facts', I conclude:

- We as humans are an evolutionary experiment which has yet to be deemed a success.
- Just as cells are a building block of life, we are perhaps designed to be a building block of something bigger than us.
- Ants have something to teach us.

Colonies made up of argumentative and selfish ants do not exist today because that approach did not promote the mutual survival of the colony.

We as humans are highly social by nature, but some societies have become highly individualistic. This is more apparent when the population is well off. Consequently individuals:

- Develop a sense of invincibility that they will never want for food or shelter.
- Take for granted that their police force and military will maintain the protective cocoon that enables them to live out this fantasy.

In the extreme, this lack of social reliance, and perhaps even a lack of social contribution, are markers of societies that will not make it in the long run, given the likelihood of both natural and manmade disasters occurring. The Japanese cultural tendency to care more for the community than the individual no doubt accelerated its recovery from the catastrophic 2011 tsunami.

But being social has a cost. There is what is called a cognitive load incurred in getting on with others, particularly those whom we wouldn't choose to spend time with. This load requires social animals to have bigger brains. Thus a simple test for an organisation wanting to ensure their prospective addition to the team will fit in would be to measure brain size. I will leave this to the recruitment industry to work out how this is measured in a non-invasive manner during the interview process.

Bottom line: Those workers who are most adept at collaborating are most likely to do well in the digital economy.

Thus those organisations that can create the conditions for the 'colony' to behave as one super brain will prevail.

It may not sit neatly with our egos, but consider the possibility that the arrival of our neocortex signified a point in time when complete self-interest became an indicator of an upcoming genetic cul-de-sac.

Possibly this is why we have tolerated the industrial era for so long. Even though the work was largely tedious and against our natural tendency to roam and tinker, at least it satisfied our need to be part of something bigger and to some extent be protected (economically) by being part of this industrial colony.

So whilst I am advocating that we become less cog and more diva, we need to get the balance right between quirky and uncompromising brilliance and, say, sharing a dressing room and performing in harmony with other equally quirky and uncompromisingly brilliant individuals.

This may well be an argument for embracing diversity. You may be different from others both physically and in worldview. But if we all bring capabilities to the table that can be harmonised into a common goal this will surely lead to superior outcomes. In a volatile market, it is likely that the super brain, comprised of brilliant cooperating individuals, will morph on a daily basis as different challenges requires different diva configurations.

So organisations need to develop a less rigid perception of themselves and be designed such that they can adapt their 'super brain' in line with the changes in the market.

The key point for you is that being collaborative is critical, as is being flexible.

A dogged determination to keep to your mastery path, despite the evidence that you are diverging from what the market actually needs, will get you full marks for focus and no marks for smartness.

Summary

The digital economy requires creative artists and not process workers. Artistry requires hard work. It requires us to take up a path that leads to mastery. Some of us:

- Will need to shake off the industrial conditioning brought about by our schooling.
- May have to learn to play nicely with others.

Occasionally I receive pushback along the lines that not everybody can be a rock star/artist. I think what they really mean is that not everybody can imagine themselves being creative; or they are uncomfortable with the notion that they will not have a boss/set of procedures to tell them what to do.

Perhaps look at it another way. If a computer can do your job, it will do your job.

If the term artist grates with you, then just substitute it for a term that embraces a capability that cannot be delivered by a piece of technology.

This shouldn't be an issue. We were designed for the digital economy. In many respects this is simply a return to our true pre-industrial nature. But again some of us have some industrial unlearning to do.

An important skill, which we will explore in due course, is in ensuring that our mastery path does not veer away from what the market needs.

Take action

- Create a number of future scenarios where you have attained true mastery. Perhaps you are the Head of Astrophysics at MIT? Or an economic adviser to the United Nations? Or even the next Bill Gates or Lady Gaga?
    - Do any of your future-you scenarios fill you with passion?
    - Can you now start to eliminate certain career paths, eg. academic or political?
    - Might a blended version of a few of your most exciting scenarios be most appealing?
- Actively look to improve things.
- Actively look to work with others.

5 Career Path

Overview

In this chapter, we take a broad brush view of your career options.

But first take this little test. Which of the following best fits your situation:

1. You live within your means.
2. You live in constant fear of being socially excluded from, say, an exclusive country club, where your 'must keep up the payments' performance car barely passes muster in terms of its suitability for the club car park.

If you chose 1, then you will have the option of choosing something that fills you with passion. If you choose 2, then you had better focus on what I describe as an economic career.

A career path

I have repeatedly used the term career path, but am conscious that its industrial branding can be taken to mean either a set of jobs that broadly leads to increased responsibility and/or increased remuneration over the course of one's working life.

The implication being that there was some form of progression in a given field with perhaps some drift along the way. For example, you start out as a software developer in the Defence sector, but over time this evolves to becoming a CIO (Chief Information Officer) in the Retail sector.

Those who have stuck with stacking shelves, being a postman, or a chartered accountant, despite the promotional opportunities to move 'up', will be less likely to talk about their career and more likely to talk about their job.

Career typically implies a path from 'hands on' operative to manager of people. Though increasingly, people are bucking the social pressure to move up the ladder in respect of management roles and are pursuing a 'technical' career. In effect they are deepening their technical skills. So:

- The shelf stacker progresses to shop window layouts.
- The postman progresses to delivering sensitive parcels (human organs, combustible materials).
- The accountant moves from working with small family run businesses to publicly quoted enterprises.

But people also have fulfilling 'horizontal' careers. The postman changes his geographical coverage. The language teacher adds adult students to her traditional market of pre-exam teenagers.

I prefer the notion of mastery over career, as I believe it better captures the idea that our working lives are becoming less about economic survival ("please don't send me back to the village") and more about self-actualisation ("let's make a difference"). I also see people developing portfolio careers that embrace both high economic return and high societal contribution. They are so good at what they do on the economic front that they set the terms with their employer/clients in respect of how they allocate their time.

I make this point so that you understand that those born last century will likely have a different take on what constitutes a career.

They are likely to see it as a linear activity that goes from physical/technical through management to ultimately (if you play your cards right) a leadership role. A big point here is that many traditional career paths see the technical piece, eg. programmer or graphics designer, as an entry level role. A sign of progress for many is when they take on a people management role. The consequences of this are that there aren't many genuinely good technical people, ie people who get things done, rather than getting others to get things done.

Social pressure and the low value organisations often place on 'worker bees' have driven potentially good (by that I mean experienced) people to abandon the technical path. Thus, many industries have very few people who have achieved technical mastery.

The IT industry is a little ahead of the game on this, and for over twenty years it has been possible to pursue a career that remains technical to the day of retirement. But even so, they are relatively few and far between. Many technically-inclined people have taken matters into their own hands and become freelancers. They only take on roles that satisfy their passion in this respect.

Silicon Valley inadvertently promotes ageism in respect of technologists. It is largely populated by under thirty something tech 'wizards'. Though this is largely because beyond a certain age:

1. They have sold their company and live a life of leisure on their own private island.
2. They have been absorbed into the hierarchy of one of the major tech brands as a result of their start-up firm being sold (leaving the founder to buy his own island (see above)). These once young technologists (aka acqui-hires) are no longer pulling pizza-fuelled all-nighters, as they are now primarily middle aged managers who spend their working day in meetings.

My main point is that many industries and many societies have yet to acknowledge the value in a technical career. Again, by technical I don't necessarily mean technologist. It implies anybody who produces or fixes something, tangible or intangible. Stacking shelves is technical ('labels always facing outwards'), as is being a doctor, portrait artist or bricklayer.

In many industrial organisations, if you are not presiding over others, you are still on the bottom rung. The digital economy changes that.

> *If your primary skill is management (making sure subordinates follow the processes), you have a career problem.*

The digital economy needs doers and leaders only.

Though be aware that the digital economy is not going to be 'The rise of the shelf stacker'. Many technical roles will experience a period whereby humans work alongside robots with the same functional capability.

> *Over time, if your job can be done by a robot, it will be done by a robot.*

So to remain relevant in this Darwinian digital economy, we need to stay 'functionally superior' to technology alternatives. This is a particularly important point.

Now looking at career options. They can be broadly categorised as follows:

- Economic.
- Discovery.
- Creative.
- Societal.
- Social enterprise.
- Entertainment
- Hybrid.

Let's take a look at these in turn:

Private / Economic

Economic career paths are pursued by those who are in some way focused on good economic outcomes for the employer/client, and in turn themselves. Such careers are characterised by working for profit-focused organisations. At the big end of the spectrum, we have companies that are publicly quoted on high profile stock exchanges, such as the London Stock Exchange or Nasdaq. There are second tier exchanges for smaller firms. The main difference between the main and secondary exchanges are:

- The value of the companies.
- The volume of trade in their shares.
- The degree of regulatory compliance (proof of good behaviour) the companies are subjected to.

In essence all quoted companies have sold all or part of their ownership to the public (individuals, corporations, governments and financial institutions). And these public owners expect their investments to be profitable.

Not all companies are quoted. There are start-ups that do not have a sufficient trading track record to be admitted to a stock exchange. Plus there are organisations that are substantial in size but remain under the founder's (or the founder's family) ownership.

You may choose to work for a large confectionary conglomerate, because you have a vision for a world where everyone has equal access to type two diabetes. As much as the organisation's management might share your vision, if healthy snacks turn out to be more profitable, they will change strategic direction without flinching.

It's all about the money.

There is no ambiguity about profit.

Much like your personal best hundred meter time, it is an absolute that can be compared with everyone else. In economic organisations, all meetings, interactions, products and services have profit in mind. They may talk about customer experience, but only in as much as it serves to plumb the customer's wallet into the organisation's bank account.

I am painting a grim picture of this career path. Of course you can work for companies that are doing good things, whilst endeavouring to make a profit. But you must understand that profit trumps 'good things' if it comes to a trade-off.

The clarity that profit brings helps oil the wheels of capitalism.

If you have the requisite skills to help organisations be profitable, then you can sell yourself to the highest bidder. In a world where outcomes are increasingly valued more than labour, there is no reason why you cannot make a lot of money for very little physical effort or investment of time.

Most of us, including our forefathers, did not have the luxury of pursuing non-economic career paths. Bills have to be paid. Eviction has to be avoided.

There is no reason why you should not pursue such an economic career. Some people spend a decade or so acquiring the wealth needed to pursue something more altruistic in the latter part of their career.

With mastery in a 'high demand – low supply' market, one can even mix an economic career with other paths. Or just go all out to get the highest score.

There are a variety of films with titles containing the phrase 'Wall Street' that explore this approach.

Discovery

Discovery as a career path covers invention (combustion-engine car), innovation (driverless car) and revelation (Neanderthal man hunted using a fleet of 4 by 4 vehicles equipped with high fidelity sound systems).

In the main, discovery careers are often funded by economic organisations. If you were working in the research and development function of a pharmaceutical giant, your role may be to harness the curative chemical properties of naturally occurring alpine daisies into a synthetic drug that can be patented and sold for profit. It is not science for science's sake.

Academic institutions often have their research funded by commercial organisations. Though the organisations will likely be less focused on a short term gain and so will give the researchers more latitude in what they explore. Still there will be parameters, and so the scope of research will be constrained.

Intellectual property is becoming the weaponry of choice in the digital economy.

In turn, research organisations have sprung up to meet the demand. They don't have a specific commercial goal in mind in respect of, for example, creating an alternative to Velcro or Post-its. Think of these organisations as playgrounds for scientists.

They are given relatively free rein with the hope that, through their curiosity, they will stumble across something for which the associated intellectual property can be sold to a commercial organisation for a healthy profit.

Some areas of discovery, for example, in the field of cosmology, are not undertaken with even the remotest of commercial intentions. I once worked on a project to establish the weight, size and age of the universe. Some things are simply driven by man's curiosity, whether this be in respect of outer space, the Galapagos Islands or the Amazon rainforest. Read National Geographic magazine for a mind opening dose of what awaits you in the big wide world.

Though if you happen to discover a jelly fish that excretes confectionary (eg. Jellybeans) and word gets out, then you can be sure that a 'scientific expedition' will be dispatched double-quick from the headquarters of the 'Imperial Sweet Corporation', or similar.

Afterthought: In such circumstances it would be wise to become the jellyfish's agent before the commercial snatch squads arrive.

Creative

Creativity cannot be confined to one category. Commercial marketers are creative, as are scientists. And even some accountants. But there are those who are driven by nothing more than the creation of art.

> *Such people help evolve society by causing us to reflect on our condition or be inspired by the capability of the human brain.*

Creativity does not need to be so profound. Some people rightly describe the digital economy as the attention economy. Every advert you encounter in a single day, along with every text and email in your inbox, is essentially someone or some organisation trying to steer you in line with their agenda. You can include online and offline content in the form of games, publications and broadcast media as tools to acquire your attention as well.

These attention seekers are under increasing pressure to get your attention and so need to employ more sophisticated techniques to achieve that, whether it be more zombies, sharper fangs, bigger explosions or more bells on the app. Thus the creative industry has emerged to provide the brain power to address this challenge.

Creative organisations are, not unsurprisingly, staffed by creative people. You will recognise 'creatives' because ironically they have a uniform comprising turtle neck jumpers, solid rimmed glasses and a ponytailed/hairless dome. Unconventional behaviour in comparison to their industrial economic workers is the convention. I am being a bit harsh, but only for the sake of my own personal amusement. You can draw your own conclusions.

> *But most importantly, creative people, whether purists or attention grabbers, get to use their brains in a potentially satisfying/rewarding manner.*

I say 'potentially' because you may not regard the application of your creative capacity to gain the attention of those so in need of a short term loan that they are interest-rate insensitive. Again, we all have bills to pay. So perhaps building a cash molehill by selling your skills to the highest bidder will enable you to eventually pursue creative endeavours that are neither constrained by economic necessity nor are morally questionable. Best of all would be to find an overlap between what you love to do and what the market requires. We will explore this in a later chapter.

Societal

Not everybody gets up in the morning with the primary aim of chasing the 'shiny shiny' or with a burning desire to express themselves through pastel shades/poetry.

There are those that are motivated purely by the greater good. The public and voluntary sectors provide ample opportunities to dedicate one's professional life to the wellbeing of one's fellow citizens, locally, nationally or even globally.

Many of those working for the benefit of society could easily make more money by working for a profit-focused firm, but they prefer to trade personal return for serving others.

I would not for a second suggest that this corner of the world of employment comprises solely Mother Teresas and Mahatma Gandhis.

Even in the societal sector, human nature being what it is leads to competitive behaviour.

Typically those working in the public sector are paid less than their profit-sector compatriots. Thus public sector workers cannot use remuneration as an absolute indicator of their status and power. Though admittedly they can, in some cases, use anticipated pension pot/retirement date as financial proxies.

So public sector workers tend to play a more subtle game that is measured by a combination of control over resources and influence over others. Consequently, the public sector tends to be more political in terms of how it operates. Those who have moved from the private sector to the public sector are often shocked by the importance of 'scheming skills' in getting things done.

To the outsider, it might appear that some people working in the public sector see helping the public as a secondary goal to building their own empire.

Such political behaviour is no doubt influenced by the politicians that pull the strings of these civil servants. It's important to point out that politics is neither good nor bad, it is simply in our nature.

The private sector is not immune from this. There are some companies that operate like a corporate version of the Medici family. Their CEOs believe that such internal competition actually stimulates productivity. It may also serve to weaken challengers to the CEO position from within the corporation if the contenders are consumed with fighting each other. But the clarity of profit coupled with a shortage of talent means that smart organisations today tend to promote a collaborative rather than combative culture.

Given that the public sector can be used as a political tool to massage the employment figures ie to create jobs, the pool of talent that public sector leaders can call upon tends to be quite large and not necessarily comprising the best and the brightest. Couple this with relatively strong employment rules, which makes getting rid of deadwood difficult/impossible, then the idea of operating as a slick dream team becomes almost farcical. Not all public sector departments are staffed by self-absorbed career protectionists, but it is a risk, and so you must choose a societal career path carefully.

But the public sector has the capacity to deliver great outcomes for society, and often does.

Bright and motivated people, disillusioned by the dynamics of the private sector, have moved into the public sector. This in turn is having a dilutive effect on the public sector being a poor second option to having a private sector career.

Plus, the public sector is not as subject to the economic cycles as the private sector. So there are times when it is the only 'game in town'. But, be aware that the public sector is not immune from economic reality.

Thus many governments are undergoing transformative change as they adjust to the digital economy. This is an opportunity for digitally-savvy workers.

However, if you are looking for a place to lie low until a generous retirement package kicks in, then with a rudimentary grasp of employment law, coupled with paid-up subs to a Trotskyite union, you will find the public sector to be a second home. Though this 'option' is dwindling, as the digital economy shifts into top gear.

Those genuinely trying to benefit society have to be very skilled at achieving outcomes despite these obstacles. Nonetheless, the public sector provides an avenue for those who want to make a positive impact on society.

For those who would like to combine doing 'good' with the commercial constraints associated with the private sector then the voluntary sector is the place to be.

> *It's a hypercompetitive market. There is no shortage of charities looking to harvest the consciences of those who prefer to donate money rather than time to charitable causes.*

Certain causes, for example cancer and children, can be considered industries in their own right because of the volume of players. To survive, let alone thrive, they need to be operationally efficient, marketing savvy and impressive 'sales' closers. My experience of working with business developers in the voluntary sector is that they would have no problem being very successful in the private sector.

To help people part with their discretionary funds, when there is so much competition, including the more selfish options of for example buying the latest tech gadget or upgrading their holiday hotel booking, is no mean feat. In some cases, this is because they in fact learnt their trade in the private sector.

I am not suggesting that the private sector lacks a heart, but the public and voluntary sectors offer a clear path for those looking to help their fellow humans.

Though admittedly, if you opt for a military career you may be forced at some point to make a decision over which group of humans you help.

Social enterprise

It is interesting to see the emergence of private organisations that are both driven by profit and making a positive societal impact.

This strikes me as a very happy medium. Economic security coupled with making a difference.

I might be overstating both these outcomes because there is tremendous skill turning an altruistic vision into a profitable enterprise.

This is a growth area. I sense it is one that will appeal to young people, particularly those who see humanitarianism as an important part of who they are.

Third world economies tend to be fertile territory for this type of work. But of course most of us don't have to travel too far to see the opportunity for, say, turning disaffected 'locals' into economically active contributors to society.

Or through building a micro-finance platform, provide those on the periphery of economic society, who cannot get a mainstream job, with the funding to start their own enterprise.

Entertainment

People often talk about so and so being a programming 'rock star'. Increasingly we hear of individuals who are rock star consultants or rock star leaders. Such a sobriquet suggests they are well known and in demand.

It might also suggest that they are arrogant prima donnas. (Note for aspiring 'rock stars': This is not the bit that clients are happy to pay for. So do not feel obliged to develop such behaviour.)

Traditionally being a rock star was limited to the entertainment industry; specifically that genre called rock music. Today, we can broaden that adulatory labelling to House DJs, boy bands and, country and western singers.

In fact we can broaden this to jugglers, mime artists, ventriloquists and hypnotists. Such people make a living by entertaining others. Their role is to entertain you. We can widen this category further into acting and professional sports.

If they can capture our attention then they have a value proposition. Their value may be released in the form of saleable content, events and endorsements. Those with mass appeal typically draw the most attention.

The more attention you can deliver the greater your value.

The world's fastest man might be more athletic than most professional footballers, but footballers generally attract a wider audience than track and field stars in most countries. So the footballers get paid more.

If you derive great pleasure from being watched, then the world of entertainment is a natural environment in which to develop your career.

Entertainers know that it isn't just what you do, but how you do it.

Top athletes that have a stylish graceful manner will command more than top athletes who have a particularly un-aesthetic manner of winning. Top athletes that have engaging personalities make more than monosyllabic winning machines.

The entertainment industry is Darwinian. If your offbeat emu (animal rather than policy-focused) ventriloquist act captures the public imagination, then you will float to the top of the entertainment food chain with ease and stay at the top for as long as you can keep the public engaged.

The competition is steep for those of us who decide to step into the mainstream as, say, a marathon runner or actor. You might subsequently discover that:

- Your lungs are too small.
- You are not attractive/visually interesting enough.

You have two choices:

- Settle on being a journeyman (pace maker, adverts and bit parts), so to speak.
- Find another career path that better fits your natural characteristics.

But it is important to point out that whether you have big lungs and/or beauty, there is still significant competition and so hard work is required to gain the attention of those that procure talent.

Even if you do not feel inclined to pursue a career as an entertainer, it is an industry worth researching. Reading the biographies of top athletes and famous actors will give you a sense of the extent to which focus, hard work and a pinch of luck are required to reach the top.

I would say that this is true for all of us who seek mastery in our career. Though some of us will have designed our paths such that we are in a market of one.

The upside of a market of one is that you are the natural choice. The downside is that most of your potential buyers may not even know that the services you offer exist, and thus they may struggle (at first) to understand why they should need your services.

Whilst you may not consider yourself a track athlete, it would be wise to design your career path as if you were one. Breaking the goal down into a set of discrete tasks, whereby each day you are able to take action to move you towards the Olympic gold, is a systematic approach.

From a career perspective, you want to ensure you end up with circa fifty years of rewarding experiences, rather than one year of experience repeated fifty times.

Hybrid

So far I have compartmentalised career options. The implication being that if you enter the public sector you cannot do research, or if you enter the private sector you cannot be an entertainer. Of course this is not true. Hybrid careers are common. Here are a few examples:

- Creatives in the public sector – Developing citizen-friendly apps optimised for dysfunctional families.
- Entertainers in the private sector – Public speakers specialising in leadership or the future of work.
- Discoverers in the entertainment sector – Scientists looking to create optimised sleep and nutrition plans for international athletes.

The possibilities are endless. Sometimes such careers are pursued by design. Sometimes they happen by chance. You might reflect on your career after, say, ten years, and notice that your seemingly random career path of working as a regulatory officer in the finance sector and technologist in the aviation sector could be repackaged.

It might turn out that you have the perfect credentials to be a technology compliance officer in the nascent space tourism industry.

There is no reason why you cannot segment your career life into a sequence of distinct career experiences. For example, you start your career on an accountancy apprenticeship on leaving school at 16. Ten years later, you are making great money, but feel that there is more to life than preying off those who do not understand basic arithmetic (This is a relatively controversial point to make. I have glossed over some minor details for both the purpose of amusement and to serve as a big red career warning sign).

You now want to engage your brain more deeply, so you become a research science assistant in the area of astrobiology. Over the next ten years, you acquire a doctorate and discover how to apply biosignature methods to retail marketing.

You patent the discovery and sell the patent to the world's largest advertising company. You are now financially secure for the rest of your life. You recognise that part of your good fortune was luck, so you decide to prove it wasn't a one off by becoming a venture capitalist with a view to investing in up and coming high tech companies.

Money seeks money. So you find yourself embarrassingly rich. You now feel a little self-conscious about your good fortune, so you decide to spend some time working in the outer reaches of the planet teaching arithmetic to tribal youngsters.

You realise you are a very limited resource, and so you create a small group of 'missionary arithmatists' (mainly former accountants who could no longer look at themselves in the mirror) to work across the five continents. It turns out that many of these tribespeople have cottoned on to the market value of their herbal remedies and other natural approaches to life. They want to take their local businesses global and public. This requires some serious financial skills.

Consequently and inadvertently you have developed the world's fastest growing accountancy practice. You are now ridiculously rich. Though out of jealousy, some people may remind you that, strictly speaking, you are still an accountant.

An alternative is to run parallel careers. Difficult but not impossible to do from day one. By day, you are a civil servant, By night, you are a stand-up comedian, novelist or emerging economies day trader (or a combination of all three).

The beauty of pursuing a path to mastery is that there comes a point when the market perceives you as a master, and at that point you call the shots.

You perhaps enjoy creating hats for the well-heeled, but you would like to spend a few days per week doing other things. The beauty of being in demand, and thus being increasingly exclusive, is that you will be able to charge more for your hat building services.

Exclusivity really does mean 'less equals more' from a financial perspective.

Demand may be such that you have to scale up your sole trader operation. You don't see yourself as a chief executive or business leader, so you hire one in. You now have a growing money machine, where you spend as much or as little time as you like influencing the creative direction of your headwear range.

You can now more comfortably pursue other career avenues in parallel. I have given you a couple of plausible journeys to illustrate the possibilities of a variegated career path.

Of course, these outcomes are not guaranteed. Subsequent chapters will show you how you can maximise your chances of engineering a highly desirable career journey.

A word of warning

Remember when it comes to man versus nature, nature wins. And when it comes to career versus market, the market wins. So I encourage you to stay open to opportunities. Just because your parents were highly in demand architects, it does not necessarily mean that once you are qualified the market will be equally welcoming.

Think of yourself as a surfer, who cannot control the waves, but can capitalise on their motion to broadly get where you want. Or you may simply be happy to just see where the waves take you.

Summary

Be aware that that there is a variety of options in respect of career paths. Your options may be limited by the fact that your town has only one main employer, which may be a tax office or car door maker, so there is economic and social pressure to follow the path of your friends and family. But these days, having access to the web enables you to pursue other career options in the evenings, rather than just pursuing activities after work that purely serve to dull the pain of being a factory cog.

The nature of careers today is that you are not obliged to pursue just one. You may have skills that buyers will pay for today, but if there is a big enough demand, someone will likely automate or industrialise your skill and thus puncture your value proposition.

We all need to keep acquiring new skills to remain economically relevant. Perhaps more importantly, we all need to keep acquiring new skills to simply enjoy a life of greater fulfilment.

Take action

- Get as many perspectives as you can on your career options, but do not treat any of them as being necessarily good advice. None of us really knows what lies ahead, but like great chess players, your next move needs to keep your options open for when you need to move again.

- Mentally visualise yourself pursuing various career paths. Does being an opera singer fill you with passion or does the idea of lifting a major trophy give you an adrenalin surge? Maybe helping those less fortunate than yourself is what will truly inspire you to jump out of bed each day? In any case, the more you can mentally simulate your career options to see how they feel emotionally, the more time you will save by not pursuing careers that whilst seeming socially attractive do not light your fire.

- Once you begin to get a feel for what you would like to do, start to conduct some research. Read the biographies of people who have successfully taken the paths you are considering. Try to really understand what the role comprises and how you acquire the necessary capabilities (knowledge, skills and even attitudes).

6   Career Frameworks

Overview

Having looked at career themes, we will now look at the different ways in which you can engage with the market. Ultimately, a career requires that someone pays in return for the value you deliver. If that part of your career is missing, you are in fact pursuing a hobby.

Let us now look at the pros and cons of the career frameworks open to you.

Permanent employment

This was the standard career path for the bulk of the industrial era. You were on the payroll of the employer, and in the earlier part of the industrial era it was unlikely that you would change employer throughout your 'career'. The majority of people in the developed world are in permanent employment.

There are some real benefits to permanent employment. These include:

- You can often focus on what you are good at. If you are an engineer who doesn't like sales, it is possible to focus your time on design and service provision, rather than convincing people to buy the service.
  - Similarly, if you are a sales person who doesn't like delivery.

- In well-established organisations, they will most likely have a slick on-boarding/induction programme that will give your productivity a boost when you are released onto the shop floor/live environment. From a chronological perspective, this is a very concentrated way to acquire the knowledge and skills needed to be of economic value to the organisation. All parties benefit from you being competent.
  - Such programmes may only be available to those leaving school or university. If you already have relevant work experience, you may well be expected to pick up any new skills required 'on the job'.
- Certain established brands look good on your resume. If you have spent time at a global brand, it typically makes you attractive to subsequent employers 'down the food chain'.
- Often there are well defined career structures, so you have a sense of making career progress.
- Big companies, in particular, can offer an ecosystem that enables you to explore many roles and work in many parts of the world.
- The remuneration package can be very attractive. But one must remember there is usually a correlation between package size and anxiety level.

There are downsides:

- It is sad to see people who have devoted their career to an employer being cast out after several decades. Such people have become institutionalised. They don't quite know how to operate beyond the confines of their sole employer. Possibly they have tied their career too closely to a product or a service that is now obsolete.
  - Remember employment is not like marriage, it is a ruthless commercial agreement (I may have this the wrong way around).

- Increasingly volatile markets make it difficult for employers to forecast their staffing needs. So even if you are a new arrival, you should be under no illusion that you are all set for a long career with your new employer. Don't take it personally if you find yourself back on the street. At worst, it was a resourcing mistake. Though it might have been that they were looking for a compliant corporate cog, but by acquiring you, they inadvertently took delivery of an inquisitive, challenging and boat-rocking free thinker.

- Large corporations, in particular, are naturally conservative. They became successful through taking chances, but are now more focused on protecting the status quo, as they now have something to lose (eg. share price, brand value and/or customers). Thus a focus on operational efficiency dominates, and innovation, beyond the realms of improving operational efficiency, is frowned upon. The end game for such organisations is to achieve more or less one hundred percent automation. At best you would be a placeholder for a piece of software/robot.

- The shininess of the remuneration package may be too compelling. If your ego/self-worth is tied to your remuneration, you will be susceptible to the 'come hither' draw that plays on your need for social affirmation/greed. Before you know it you have acquired the property, land and chattels of 'success'. In the short intervals between working, you will be 'living the dream'. However, once you get on this particular treadmill, it is difficult to dismount. Your souped-up lifestyle requires you to make your primary focus in life continued employment with your high paying employer. The idea that a recession might be around the corner would be too much to even consider. I recall working at an investment bank as a freelancer. I sat alongside people whose first item on their daily to do list was to cross off yesterday's entry on the calendar (there was a time when calendars were tangible, fixed location tools you could actually write on), thereby highlighting they were getting ever closer to their next holiday. They literally hated their job, but they were addicted to the remuneration. Software eventually put them out of their misery.

- Consolidating markets can lead to frequent acquisition. Each acquisition is a source of stress, as you wait to establish whether you have 'survived' the restructure. Today it is possible to have a career, whereby through most of it, you are escorted by this dark cloud of uncertainty.

Freelancing

Freelancing is an employment model, whereby you engage with the employer as a supplier rather than an employee. That is to say, you are selling your capability and not your loyalty. The loyalty piece is perhaps inaccurate. Not all permanent employees are loyal to their employer, but it is hoped, by HR at least, that permanent employees will feel part of the team.

As a freelancer, you do not always get to enjoy the perks of being a permanent employee, eg. having access to the company sports centre or attending the annual company bash. Though in some jurisdictions, employers have to offer the same benefits to freelancers as to their permanent staff.

The benefits as I see them:

- You are paid to do a job and so can get on with it without getting caught up in office politics. Ambitious permanent employees need to devote a percentage of their working day to politics/'pecking order' matters.
- Whilst many perceive being a freelancer as riskier than permanent employment from a financial security perspective, the reality is that it is not. As a freelancer, you are a hunter gatherer. Over time you become skilled at securing food, or starve. Permanent staff get used to having their food delivered, so to speak, and thus when they are released back into the wild they are ill-equipped to survive.

- Companies used to limit their use of freelancers to low level administrative work. Over time this has extended into skilled work such as software engineering. Today the CEO can be a freelancer (though the term 'interim' is preferred at that end of the market). Thus there are very few roles for which freelancers are banned. Though this does vary from country to country. The UK, for example, embraces freelancing wholeheartedly. Whereas other developed countries still correlate a permanent career path with social standing, and so freelancers are akin to drop outs (though typically very well paid drop outs).

- Freelancers tend to get paid considerably more than permanent staff, though various governments are doing what they can to reduce the advantage. This is poor policy and will simply drive talented people to economies where their value is valued.

- If you are good at what you do, then you will have no trouble finding work. Thus, you can cherry pick the opportunities. Not all freelancers want to find their own work. They just prefer to turn up, do it well, and get paid very well for it. Essentially this is the service recruitment agencies provide, and so many freelancers will use them to secure their next gig.

Of course there are some downsides too:

- As a freelancer, you are a resource to get something done, whether that be design a new IT system, write a series of white papers, train the sales force, or upgrade the customer database. You are expected to be able to do the job well. Think effective and tidy plumber, though ideally without the cheerful whistling.
  - o Actually I like this reality, as it provides clarity in terms of expectation. If you do a good job, you tend to get more jobs to do. The client also tends to treat you more respectfully, if you are more central to their objectives. But at the other extreme, there are clients that won't even offer you a cup of tea, when you arrive to fix their bathroom tap. They would rather you were not there and are keen for you to go as soon as possible.
- Circumstances can change quickly for the client. So unless you have a contractual agreement that includes cancellation clauses, you could find yourself out on the street with little notice.

- o Many freelancers operate on a time and materials basis. "I will be paid for the time I apply to your requirements along with any expenditure I incur in the process". I personally don't like this model, as it encourages freelancers to string out assignments, rather than focus on getting the job done.
- Clients do not care about your career path or personal development goals. You are expected to arrive fully competent. They are not expecting to invest in your skills, unless it is critical to the task at hand. So you need to be prepared to plough back some of your earnings into your own development.
  - o And development is costly for freelancers. Not only do you have to pay for it, but whilst you are acquiring these new skills, let's say on a training course, you have lost the opportunity to do paid work. Permanent employees do not have this concern. They are getting paid whether they are doing real work or sitting in a classroom.
- When the market turns south, there is no economic umbrella to hide below. Permanent employees can often ride an economic storm because they are in an important role, or the organisation is creative in how they keep their people on board. Though redundancies are a reality for everybody in a downturn.
  - o Again freelancers will be the first out the door, unless you are in some way critical to the organisation's survival.

Hybrid freelancer

There is also a hybrid freelancer. This is a model whereby you are engaged as a freelancer (from the client's perspective), but you are in fact a permanent employee.

Consultancies, software houses and accountancy firm are examples of hybrid employees.

Such firms trade in brainpower. This ranges from selling individuals on a 'time and materials' basis (good old fashioned labour), to selling complete teams on a fixed price basis. In the latter case, once the price is agreed, the agreed outcome will be delivered, regardless of the number of people required.

This hybrid-freelancer approach offers a number of advantages:

- You work for an organization, which, through its size and reach, can assign you to work that you would never encounter through your own marketing activity or via a recruitment agency.
  - o Though initially, the recruitment agency might find you this employer.
- You have some security. You will be paid even when you are not on assignment (ie hired out to a paying client). Though if you spend too much time 'on the bench', you will be shown the door.
- You enjoy the benefits of permanent employment in terms of paid holiday, pension plan and so on. Plus you get to attend company social events.
  - o Though such events are really designed to ensure that the field operatives (ie. you) do not go native (ie. take up permanent employment with the client) as a result of spending too much time in the client's environment. Think intelligence agency that, from time to time, calls its spies back to headquarters.
- You typically get paid better than those on the client-side who are doing a similar job.
- The employer will invest in your personal development. Though this can drop to zero during market downturns, unless the investment is very likely to improve your saleability.
- In a relatively short period of time, you can gain a great variety of experience. I worked for an international system integrator for seven years. It felt as if I gained twenty years of experience in the process.

The downsides:

- Your employer takes the lion's share of the fee. This is understandable. They have infrastructure and a salesforce to maintain. The role of the latter being, in effect, to find your next assignment.
- You get treated by the client's permanent employees with the disdain generally reserved for genuine freelancers. So the 'remuneration to disdain' ratio is unfavourable compared to being a genuine freelancer.
  - Not all clients behave in this way, but some do.
- You can be sent anywhere in the world. As a young person, the travel bit is exciting. Less so if you are a home bird or have a family with whom you like to spend time.
- You could be assigned any job. Again, as a young person, almost any experience is good experience. This hybrid model has the potential to enable you to try a variety of career appetizers before you decide which one really appeals. However, it is equally likely that you could be assigned to a soul-destroying role, with a septic client, for the full duration of your time with your employer. That's the nightmare scenario. But I have to say that it is at least worth having one such experience in your career (for a limited time). If only to appreciate how generally lucky you are.
- You are often pushed into situations where you have been sold in as the expert. That is why the client is willing to pay the big bucks for you. However, on day one at the client's premises, you may well be the least qualified worker in the building. This happened to me on a number of occasions. However, the risk of being found out was a natural accelerant to getting up to speed very quickly.
  - This can be very stressful. But some would argue that getting such exposure was a hyper-efficient way to acquire new skills, and so such situations are really opportunities. On reflection I would agree. Though at the time, at best, I would have considered them the perfect cure for constipation.

Most young people will stay two or three years, tops, at such firms. The nomadic existence does not appeal to everyone. People will typically move on to something more permanent using the brand of their departing employer as a lever to gain a healthy salary in their new role. I stayed for seven years, because I was gaining great experience and knew that I could cash in my experience chips at some point in the future. On reflection this was a good move.

Something to keep in mind about the hybrid freelancer role is that employers in this field like young people because:

- They generally have lower salary expectations. Typically they have yet to settle down or to have a personal divorce lawyer on short-dial.
- They are more malleable and thus easier to manage.
- They are more likely to consider it cool to receive a phone call on Sunday night to say that they need to be at the airport tomorrow morning at 6am, where they will receive more details of the assignment.
  - o Woe betide the consultant who mentions 'school play' during that conversation.

However if you are experienced and very good at what you do, you can call the shots. But if that really is the case, you do not need an employer of hybrid freelancers to find gigs for you.

Entrepreneur

It has never been easier to set up a new business from an infrastructure perspective. There are tools available on the web to cover the majority of things that all businesses need. Increasingly these tools are available on a utility model basis, so you just 'pay as you use'.

There are a variety of online services that enable you to acquire expertise and to pay for it on a project by project basis.

Some jobs are so relatively trivial that it is not worth engaging a recruitment agency to source the talent you require. They won't be interested in running a campaign to build a shortlist of candidates who are all vying for the opportunity to produce a cartoon for your home page.

Twenty years ago the decision to become an entrepreneur, and start your own business, was fraught with risk.

Is it the right move to leave your safe corporate job? Will anyone buy my product? How will I manage the IT side of my business? Today, you can set up your business in a few hours at the weekend and test drive the market appetite through a variety of low cost marketing techniques, without having to take any of the above risks. If it turns out your great idea is not so great, then you simply abandon the project and try something else.

I would suggest that everyone tries at least once to be an entrepreneur. Don't expect to be a billionaire unless your proposition is naturally viral and capitalises on human behaviour. Keep in mind that the other key conditions of timing and luck must not be underestimated. Though the harder you try, the luckier you will likely get.

Not all entrepreneurs start out as specialists. Unlike freelancers, they often do not have expertise in what the market needs. But they do have expertise in spotting a market need and rallying resources to capitalise on that need. Some of us find managing people stressful. Good entrepreneurs are experts at achieving results through others and making those others feel good about being involved.

But freelancers can be entrepreneurs too.

Once they migrate away from doing what is asked of them on a client by client basis, and start to package up their capability into a series of services and/or products, then the freelancer is in effect a one person entrepreneur. I would encourage freelancers to strive towards this, as it leads to a better financial return on your time/expertise.

One might say that the difference between a freelancer and an entrepreneur is that, over time, the latter focuses less on the operational parts of the business and more on growing the business. When recruiters call to sell you people, rather than to buy your capability on behalf of their clients, you will know that you have moved from freelancer to entrepreneur.

Again there is no reason why those pursuing a 'permanent' career path cannot explore entrepreneurism. When I first started out, my conditions of employment stated that not only could I only work for my employer, but any free thinking in my own time that led to something of value would also be owned by the employer. Do not be so commercially innocent. Looking back, I do regret:

- Not patenting my idea of hyper-texting online documents across a network using the TCPIP protocol.
- Sharing the idea with an English scientist based at Cern.

Semi-retirement

The notion of retirement is disappearing with the industrial era. Semi-retirement is a more realistic path, because it is unlikely that your company pension will fully meet your needs in retirement. In any case, many people retiring today are at the top of their game from a wisdom perspective and so look to keep their hand in by doing occasional assignments that fit in with their post-work lifestyle.

My view (and approach) is that semi-retirement does not have to commence once you reach the retirement age decreed by your employer or government.

There is no reason that if you have managed your path to mastery carefully, you cannot semi-retire whilst still young. You may need to reconsider your discretionary spending habits and social aspirations. But if you value your free time, then semi-retirement will enable you to have three, four, five, or even six day weekends.

Some smart entrepreneurs build their own empires and appoint a CEO to manage them. This allows them to sit by the pool all day sipping pina coladas and occasionally tapping into their online banking app to monitor their growing fortune, in real-time. Some entrepreneurs, who perhaps started off as freelancers, appoint themselves head of research and development, so that they can continue to innovate and do what they really love.

Recruitment agencies

I have commented on the recruitment sector in earlier chapters. They are under pressure to raise their game, as both clients and candidates have ways of disintermediating them.

As the talent shortage becomes more acute, I anticipate the recruitment agencies shifting their loyalty from the clients to the candidates.

I am also seeing agencies enter the hybrid-freelancer market. This requires them to hire talent on a permanent basis in order to have greater control over their talent pool. The difference from their traditional model is that the talent will continue to be paid in between assignments. Recruitment agencies, like consultancies, will strive to achieve 100 per cent utilisation of their talent pool.

As mentioned, some recruitment firms are moving beyond the body shopping of individuals to taking on multi-person projects. This requires a different operating model, and not all firms will be capable of embracing the riskier fixed-price approach. However, for those that get this right, there is a good chance that they will be more generous in sharing the spoils with the talent.

Recruitment firms typically operate very lean business models and so can offer more competitive pricing than the big players, with their large overheads. It's too early to say how the recruitment industry will evolve. Currently, they are an important part of the work eco-system. So you are encouraged to get to know which firms have both a good reputation and can demonstrate, through action, what they can do to add value to your career. Visiting employee feedback websites and looking at the organisation's corporate and social responsibility report/statements are good starting points.

Summary

You have a variety of career frameworks to choose from. The popularity of these will change as the digital economy evolves. There is no reason why you cannot sample each of these throughout your career or even run some of them in parallel, eg. allocating three days a week to permanent employment and the rest to freelancing.

Do not be put off by the prospect of being an entrepreneur. Growing an empire enables you to deliver value on a larger scale. It has never been easier to explore this path, and I would go as far as to say that in the digital economy it would be foolish not to try.

Take action

- If you go down the permanent route, look beyond the pay and establish whether the organization you have in mind as an employer provides an induction programme. Establish what their general philosophy is in respect of developing their people.
  - Consider whether the job will take you further along your path to mastery. The experience you gain today should lead to greater remuneration/options down the road. So the financial package, above what is needed to live comfortably (ie not fretting about making ends meet), is a secondary consideration. At least for those at the outset of their career.
- Much like visiting the emphysema ward as a shock therapy approach to quitting smoking, I recommend you join the commute into any of the world's leading financial centres for a day or two, and register the well-heeled, yet dead-eyed commuters. You won't be able to see the golden handcuffs, but they are there. Appealing?
- Take a look at what tools are available to entrepreneurs. There is also plenty of content online on how to become an entrepreneur.
  - Beware: There are also a lot of sharks selling services to would-be entrepreneurs. Their websites tend to comprise very long sales letters, designed to convince you as to why you need their services. Words such as 'bonus' and 'cha-ching' (or any textual representation of the noise a cash register makes) are red flags in respect of such predators.

7 The Magic Triangle

Overview

If you have patiently read the previous chapters, you will be developing a strong sense of the environment in which you will be navigating your career path. Now we are going to explore how you can load the dice to ensure you enjoy a successful career.

There are three key elements we need to consider in terms of a successful career. Let us look at these in turn:

Demand

There are two schools of thought on demand. By demand, I mean whether there is a market for your value proposition:

- If there is a demand for your capability, you are more likely to convert that capability into money than if there is no demand.
- A lack of demand is no indicator of the absence of a potential market. Nobody wanted a tablet computer before the iPad, or car before Ford started making them.

In reality, whilst demand might be a good indicator of a fertile market, unless there is a sufficiently high demand, or a sufficiently low delivery capacity, your income will be low.

There is a big global demand for burger flippers. However there is a surplus of suitably qualified burger flippers.

You might go with Henry Ford's or Steve Jobs' approach of igniting market demand. That is typically very expensive. Not all new products gain instant traction with the market. (Read up on the Apple Newton).

Do not enter a new market unless you have some evidence that there is a demand. Just because your first job paid you for your unique ability to code Java and juggle chainsaws, it would be unwise to market that unique combination of skills unless you were sure that the market was substantially larger than one buyer with a one-off requirement.

Increasing globalisation is leading to increased market competition. If you want the best jobs in your field, you increasingly need to be the best in the world. If that seems like a tall order, then 'niche up'. By uniquely combining skill sets, you can in effect create a new market in which you are, by default, the top player. As discussed this is risky. But you may already have acquired the skills, so all that is needed here is to test demand by playing around with how you position yourself (ie how you label yourself in your LinkedIn professional headline).

An alternative niching approach is to descope your target market.

Perhaps you have decided that you would like to be an oncologist. The food industry is creating a great demand for your services, but there is a glut of cancer specialists. So you take a look at the statistics and note that bowel cancer is underserviced. So that becomes your speciality. If that market becomes saturated because people start eating more healthily, you may need to niche further into, say, a focus on people under the age of 30. This may not be the best example. The point being that you must specialise to the extent that your focus (and associated competence) is sufficiently in demand to meet your economic/career satisfaction needs.

Most people have economic needs. So you need to ensure your job funds your chosen lifestyle. I would say that economic needs is a shrinking subset of career satisfaction.

Other factors include the extent to which:

- I am benefiting society/humanity.
- The work is stimulating.
- The work I do takes me along my path to mastery.
- I get to engage with interesting people.
- I get to experience different sectors and cultures.

I cover this is some detail elsewhere in terms of what workers increasingly expect.

Keep in mind that an indicator of market demand is the extent to which you sense the power lies with you or the buyer/employer. A high remuneration package is the industrial era indicator of demand. In the digital economy, Twitter followers is a rough indication. Study your competitors (I have given up on challenging Lady Gaga). That will give you a ball park sense of the follower count you should use as a benchmark. Keep in mind it is better to have a low number of potential buyers following you than a high volume of sociopathic trolls. Also follower measure doesn't apply to all career paths, particularly if social media is banned in your geo-market.

Be very clear as to the difference between what the market needs and what the market wants. As a subject matter expert you may have great insights into what your target market genuinely needs. But if your market doesn't share your view, you will find it very difficult to move forward career wise unless you have the evangelical skills and energy to turn that need into a want. Ultimately it is easier to sell people what they want.

School children, transitioning into the world of work, might typically seek the advice of their school's career advisor. Possibly they would be driven by what their parents thought best or perhaps by a teacher who inspired them to pursue a certain path.

I am amazed/terrified/uplifted by the extent to which quality TV is influencing the next generation; 'Silicon Valley' (IT professionals) and 'The Big Bang Theory' (physicists and engineers) come to mind.

These different approaches towards career assessment can be considered as events or, as some of my examples suggest, literally a series of events (plus repeats). My view is that in the digital economy, these career pre-embarkation activities need to turn into career long habits. In the extreme, we need to sleep with one eye open. In other words we need to constantly monitor the market. Are there new apps emerging that will reduce your capability to a 99 cent investment, or are there converging trends that, with a little up-skilling on your part, might make for an even more rewarding career path?

If you do not monitor market demand, you will by default have chosen to hermetically seal yourself from reality. Never good.

Competence

Your ability to deliver value will have a direct bearing on your reputation, which is the key currency of the digital economy. You may be able to fool a few buyers of your services, but eventually you will be found out.

In my experience, large cities tend to attract the incompetent, because the pool of buyers is so large that you can move from one to another delivering poor service for quite some time before you run out of victims, or before the word spreads. This doesn't work in small cities or towns where everybody knows everybody, and where once you 'blot your copybook', you are damaged goods. In fairness, big cities also attract the highly competent, because that is where the big paying buyers tend to reside. But as more and more business is conducted via the web, geography becomes less of a factor.

In the social economy, regardless of whether we live in a big city or a McDonalds'-free hamlet, for all intents and purposes we live in a virtual village. Gossip spreads like wildfire online. In the social economy, social success begets professional success. Your reputation determines whether your career accelerates or comes to a screeching halt.

In the introduction we talked about your value proposition. In summary it comprises:

- Your skill.
- Your experience.
- Your behaviour.

Your path to mastery should address all three of these.

Buyers of your capability want to know that you have the skills to do the job. They also want to know that you have had relevant experience, so that if things don't go as planned, you will bring that experience to bear to recover the situation.

Most roles have a social element to them. For people under a certain age, that is not the same as having a Facebook account. So the manner in which we engage with others, including our boss, colleagues, subordinates (a great industrial era term right up there with minion) and clients is a significant element of our competence set.

The path to mastery is the path to improving one's competence. Though the field boundaries may shift as macroeconomic forces and fashion impact market demand. It is all very well developing your sword skills as a Samurai warrior, but they are of limited value if the competition carries an MP5 or an AK-47.

Charting your competency growth through the turbulent market tempest is a challenge. Like all seafarers in such situations, it pays to always keep at least one eye on what is happening around you (soft focus) and one eye on what lies ahead (laser focus). Health warning: Qualified opticians would likely add a caveat that one should not simultaneously use each eye for different purposes, but rather flit between short and long range usage of both eyes.

In the digital economy, career planning is a daily habit not an 'event' that is attended a few times in your life. We will explore career agility in more detail, later on in the book.

Passion

Passion is a tricky one. Unlike competence, you cannot attend a course that specifically turns your interest in, say, physics into an all-consuming passion, whereby eating and sleeping become secondary considerations.

Course objectives:

1) You will understand the practical applications of quantum entanglement.
2) You will feel strong and barely controllable emotions whenever the topic is mentioned.

Though inadvertently, you might attend a lecture or read a book that ignites your passion for a given subject or career path.

Passion is the propellant that will fuel your career journey. If you lack passion, you will be dragged along career wise by your economic requirements. If you feel real passion for your chosen field, then all sorts of amazing things happen:

- The quality of your work improves.
- You progress much quicker along your path to mastery than less passionate people on the same path.
- People want to support your progression, because we tend to empathise with the passion of others and are often inspired by that passion.
- Buyers feel more inclined to buy services from people who are genuinely passionate about their 'art'. The buyer knows that you are unlikely to require significant management if you are self-motivated and live to do great work.
- You tend to be happier, or at least you spend less time reflecting on whether you are living your best life. As you get older, the cognitive burden in this respect can become significant.

A search for passion may well also take you off the career path groove you have settled into. King Edward the Eighth of the United Kingdom comes to mind.

When I engage with passionate service providers, I sense that their focus is not on raiding my wallet, but more on working with me to deliver a great outcome.

As an example of the significance of this: I often work with very large technology firms. They are undergoing an existential crisis, where their business models are under siege. Some of these firms have been traditionally sales rather than service driven. They send an army of sales people out into the market with the objective to seek out opportunities and convert them into sales.

They have to make their numbers, so the closer they get to the end of the current reporting period (end of quarter, end of year), the more aggressive/desperate their sales approach. Sometimes buyers are manipulated into buying what they didn't need. But that wasn't an issue, because once they were signed up, it didn't really matter whether they used the software licences or installed hardware.

But the world has changed, and increasingly buyers are demanding a more utility based approach, ie "we will pay for what we use".

If we don't use your hardware or software this week, we will pay nothing. This model is gaining traction. So the vendors are now focused on utilisation. This shifts the focus from sales to service.

Engaging with clients is now moving from a 'hit and run' sales model to a consultative service utilisation model. Smart tech firms are coming up with new and helpful ways in which their clients can consume their service. Again the more they consume, the more they pay.

Those that service the clients after the deal is done will determine, through their consultative skills, to what extent the client uses the service. Competence will drive utilization, as will passion. Sales/service professionals, regardless of sector, who both know their stuff and are genuinely excited about how their offering can help the customer are the most likely to garner trust, and consequently encourage greater utilisation.

Bottom line: Service is the new sales. Passion is key.

Think of all the service encounters you have had from restaurant waiters through to call centre operators. How many of them have you dealt with who clearly hate what they do and are disengaged from the experience of serving you? Whilst at the same time, there are people who radiate passion and who by virtue of that passion lift the spirits of those they encounter. Not all of these people are faking it to boost your spend/tip.

Some people have the ability to commit to what they do and do it to the best of their ability from a competence and passion perspective. Being social animals, our level of passion will determine how attractive we are to others. Are you a 'new battery' that charges those who come into contact with you? Or are you an emotional sink that drains down the spirits of those unfortunate enough to cross your path?

Passion sharpens our senses. We are more likely to see opportunity and threats. Whilst everyone might be aware of the pile of old magazines in the doctor's waiting room, you spot a reference to a career-relevant article on the cover of one of the magazines. Passion increases the likelihood that we will spot opportunities that propel us along our career path. Maybe passion is the key to 'making your own luck'?

Those with the greatest passion tend to get pushed to the front of the tribe. Those that lack passion (or are passion-negative) get drummed out. I would argue that passion kept our ancestors alive, and passion has, no doubt, played a role in our continued existence as a species.

If you lack passion for what you do, even though you are both in demand and highly competent, I would encourage you to explore ways of reframing what you do to ignite the passion. Alternatively find something that causes you to attack each day with a deep sense of purpose.

Employers also have a responsibility to create the conditions to ignite and grow passion. Smart employers get this.

2 out of 3 will not do

Many people have two of the three conditions required for career success. Looking at these in turn:

Competence and passion: The absence of market demand implies that, at best, you have an engaging hobby. This is not going to pay the bills.

Again, creating demand requires resources. I suggest you look for genuine market demand that overlaps with your competence and passion, and package yourself accordingly.

Passion and demand: The absence of competence suggests you are incompetent. Something of a deal breaker when it comes to selling one's services.

There is a variety of approaches to addressing this, including studying, mentoring, volunteer work and shadowing competent colleagues.

Competence and demand: The absence of passion probably earns you the nickname 'Buzzkill'. That is perhaps an extreme reference. But it is quite likely that if you are not really into what you spend most of your life doing, then the chances are that you are heading that way.

You need to be clear as to what 'makes you tick'.

It may be that by just mentally reframing your role, you will create the necessary congruence to ignite your pilot light.

A successful career requires all three elements to be in place. If you have chosen a career path and it's not going well, the chances are that you have one or more of these elements missing.

Summary

Ignore the magic triangle at your peril. It doesn't take too long for people to detect incompetence. Each one of us starts from a position of incompetence. If your path to mastery is not moving the dial in this respect, then you had best re-evaluate your learning plan.

Many people try to impose their will on the market based on their perception of what is best. Often, this is based on genuine insight. But, if the market doesn't respond, then it would be better to swim with the tide, ie. quickly establish what it is that the market wants that you can deliver on a professional basis. It took me a while to realise this.

Regardless of whether your work is challenging or not, or highly paid or not, if it drains you emotionally, it may be time to rethink your career plan, or even your attitude. I recall a period of my career where I spent a considerable amount of time delivering classroom training. It wore me down.

1. ... 10:37 here comes the open source joke
2. ... Pause
3. ... Delegates laugh...

I could hear myself going through the motions and was regularly in danger of wearing out the classroom clock. But eventually I realised that my perspective was self-centred and that I had a great opportunity to help young people at the outset of their careers and make a real difference to the quality of their professional lives.

Having reframed the situation, from then on I was genuinely fired up when I was in the classroom. I even started to laugh at my own jokes again. Good times.

Take action

- Choose your career path carefully. An absence of demand is a bad sign. The situation may change next month though. Or in two decades. So base your plans on today's realities. If that changes tomorrow, then you change with it. Careers need to be conducted in real-time.

- Reflect market demand by ensuring you refine your craft and how you promote your craft, so that you are known to be highly competent. Again, not just highly competent, but known to be highly competent. Self-promotion, as we will cover in a later chapter, is a key competence for those pursuing post-industrial careers.

- Many musicians fail to find commercial success, despite the quality of their work. This is a competence issue. Specifically, it is a marketing competence issue. In the digital economy, we are all brand-sensitive micro-corporations. More specifically, we are all brands.

- You may not be passionate by nature. There is possibly a correlation between the latitude of your homeland and the extent to which you are overtly passionate. But by passion, I don't necessarily mean your tendency to throw crockery around the room, shout, cry, or embark on frantic upper limb gesticulation marathons. If you live near the North Pole, passion may take the form of quiet determination coupled with a faint smile. No doubt a characteristic of successful Siberian parcel delivery staff. Our professional lives will increasingly be entwined with our personal lives. A lack of passion is going to taint your life. Passion is your career propellant. Ensure you have a full tank.

8 The Way of the Warrior

Overview

I make reference to both mastery and the path to mastery throughout this book. In this chapter we explore the process of becoming a master.

What is mastery?

Mastery implies great expertise or capability. An experienced person might even say that they have mastered the skills associated with their professional value proposition. They have conquered these skills and subjugated them, such that they can be applied to the delivery of the outcomes they and their clients expect. This of course may equally apply to a Norse god. And perhaps to some onlookers, watching an expert do their thing can create feelings of awe.

Certain professions formally confer the status of master, for example, master baker or master chef. In other areas, mastery is achieved through a formal system as found in say chess (points) or martial arts (belts).

One can even achieve academic mastery by studying a master's degree. Though very few people who have recently taken possession of a master's degree will claim to be a master of their subject. Master's degrees are often a stepping stone to a higher level of research or study that leads to a doctorate. Some may acquire such a qualification as a career-boosting investment. So a master's degree, or a doctorate for that matter, for all their academic and social value, usually happen at the apprentice-end of the path to mastery.

For some of us, mastery will be reflected by the demand for our services, and the price people are willing to pay (any Hollywood star). Or it may be in the impact we make on humanity as a whole (eg. Mother Teresa, Genghis Khan).

Mastery and recognition do not necessarily go hand in hand. Being a world authority at what you do does not mean you will become a household name. Very few people can name the world's top ten all-time cross country runners, despite their superhuman endeavours and cruel training regimes.

Being a master in what you do may be something only you truly recognise. But that doesn't matter, as you have taken this path because it is important to you, and you alone. You do not choose your path to give your parents something to boast about or to appear interesting to those you are trying to impress.

The path to mastery is not necessarily the path to fame or even fortune. But it could be.

Best to think of your path to mastery as one that leads you to acquire the capabilities you need in order to be the best at something that you find meaningful, and the market finds valuable.

The idea of choosing a profession implies that you would like to enter a career structure that already exists. You hope that your chosen profession exist for the duration of your working life. Or at long enough for your associated effort investment to deliver a substantial return beyond its cost.

We have needed doctors and soldiers for a very long time. Architects, lawyers and hairdressers for quite some time too.

But there is no guarantee that these will be flourishing career options in the next decade or two. In part because they may well be either automated or simply unnecessary.

Off the shelf?

If you choose to become the best military leader in the world, it is very likely that your nation has at least some of the following career paths in place:

- Navy.
- Air force.
- Army.

Nationally you have 'arrived' when you earn the title, General or Admiral. You probably have to have actively engaged in a war or two. Taking control of the enemy's military definitely makes you promotion material. For older people, world wars come to mind. For younger people, think team-based Hunger Games.

There are also structures of progression for lawyers, doctors and other established professionals. Thus, they offer you an 'off the shelf' mastery path. As such, it is all neatly laid out. You simply have to achieve the criteria to move from rung to rung up the ladder.

However many of you will have to design your own path to mastery because:

- Your chosen profession is not sufficiently evolved to offer a formal path.
- Your chosen profession doesn't exist yet.
- You haven't chosen a profession.

The IT industry is an example of an industry that is relatively new, circa 50 years old, and has yet to develop a clear path to mastery.

Some countries have frameworks that involve examinations and experience. But there is no global standard. And in any case, does becoming a master in IT mean being the smartest techie, the most operationally effective CIO (Chief Information Officer), or the most well-paid CEO of a technology firm? Possibly there should be three mastery paths for IT. But even techie roles can be subdivided into specific programming languages, information security, data science and so on.

But most importantly, does anybody care? Where there is no formal mastery path, employers are unlikely to ask where you are on your path. They will take a view based on your alleged experience/track record and pay little attention to qualifications.

This dawned on me around three years into my path. I was in transition from an engineering company, where I was involved in naval ship systems, to one focused on general IT services. The latter focused on whatever the market wanted and so had divisions that mapped onto the main industry markets (finance, utilities, government and so on). In the engineering firm, we went through an 'apprenticeship' of circa eighteen months.

There was a degree of formality in this process, because they could not afford to have substandard programmers 'contaminating' the mission critical systems they were selling. With the service provider, they just shoved you onto the client's site. As I mentioned earlier, you either got up to speed pretty quickly or drowned in a pool of your own humiliation. That business model worked well, because they generally employed very bright graduates or people with some experience (me in this case).

Not long after I started with my second employer, I broke my arm in a public demonstration of how NOT to do judo. More Johnny English than James Bond, a stomach throw resulted in me redirecting all my bodyweight onto my forearm causing it to crack in half midway down. A messy business involving a torn artery, a haemorrhaging arm and my plans for the evening going out the window.

Fearful of losing the arm, I endeavoured to stay alert as I arrived at the hospital. The long queue to be examined was offset by the 'all you can inhale' morphine tank (with user interface attached) that was propped up against my stretcher bed. Four operations and several hospital stays later, I was fully functioning from a damaged arm perspective.

What really struck me during my time in hospital, was that both the doctors and nurses, who worryingly at the time seemed to be about my age, conducted themselves very professionally. They were both very knowledgeable and had a very good bedside manner. I felt safe and in good hands. At the time, it made me think how I wanted to conduct my career as if I was the equivalent of a medical professional in my own industry (IT). But as we didn't have the formal steps, I would have to create my own path.

Working for an organisation that could send you anywhere in the world at short notice, to do anything vaguely related to IT, it was unlikely that I could design my mastery path down to the level of determining which experiences I would acquire, and in which order.

However, I decided that at least I could control my attitude and service ethic. And regardless of what I was working on, I would develop a world view that would give both my clients some perspective on why they needed to invest in new technologies.

Beyond that, my career to date has had a Brownian motion feel to it. Such is the nature of moving with the market. But I do believe I have come some way in respect of my intended objective.

As I enter my fourth career decade, I notice that I am paying more attention to the remaining part of my journey. What might have started out as hacking through the career jungle, has now become more akin to 'career topiary'.

My long winded point being that just because a mastery path doesn't exist, it doesn't mean you cannot create one.

As bulleted above, many of tomorrow's key roles do not exist today.

Some of us will be doing things for the first time in history, eg. managing a team of robot garbage collectors, installing 3D printers/teleporters, or proofreading the output of software generated news content. Maybe you will be an architect of subterranean urban parks or a musician whose work is based on the natural occurrence of fractals. Maybe mastery means leading a bigger team or designing bigger parks. Perhaps it is more humanitarian? Perhaps it is to make the world a cleaner place or reducing crime through better urban design?

You will have to identify which path you will take. And much like the smart woodchopper who spends most of the allocated time sharpening their saw, you may spend the majority of your career trying to establish what it is that truly gives your life meaning. But of course, all the better if you can make the discovery early on in your career. Hopefully this book will encourage you to make this a priority.

Not having chosen a profession is not an issue. Sitting around all day gorging on box sets and YouTube is. Get stuck in. Most experience is good experience, particularly if you learn how to collaborate with others and engage with customers. Like Thomas Edison with his 10,000 attempts at creating a light bulb, if your initial choice of work repels you, then you have successfully narrowed down the search for your ideal career.

Increasingly, career paths will be tailored and will require regular reviews and pivots. Perhaps this is an opportunity for the recruitment industry – 'bespoke career paths for those going places'.

From zero to mastery

Assuming you have identified a market where your passion is matched by market appetite, you must now acquire the capabilities needed to service that market in return for payment.

Growing yourself into a position to service the market is not simply a case of acquiring skills.

It also involves developing a reputation and being known to the key people in your chosen market.

Author Robert Greene has written what I would consider the definitive work on mastery, unambiguously entitled 'Mastery'. In broad terms he presents three steps:

1. Learn how the game is played.
2. Gain experience through playing the game.
3. Change the game.

Greene acknowledges the role of mentors in accelerating the journey and the need for social skills to minimise the emotional drain on our limited resources. Thus, enabling us to allocate more of our mental bandwidth to the pursuit of mastery.

As mentioned, increasingly there will be no arena to observe 'the game', as many of the digital economy games are still being formulated. The challenge then for you as an apprentice is to develop your ability to influence the rules of the game so that they favour your strengths. Thus influence has to be considered a key skill. Again, in respect of influence, you might want to turn to Greene's 'The 48 Laws of Power' for an in-depth primer.

Finding a mentor

You might as well 'go large'. Who is the top person in your field?

Study them. What is it that makes them great? What path did they take?

Approach them. Social media makes this possible. They might even say yes. But if they don't, you can learn a lot just by:

- Studying their biographies.
- Listening to what others say and watching them do what they do, either live or on YouTube (but not all day).

Your mentor or the virtual equivalent is just a few key presses away. It's never been easier to learn from the greats.

If your chosen field of endeavour is in its infancy, then you may have to identify several mentors and extract what is relevant from each of them. Even if you cannot meet or speak with your mentors, you can often learn enough about them to generate a reasonable response when you ask, "what would <world class mentor> do in this situation?"

I often use this approach more generally. For example, when I am the subject of road rage, I ask, "What would Vlad the Impaler do in this situation?"

At the other end of the spectrum, seek out somebody who is closer to you on the journey. Perhaps they are two to five years further down the path than you. It is likely that they will be more accessible and better able to relate to the issues you are facing at this stage of the journey.

You might even consider outsourcing your career to a career coach. You both agree the target, and they create the associated programme and ensure you do not shirk. Given the increasingly volatile nature of the market, what constitutes the target will need to be reviewed on a very regular basis.

Whether you go for a physical mentor, or a coach, or whether you have a virtual executive board that advises you from within your mind (not as weird as it sounds), you are likely to make better progress than discovering what works and doesn't work the hard way.

We have a limited lifespan, so we need to learn from other people's mistakes, and mastery hacks, where we can.

Mastery habits

Do you wake up each day in a grouchy mood, in part driven by the fact that as soon as your feet hit the floor you are already behind schedule? Do you spend more time in the gym using your smartphone, to alert the world that you are in the gym, than actually doing any exercise? And you wonder why you are not in possession of 'buns of steel'?

One more. As a child, did you expend considerable energy arguing with your parents/coming up with innovative ways to avoid doing homework and now find yourself doing process cog work for an 'also ran' boss in an organisation whose ethics you detest?

Okay. I laid it on a bit thick with that last example. My point is that bad habits lead to suboptimal results. There is an abundance of content out there to guide you to better habits, ranging from 'turn that frown upside down' through to more empirically robust neuroscience papers.

The bottom line is that to develop good habits, you need to actually start practising the desired behaviours until they become a habit. You need to reach a point where for example there is no cognitive burden/dilemma when faced with lemon meringue pie on the menu or where getting up in response to your alarm every morning does not trigger an existential crisis.

I appreciate that this level of advice might be somewhat disappointing/lightweight for those readers trying to shake off, say, a heroin habit. But at the other end of the spectrum, if career mastery is your goal, you need to weave good habits into your life. They will propel you forward and release the mental energy that would otherwise be tied up in unnecessary decision making/regret.

What constitutes a good habit is something for you to decide. Some people get more done by rising at 5am. Others by going to bed at 5am. If having five boiled eggs for breakfast gets your creative juices going, and you have the option to work in a well-ventilated room, make it a habit. But do seek the advice of a medical professional beforehand. Or for younger readers, at the very least, a parent or guardian.

In essence there are three types of habits in respect of your path to mastery:

- Those that impede your progress.
  - o Donuts: if you are a professional athlete.
- Those that have no impact.
  - o Zumba: if you are a museum curator.
- Those that accelerate your progress.
  - o House of Cards (Netflix): if you are politically ambitious.

The trick is to minimise the impeders and maximise the accelerators.

There is plenty of literature on habit formation, now that the neuroscience community is on the case.

Habits is the most critical aspect, in my view, for career mastery or for just living a fulfilling life.

Habits lie at the core of your success, particularly the habits needed to enable you to acquire the skills and experience your path to mastery requires.

Summary

Mastery is not for everyone. It requires discipline and resolve. Your path may cut across the objectives of other people. Each day, others will place demands on you.

If these demands propel you both along your respective paths to mastery then great.

I am not suggesting you should be single minded to the extent that you alienate yourself socially, but you should consider each demand on its merits, rather than ploughing through your inbox because it is easier to do what others ask than to think through what you need to do.

Regardless of whether you see yourself as an artist, athlete, humanitarian or captain of industry, it just feels better if you know your habitual behaviour is supporting your ambitions, regardless of how grand or modest they may be.

Take action

- Create your own mastery plan. If you are not overly ambitious or have a fear of failure, then start modestly with a view that you will live more 'outside your comfort zone' as your confidence with being unconfident grows.
- Identify mentors. They need not be accessible in person or even alive. Their body of work, however, might help you capitalise on their wisdom.
- Conduct a habit audit. Identify which ones are inhibiting your career progress. And identify which habits you need to embrace.
  - As I imply in this book, mankind is probably moving to the next stage in its evolution. This will raise the bar significantly in terms of what mastery means in some endeavours. Technology will play a role in most cases, so ensure you develop the habit of keeping up with human performance technology developments as they relate to your chosen path. Wearables, decision making, social and mobile technologies come to mind.

9 Key Skills

Overview

Whilst it is not possible to list every skill that will be needed in the digital economy, there are certain skills that will likely serve you well whichever path you take. There are also skills associated with mastery/maximising the quality of one's life that are worth noting and embracing.

Let's look at each skill in turn:

Creativity

Disruption and transformation are key themes of the digital economy. Whether you are the disruptor or the disrupted will determine whether you are in demand or 'on the bench'.

Disruption will largely be fuelled by organisations wanting to gain a step-change advantage over their competitors in respect of creating a positive customer experience. That disruption might blow away the competitor, or it might even blow away the industry.

Looking at ways to radically transform an organisation through disruption requires strong creativity skills. It requires the ability to really understand what the customer values and the ways in which they prefer that value to be delivered.

Creativity is the seed that grows innovation. Innovation represents new ways of doing things. A creative mind can result in creating new industries and destroying old ones in the process.

A creative mind can also solve a customer's specific problem by looking beyond the documented response process and developing a more empathetic solution.

As mentioned in an early chapter, everyone will be a 'creative', not just a small percentage of the workforce. Human workers will increasingly be replaced by robots. So creativity is perhaps the last domain where we can still outperform our cyber colleagues. This edge should keep us in play, despite our relatively high maintenance as employees.

Sparks of creativity often come about because a link is made between two seemingly unrelated domains. For example, one could examine some natural phenomenon, such as animal swarming behaviour, and apply it to customer communities, or say, apply cosmology to urban planning.

Creativity also comes about when one is constrained in respect of resources. How can I prepare a palatable lunch for my family given that the cupboard is almost bare?

That necessity is the mother of invention is very true. When there is no option, and the stakes are high, our brains tend to operate in a heightened state. Often, this can lead to highly creative lifesaving/family-protecting 'solutions'. Organisations are increasingly entering the necessity phase and so will value those with strong frugal innovation skills.

Service

There was a time when customers were the victims, and it was the sellers' duty to capitalise on this imbalance.

The victim status was often driven by ignorance, "But Doctor, the advert said smoking is good for you". Increasingly, today the customer is very well informed, has options, and is thus in the driving seat.

Smart organisations are reengineering themselves around what their customers want (eg. reliable information management), as opposed to what they have to sell (eg. servers and databases). Such organisations do not have a service desk, as every employee is expected to behave as if they are a service professional.

This means that developing a service ethic (I love to help people) and the service skills (I know how to help people in a manner that they appreciate) is very important.

A technically good doctor with a bad bedside manner is the equivalent of a bad doctor in the eyes of the patient.

She may have solved your urinary problem, but there was no need for the bladder joke. And leaving the surgery door wide open during the investigation was also a little insensitive.

We all like to be treated with respect, and so it should be no surprise that others like that too.

Respect includes knowing your business and delivering customer value through sharing what you know in a manner that is both relevant and understandable to the recipient.

'Service is the new sales' for smart organisations. That also applies to us as individuals looking to maximise our career options.

Brand management

We all have a brand. People perceive us in a particular way, whether we engineer it or not. Celebrities understand the importance of brand, and they typically manage theirs carefully.

I pity the poor aging rock stars who have an image to maintain. After an exhausting stage set, more often than not, they prefer to return to their hotel, have a light salad and perhaps watch some TV before hitting the sack. But unfortunately their market appeal is based on them being a 'bad boy'. So, despite being a doting family man, they have to 'entertain' an entourage of adoring fans, in what the press will document the next day as a 'drug fuelled orgy'.

Next day, despite their innate placidity, they are contractually obliged to throw their phone (sponsored by <phone brand>.) at the concierge, as they make their way through the paparazzi-filled hotel foyer.

You may do all of this as a natural part of your lifestyle. That would work well if you too were a celebrity bad ass. But if your path to mastery is centred on motivational speaking, childcare or building a chain of yoga studios, then this behaviour will likely detract from your brand.

The point is that you have to become skilled in behaving in a manner that reinforces your credibility in your chosen path. Depending on your career path, brand can cover everything from what you wear to what you say.

If our natural tendencies are not aligned to our professional path, then we might consider whether we are on the right path. Natural characteristics matter too. Olympic standard high jumpers tend not to be short.

Panic attacks are rare in bomb disposal experts (or at least in experienced bomb disposal experts).

There is a good chance that we have already acquired some 'brand equity', including:

- Typically late for meetings.
- Doesn't take responsibility.
- Good if you need help setting up your tablet.
- Rubbish at boxing.

These may or may not matter.

- Typically late for meetings.
  - o Not good if you are a public speaker (note to self).
- Doesn't take responsibility.
  - o Difficult to imagine where this would be a valuable trait. Captured criminal, perhaps?
- Good if you need help setting up your tablet.
    - ▪ Not good if you want to be seen as the Chief Innovation Officer in your organization, rather than an IT operative.
- Rubbish at football.
  - o Not an issue if you plan to be a novelist. And great if you plan to write a biography entitled, 'Why I never played professional football'.

So it is worth defining what brand attributes you need to acquire, and then acquire them. These might include:

- Dressing like a Dandy (Well it is the 'attention' economy).
- Be an expert on fossils.
- Insisting on rose petals being sprinkled throughout your hotel room prior to speaking engagements (Note to self).
- Deliver early.
- Understand quantum discord.
- Return calls within 2 hours.

If people primarily think of you as 'the person who fixes PCs', and you want to become an expert in organisational transformation, you have a brand migration exercise to undertake. Harvard Business Review covered this topic and broadly suggests the following steps:

- Define your brand.
- Reengineer your history, eg. LinkedIn and resume to highlight those points that support the 'new you'.
- Live your new brand. Use terms that convey it, and focus on work that increases your brand credibility.

The Harvard article goes into a little more detail.

New people you encounter will only know the 'new you'. Those that knew the 'old you' may ridicule your transformation or continue to treat you as before ("fix my PC"). With such people, you need to persevere. Eventually they will come round.

Some people regard branding as fluffy and the stuff that only marketing people care about. On the contrary, it is the most critical element of your value perception. So ensure you develop the ability to cultivate your brand to achieve your objectives.

Tech savviness

In some cultures, an understanding of technology and how it can increase productivity, support better decision making and empower people to live a 'real-time' life is recognised as a valuable skill. In other cultures, some otherwise smart people wear their ignorance of IT as a badge of honour. This is most acute in the IT industry at the 'sales end'. "I close big deals, despite my tech ignorance, because I am one helluva guy."

As the next generation of workers arrive in the workplace, they will regard such an attitude to be no less incongruous than boasting about one's inability to read.

Having stated that, knowing your way around Minecraft and having the latest Samsung phone are not in themselves signs of tech savviness. Again, tech savviness is understanding how new technology can support positive outcomes.

A note for policy makers: Those nations that are culturally technophobic, or worse techno-indifferent, will find themselves left standing early on, as the global economic game of musical chairs plays out.

Those left standing should brace themselves for the reality that their young people will take their economic value, and family, to a nation further up the digital food chain.

You need to ensure you understand the power of new technology. There is no need to learn a programming language, despite what some sub-informed government leaders think. Unless you are entering the IT industry as a technologist, or your role contains the following prefixes: astro-, bio-, geno-, phys- or eng-, you need not worry about the technical detail.

One of the key benefits of new technology is its ability to turn raw data into useful information and insight. Thus, it can enable us to make better decisions. Such decisions might relate to personal health or financial investment.

In general you are encouraged to get to grips with data privacy and security. In particular, you are encouraged to get to grips with personal data management, because personal data is the new currency of the digital economy.

In summary you need to understand what technology can do, not how it does it.

By all means learn a programming language, if you want to.

But, like learning a spoken language, the reality is that it will take more than a three-part newspaper supplement to accelerate you from zero to (Silicon Valley) hero.

Outcome oriented

This is more an attitude than a skill, perhaps. Some athletes enjoy training. Some dislike training, but love competing. The latter are outcome oriented. From a mastery perspective, your journey should be a series of outcomes, because that is what the buyers of your service are looking for.

Outcome oriented people don't use defensive language such as, "I am doing my best" or "I am doing what I can". They are more likely to say "I am on it" or "Consider it done" coupled with a delivery date/time.

Think of yourself as a one-person service company, regardless of your actual employment status.

The customer wants an outcome – fixed car, happy delegates, new app. Some may care about how you will achieve the outcome, but most want to let you do your magic, without a need for details.

Returning to the athlete analogy. Training is important. Racing is important. But winning is the objective.

And more than being outcome oriented, we need to be empathically outcome oriented.

For example, the client asks me to build a house. They don't specify a need for windows and doors (quite reasonably, they assume this is a given). I could literally build a house with neither windows nor doors and thus deliver what they have technically specified. Or, as I embark on the process of building a house, I actively imagine how they will use it. Consequently, very soon into the process, I would recognise the limitations of a home without windows and doors (particularly if I started building from the inside). This would trigger me into discussing the desired outcome with the client in more detail.

Most buyers will consider a well-meaning challenge to their request as consultative/value adding.

Though again, if you work in retail fashion, you need to be careful in how you phrase this. "That dress makes you look like a Christmas tree" may well be accurate, but it is in most cases unlikely to lay the foundations for a long term working relationship.

Collaboration

The ability to be a team player is very important in the social economy. Possibly you have cultivated a blended brand of brilliant and prickly. Your clients, whilst slightly fearful of you, know you get the job done.

However if you are not collaborative, your value proposition is somewhat capped. Brilliant footballers who don't pass to others receive less passes over time, thus reducing their ability to make an impact.

As the war for talent heats up, organisations will have to invest more to secure the best talent. Once acquired, the employers will be keen to maximise the value of their talent pool.

Part of this value maximisation will come through their 'best and brightest' collaborating to deliver results that are greater than the sum of the individual contributions.

Imagine a conference call with Salvadore Dali, Muhammad Ali, Lady Gaga and Stephen Hawking.

It would be difficult to predict what might emerge ideas-wise, but the chances are it would be highly unique and thus a potential source of competitive advantage. They may or may not get on socially (if chronology wasn't an issue), but they know their trade and they know what 'professional' looks like.

Admittedly, this is an extreme gathering, but it happens all the time on late night chat shows. Those celebrities that don't play ball and support the banter won't get asked back.

No matter how good you are, if you can't play nicely, your perceived value, and thus demand for your services, will be significantly diminished.

In the professional world, you are not expected to like everyone you engage with. This creates even more demand for people who are brilliant at what they do and have the ability to catalyse the group into collaboration.

Such people are social glue, and in the social economy this is a very valuable skill.

IQ (intellectual intelligence) is revered in the digital economy, but your overall value will be seen as the average of your IQ and EQ (emotional intelligence). Substandard social skills will erode your perceived value.

Decision making

The easier you find making decisions, the quicker you can progress. Plus, less of your cognitive capacity (willpower) is wasted on the decision making process. But it is important to not just make decisions quickly, but make good decisions.

Organisations that can make better decisions faster ultimately win. If my organisation spots a market opportunity before yours, we will grab the market whilst you are still having breakfast. This also applies to individual career path progression.

Decision making requires a combination of quantitative and qualitative judgement. Your decision making power is determined by your ability to find the data to support the decision making process. And then analyse that in conjunction with anecdotal information alongside your gut feeling.

An understanding of risk management is important too. What is the impact if I make a bad decision? How likely is that to happen? Can you break a big decision down into smaller decisions, so that you are able to move forward whilst waiting for some missing data to arrive? Importantly, do you have the flexibility to adjust to the unforeseen consequences, good or bad, that emerge from your decision making?

Very often in business, decisions have to be made with an incomplete set of data. How do you start a new business if you don't know for sure whether anyone will actually buy your product?

In broad terms, you reduce the associated risks by thinking big, starting small, and scaling quickly should there actually be a market appetite.

Decision making is ultimately an exercise in risk management.

How you minimise the risk associated with your decision making is key, whether that be to:

- Start your own business.
- Change careers.
- Ask that rather attractive person over at the other side of the bar in the nightclub whether this town is 'entrepreneur-friendly'.

Commercial value

Very few organisations work without commercial constraints. Outputs need to exceed inputs. If costs exceed revenues, then it is just a matter of time before the organisation grinds to a halt.

So having commercial skills, at its simplest level, means understanding that the cost of engaging you needs to be significantly less than the value you produce. Your ability to communicate that in terms the market understands will make hiring you a lot easier. For example:

- "I can write at least 4,000 words per day"
- "I average one point five goals per match"
- "I can do three hip replacements per hour, with minimal bruising, and hardly any patients falling off the treatment table".

When we are allocated work, our ability to conceptualise it as a project and to then break it down into a set of digestible tasks is valuable.

Our ability to allocate our time/client's spend against these tasks will enable us to manage the work such that we, or the client, do not over invest in this task.

Some industries such as engineering or management consulting are very commercially oriented and usually manage their deliveries with great financial care.

Entertainers are renowned for having no handle on their finances. This usually becomes apparent soon after their agent has fled the country.

Whether you are a trapeze artist, voluntary worker, impressionist painter or personal bodyguard, you need to see your career in commercial terms. You may not be addicted to money, but if your costs exceed your income, your current career trajectory will be short lived.

For those of us who have a variegated career, say a mix of corporate, voluntary and entrepreneurial activities, the key currency may be time rather than money. Though usually it will be a blend of both.

Discipline

We covered this in some detail in the previous chapter. Ultimately, discipline boils down to good habits, or at least habits that propel rather than hinder your career path.

It might be worth addressing the associated issue of focus. Watching the Big Bang Theory on your mobile whilst supposedly learning French vocabulary, is likely to result in both a reduced French vocabulary, and a superficial appreciation of the witty dialogue between the Caltech protagonists.

Try this very short experiment.

Purchase two hares.

Failing that, two highly anxious rabbits, comprising predominantly fast-twitch muscle. Take them to a nearby park, or ideally open countryside. Release them from your animal carrier; at this point they should go tearing off.

Now chase them with the view to catching them.

Unless you are standing in a 'soon to be harvested' carrot field, or you have purchased Siamese rabbits, you will discover that it is impossible to chase both rabbits at the same time.

The science behind this is that we can only engage mentally on one thing at a time. Similarly, we cannot commit all our limbs to more than one thing at any given time (no scientific proof needed. I hope).

The fact that we watch TV, whilst perusing Amazon on the tablet, whilst engaging with friends via Whatsapp on the phone may well be considered cool ("Hey look at me. I'm multi-tasking!"). But the reality is that we are doing these three things sequentially. And each time we context-switch, we impose a cognitive burden on our brain, which both wastes mental energy and reduces our ability to actually achieve anything.

In the IT world, when computers try to do too much, they end up purely context-switching. In IT department street slang, this is also known as thrashing. You are encouraged not to thrash.

The world is certainly progressing to a point where we are drowning in a torrent of incoming information, and information requests. Such mental bandwidth thieves include:

- Addictive media content.
- The need to respond to cyber bullying.
- An inbox that is filling so fast it looks like a virtual art installation.

It requires discipline to manage this deluge. If you don't, you will be swept away in a sea of superficiality. You will start to live a life where your engagement with the world is shallow at best (See Nicholas Carr's book – The Shallows (2011)). You might also want to explore the notion of Continuous Partial Attention.

With discipline comes responsibility. Developing a reputation as a person who takes your responsibilities seriously is a worthwhile character investment.

By all means use high quality Netflix content to wind down at the end of the day, but not while you are endeavouring to do great work.

Otherwise you won't do great work and will consequently drift into the career path hard shoulder/stopping lane.

Summary

Some skills are highly specific to a given role, tooth removal and reversing an articulated lorry come to mind. But in a highly-social digital marketplace, whether you plan to be a hedge fund whizz-kid or an aid worker in war-torn parts, you need to have a broader set of skills to complement those role specific skills if you are to be successful.

The beauty of these generic skills is that if you can demonstrate you have acquired them, then potential employers will be more likely to take you on, despite your lack of role-specific skills. The phrase 'Hire for attitude. Train for skill", is increasingly common in talent management circles. A number of the skills I have identified do indeed have an attitude component.

Even your recognition that these skills are important will convey the right attitude to prospective employers/clients.

Take action

1. Assess where you are in respect of these skills. Ask friends and colleagues if you feel you lack objectivity.
2. Prioritise these skills in terms of your lack of capability.
3. Systematically work through your list, aiming each time to make your worst skill your best.

Career Vectors

10 What is Driving the Future?

Overview

We can better steer our careers if we have an understanding of the major trends impacting the world of work. Exploring the impact of the industrial era on human behaviour will also provide us with further clues as to what will be the driving forces of the post-industrial economy.

Let's take a look at some of the key drivers:

Globalisation

Globalisation is not by any means a new phenomenon. Trading between nations/geographically dispersed communities can be traced back to the third millennium BCE. The Greek, Roman and Mongol empires had an accelerating impact on international trade.

European expansionism saw the emergence of various companies set up to trade with the Middle East, India and South East Asia. Traded goods included cotton, spices and opium. The most significant player was the English East India Company, which at one point controlled half of all global trade. Other European nations had similar trading models that were entwined with their colonisation objectives.

So again, there is nothing new in respect of globalisation. However, the interdependencies are now greater than ever. The tragic earthquake in Japan in 2011 had global repercussions on the price and availability of electronic goods in the homes of Western consumers.

Everything being connected to everything by virtue of global supply chains has the effect of everything affecting everything. This makes for a very volatile global market. This is a recent phenomenon.

Career impact: Be flexible in respect of where you will work. Alternatively if you are a 'home bird' be very clear on:

- Where your country sits along the global value chain.
- What skills are needed to support your country's value proposition.

But given the volatile nature of the global market and the disruptive nature of emerging technologies, it is risky to assume that the skills your country values today will remain relevant tomorrow. So like our hunter gatherer ancestors, you will need to follow the food, and/or adapt your food capturing skills based on what is required.

Economic power shift

There is a trend towards the economic power axis moving to the East and South. Brazil, Russia, India and China come to mind. Alongside these so called 'BRIC' economies, we also have the similarly emerging MINT economies - namely, Mexico, Indonesia, Nigeria and Turkey. The bottom line is that the Western economies are losing their global influence.

Keep in mind that this shift will not be smooth. Even emerging economies are subject to economic and political forces. Their leadership will play a significant role in the extent to which these countries blossom economically. As you will read later, the evolving middle classes in these countries will ultimately determine which countries will be the economic beneficiaries.

But if you live in the West, don't worry. Even if your slice of the economic cake is shrinking, the cake itself is getting larger.

So assuming that Western economies wake up to the economic tectonic shift I am identifying in this book, you should continue to, in the main, enjoy a good quality of life.

Whilst I am seeing some good responses eg. Silicon Valley and the various other Silicon <insert locational term> (eg. Silicon Alley, Silicon Glen etc), I am not seeing the infrastructural overhaul needed in terms of education to ensure that every citizen is equipped to be part of this 'Silicon economy'.

This book is an attempt to help individuals recognise what is happening and to manage their development accordingly. So again Western governments need to set policy that reflects this new reality.

And congratulations to those societies that have taken the lead on this. Whilst the concept of Chinese 'Tiger Moms' may not be totally driven by an economic vision, it does reflect a recognition that being best in class is a poor second to being best in the world.

Career impact: Keep in mind that it is almost fashionable to talk of the demise of the West and the rise of the East. Even if this is a long term reality, the paths for both hemispheres will be bumpy. There will be periods when this trend will have seemingly flipped.

So placing your big career bets on an emerging economy might well be a wise long term strategy, but at any given time in the foreseeable it could be a mistake.

Also keep in mind that learning Cantonese, Portuguese or Hindi might well be a wise career move. At the very least it will help you understand the 'wishes' of your likely future boss.

Technology advances

In a world that runs 24 – 7, where we are continuously subjected to 'mental bandwidth consuming' distractions, it is very easy to treat technology advances as akin to nothing more than the release of a new film. Interesting for a day or two and then forgotten. But, bit by bit (literally), technology is changing our lives and in turn the world of work.

Significant advances that have shaped societies include:

- The spear.
- The wheel.
- The PC.
- The Internet, particularly the World Wide Web.
- Smartphones.

The latter three, in particular, have not only allowed people to become more productive, but also to become more collaborative. So whilst the hunter gatherers collaborated as a pack to hunt down prey, so too can people today work as a unit. Such units in effect synchronise the brain power of all the collaborating individuals. This collective super brain has the power to make great scientific discoveries, solve business problems, and topple governments.

These technologies are now so woven into our societies that they are not really considered as new technologies.

As we will see elsewhere in the book, technology advances are fast overtaking science fiction in respect of their capability.

Career impact: Whether you pursue a technology-based career or not, new technology will most likely be an important tool for you. Ensure you keep on top of technology developments, particularly those that enhance personal productivity and your ability to collaborate effectively with others.

Energy security

As societies became more industrialised, their need for a steady supply of energy became more acute. Imagine your life if you simply did not have access to enough power to fuel all the electric and electronic appliances you use in a typical day. Add to that the energy that is required to maintain your home and the transportation systems you use, and you can see that a shortage of energy would have a detrimental impact on the economic output of your country, its social stability and its ability to defend itself.

Whilst from time to time we are the beneficiaries of global pricing wars, the demands are generally growing faster than the earth's production capacity. Admittedly, the increasing interest in shale gas might dilute the intensity of the points I am making.

Looking at the energy requirements of IT alone. More and more of our data and processing requirements are handled via a network of datacenters, more commonly referred to as 'the Cloud'.

If the Cloud was imagined to be a country, its energy requirements would rank it fifth in the world for energy consumption!

That is to say only four countries in the world have greater energy requirements. And today the Cloud is this is only addressing a fraction of our IT needs.

It is energy insecurity that often dictates foreign policy and causes conflict in or near energy-rich parts of the world. Exploiting renewable energy is a growing theme.

Technology intensive companies such as Google and Apple are starting to move back to the waterways to ensure that they have ready-access to the power they need.

Though, unlike the early days of the Industrial Revolution, instead of a babbling brook turning a waterwheel, they will be using engineered rivers to produce gigawatts of power (enough to power over 300,000 homes).

It is likely that most of the research and development (R&D) allocated to technology hardware advances will focus on energy efficiency. Countries and corporations need to contemplate a future where their adoption of new technologies peaks as a result of their limited access to energy.

Career advice: This will likely trigger further wars and greater R&D spend in respect of technology and energy. So military career options are unlikely to evaporate, though the weapon of choice will likely shift from machine gun to keyboard.

Developing expertise in energy management will make you very popular across the globe. This is a broad field covering everything from oil extraction through to wind powered smart phones.

Talent shortage

The planet is not producing enough talented people. By that, I don't necessarily mean people whom can sing and tap dance. Primarily, I am referring to the people we need to support the maintenance and growth of our governments and corporations in the post-industrial world.

Again we need people with the appropriate skills, knowledge and mind-set for the digital economy. It may not always seem as if there is a talent shortage, given the levels of unemployment we see across the world.

The issue is partially a mismatch between the skills the market needs and the skills the unemployed have. It is also because of the inefficiencies of the recruitment sector in matching the right people to the right job.

The talent supply chain, of which the recruitment sector is an important link, in my experience has overly focused on cost rather than value. This is in part driven by:

- An unsophisticated 'procurement mind-set' approach to acquiring talent.
- The recruitment industry's struggle to move the dialogue to one based around value.

A more pernicious issue is the fact that we are not educating our next generation of workers such that they gain the skills needed to be digital economy workers. So the demand for talent will increasingly outstrip supply, and this will eventually start to hurt economies.

Much like energy, if your country does not have access to sufficient talent, the employers will go elsewhere. In the absence of employers, economies go into freefall. The ensuing barren economic wasteland will have a detrimental impact on tourism income.

Unless of course some entrepreneur can package what remains of your country under the theme of dystopian tourism.

Career advice: The issue is not a shortage of people, but a shortage of economically-relevant people, ie people with the appropriate skills for the post-industrial economy. This shortage, as we will see, is having a profound impact on the relationship between workers and employers.

This is great news if you happen to meet the profile of the next generation of talent. This is ultimately what this books sets out to help you achieve.

Keep in mind the value that recruitment agencies can potentially bring to your career aspirations. The good ones are well connected to opportunities you might otherwise miss.

Power

Power in this context can be subdivided into hard and soft. Hard power is primarily associated with military might. Those with the best military can acquire the resources they need by force to ensure their nation's economic engine turns over/accelerates. Petro-wars in the Middle East come to mind. As business lies at the heart of economic prosperity, we are seeing a slightly more circumspect approach to war. Upsetting the global value chain is bad for business and irritates our trading partners.

That doesn't stop countries stock piling weapons under the premise of mutually assured destruction (MAD), which in short is a recognition that everyone loses should things get nuclear. But, it might put our enemies off if they believe there is a possibility we might just press the button.

So there is some correlation between military and economic might. In theory, countries with a strong military capability should be the most magnetic from a talent attractiveness perspective. There are of course other factors that blur this correlation. These include:

- Government corruption.
- The guy in charge is bonkers.
- A combination of the above.

So given the relatively limited influence of hard power, nations are focusing on what is referred to as soft power.

This can be seen as a brand offensive. "Come and work in our country because":

- We are happy.
- We are nice.
- We have the best wine.
- We have the best cultural heritage.
- We will ensure your family have a high quality of life.
- We are a growing economy.
- We speak your language.
- We do the best research.
- We have the best climate.
- We like to party.

Countries invest massive sums of money into hosting major sporting events because of the associated soft power it confers. "Look at us. We hosted a great Olympics. Despite world opinion, it will not have escaped your notice that no athletes were tortured, or had their human rights denied". Soft power is a relativistic concept. One nation can either focus on boosting its brand or focus on damaging the brand of others. Sometimes that brand damage is done by simply waking up citizens to realities that do not sit neatly with the targeted government.

Television channels such as Al-Jazeera and Russia Today come to mind. The important point is that our perception of the world, in the absence of seeing for ourselves, will be aggressively shaped by the growing use of soft power.

In the past, the acquisition of another nation's resources commenced on the beach or at the border. Today, thanks to the Internet, the offensive is taking place in people's living rooms, and increasingly in people's hands via their smartphones.

Of course, not every video on YouTube has an underlying economic power agenda. "What does the Fox Say?", was probably not produced to solidify Norway's sovereign entitlement to modify oil transportation tariffs, as the mood takes it; as far as I am aware.

Nonetheless sovereign power, whether hard or soft, does shape our present and our future. From a career perspective this is important.

Career advice: Once you establish your niche and develop your reputation, it is likely that you will have the option to travel abroad. I encourage you to research target destinations.

The chances are that they are not as good (or sometimes not as bad) as the media, in particular, might suggest.

Elsewhere in this book, I talk about the importance of personal branding. You might consider this an investment in your soft power.

Similarly I talk about the skills you need to acquire. You might think of these as a hard power investment.

Anthroeconomics

Some readers will consider the first section of this book as a side show to the main theme.

The point I am endeavouring to make is that the evolution of humanity to date is central to the ongoing evolution of humanity.

In previous chapters I have identified certain characteristics that perhaps define our humanity. Understanding these will both enable you to steer your career path accordingly, and enjoy the feeling of harmony that goes with acting in line with your true nature.

Anthropological economics is an emerging theme, which I believe yields useful insights into the future world of work, workers and leadership. Let's take a closer look.

Why is this not just an industrial era upgrade?

I raised the point in an earlier chapter that the changes we are witnessing today are fundamental, and so we cannot regard the economic changes we are experiencing as simply an industrial era upgrade.

The problem with treating the current economic step change as simply the industrial era 'on steroids' is that it misses the fundamental anthropological significance of the change. Importantly, these changes will be of interest to all of us looking to maximise our economic relevance, and not just anthropologists.

A number of themes have been covered so far in this book. These include:

- Sociality.
- Mobility.
- Work-life.
- Decision making.
- Productivity.

To summarise, prior to the industrial era, the following applied:

- Sociality – We were highly social in both work and play.
- Mobility – We were highly mobile.
- Work-life – Our work and personal lives were highly integrated.
- Decision making – This was a natural part of our lives and was based on environmental reality.
- Productivity – Our output was clearly measureable,eg. # berries picked, # sheep sold.

The following changes took place as a result of the Industrial Revolution:

- Sociality – This was actively discouraged at work. It was considered to be unproductive.
- Mobility – There was no mobility. You simply turned up to the factory each day.
- 'Work-life Integration' gave way to partitioning and so spawned the concept of work-life balance.
- Decision making – This was the sole preserve of the factory owners. Plus their decisions were more focused on the future (strategy) than the environmental reality. The majority of people were discouraged from thinking and encouraged to follow pre-defined process steps.
- Productivity – Productivity, in the sense of a worker being able to see a link between their work and a given economic outcome, was lost as workers focused purely on their part of the assembly line. Workers were now paid for their time rather than their output, and so humans became, in effect, beasts of burden.

The industrial era, despite the economic productivity gains it delivered and the improvement to the quality of most people's lives, had the impact of displacing us from our true nature.

The amount of time we spent working in the industrial era was significantly more than in prior economic eras.

Consequently whilst many humans today enjoy the spoils of the industrial era – television, cars, home ownership and access to relatively exotic food, many are so sleep-deprived and exhausted by the tyranny of process work and unreasonable work demands that they conduct their lives in a zombie-like state.

Never truly present, industrial workers are either fretting about what has happened or what has yet to be done. This condition, whether at home with the family or visiting the Grand Canyon as a tourist, ultimately means that many people are missing out on life.

Young people are increasingly noticing parallels between the zombie-centric content they watch for entertainment and the trance-like behaviour of their parents. And it's dawning on the kids that this is not the life for them.

This book exists to show there are better options. But only for those who adapt to the changing market.

Summary

Macroeconomic trends, coupled with the anthropological detour forced upon us by the industrial era, are giving rise to forces that are reshaping the nature of work. Recognising these forces will provide you with an advantage over those who are unaware of these prevailing currents.

Take action

- Develop a discipline of keeping on top of existing and emerging macroeconomic and technology trends.
  - Regularly reconsider the consequences of these trends on your career plan, and steer your path accordingly.
- Note how those whose jobs embrace all or many of the natural states that the industrial era required us to suppress, are either more or less happy in what they do compared to those working industrial/process jobs.

11 Nature Goes Digital

Overview

In this chapter, we will take a look at how the digital revolution is putting a strain on industrial era practices. In part, this is to reinforce the point that the changes we are experiencing are not just an industrial era upgrade, and in part to help you understand why the tensions you might be currently experiencing at work have come about.

A brief history of workplace tech

Let's take a brief look at the history of digital technology in the workplace.

New technologies have been changing the world of work for over half a century. They have been changing the world of life for about half that time.

Organisations have focused primarily on using technology to automate business processes (automation), ie drive humans and cost out of the building. Increasingly it has been used to make better decisions (information).

At the same time, we have seen the emergence of technologies to enable workers to communicate (collaboration). Email and the phone being two notable examples. History lesson over.

Now let's look at how nature is pushing through the cracks of this somewhat sterile and inhuman industrial model.

Mobility

Let's just dwell on the phone for a bit. This device was once tethered to the wall. You might hear the term landline used to reflect that it was connected to cables, typically embedded in the ground. Eventually we saw the arrival of mobile phones, and, in particular, phones that enabled people to make calls from almost anywhere, rather than just within a 20 metre radius of a base station. I believe phone historians refer to this limited range mobile device as a cordless phone.

We then saw the arrival of the pre-cursor to today's smart phones. It was generically referred to as a PDA (Personal Digital Assistant). The Psion Organiser and Palm Pilot were popular devices. However, they never made it into the corporate world because the IT function saw them as 'rogue devices'. Their concern related to the security issues associated with corporate information being accessible from outside the 'fortress walls'.

> *Whilst the tradition of accidentally leaving confidential content-laden briefcases on trains was well established, and more latterly extending to laptops as well, the size of these PDAs meant that it was easier than ever to lose content-rich corporate devices.*

As an historical aside, Apple was a major player in this space with its Newton product. A little ahead of its time, it crashed and burned. The nineties were the dark ages for both Apple and corporate IT. And the corporate IT function (back then they were known as the guys that put the 'no' in innovation) maintained tight control of the technology estate.

However the arrival of the Blackberry smartphone was akin to a technology tsunami. Its functionality was just too enticing for users, and so the IT function had to release its grip and allow smartphones into the organisation. This was a cultural turning point.

It represented a shift in user empowerment, and it also represented nature getting its way in that mankind wants to be mobile and not tied to a desk day in day out.

Mobile devices have enabled us to roam again. We can now work away from the factory. We can now pursue our customers across the business savannah. It was not always this way. Many employers fought back, but this heady mixture of technology and nature has prevailed.

Social

Another example of nature prevailing came in the form of Facebook, Twitter and LinkedIn. The world of social media augmented our natural desire to gossip, show off and generally bond with others. From a corporate perspective that was fine, so long as you conducted your online social life outside of work.

LinkedIn, being more focused on professional networking was seen as less of a threat by organisations. But in the early days, we saw a battle play out between the management and the employees. Smart workers built their LinkedIn contacts to lever their networks professionally. Recruiters, in particular, saw the value in widening their connections, as this increased their ability to find good candidates.

The tension arose when workers changed companies. In some cases, the former employer deemed the workers' LinkedIn contacts to be owned by the company, as they were acquired 'on their time' so to speak. Thus we saw IT functions actively logging on to the departing worker's LinkedIn account to delete their connections.

It is now generally accepted that the LinkedIn connections of the workers are theirs, regardless of when and where those connections were acquired, and as such they are part of the employee's value proposition. Smart employers recognise the power of LinkedIn in respect of brand management, sales and recruitment in particular, so it is now part of the fabric of most organisations.

But Facebook and Twitter, that's another thing. Letting the world know what you had for breakfast, or questioning the referee's parentage in last night's football game, have no corporate value, so those social media toys were typically banned in the workplace.

Slowly but surely workers grew in confidence in respect of their value and their career options, so they found ways of sharing their perspectives from their desktop computers. Employers withdrew slightly and opened the firewall to enable access during lunchtime. This required an unnatural degree of self-control. Your natural urge to stop working and immediately humiliate your co-worker, by posting a photo of them having just tipped over on their swivel chair, would now have to wait until lunchtime.

However the social media curfew evaporated once smartphones entered the workplace. Now workers could urgently tap out their thoughts on some celebrity gossip, whilst maintaining the earnest expression of a concerned service desk operative addressing a customer issue. And this happening during the breakfast team meeting.

Again nature has prevailed. Humans are social and no industrial era institution is going to stop that. Period.

Work-life

As I have mentioned, the industrial era caused us to compartmentalise our lives. There was work, and generally it was to be hated, but unfortunately was necessary to survive/maintain a certain material lifestyle. Then there was 'life'.

This was the time when we had control over how we used our time, and this was deemed as something to look forward to. "Hooray, it's the weekend", is the cry from many industrial era workers.

Having had a week of servitude, doing work you despise because of its paralysing repetitiveness or the unreasonable demands of a task-focused boss, the weekend offered temporary respite before one had to hop back on the hamster wheel.

However, the increased pressures of work and the 24-7 nature of electronic communications means that the boundary between work and life have become blurred.

Intimacy with one's partner is now something to be scheduled on an online calendar.

But even that is no longer sacred. Today, the pre-match build up often includes one last email check. However, all it takes (apparently) is an urgent edict from your boss to trigger dysfunction, and the subsequent need to reschedule.

But some workers are fighting such intrusions by announcing that they will not be looking at their emails when, for example, they go on holiday. And as if this wasn't defiant enough, they announce that they will be deleting their inbox on their return. If it is really important, the sender will need to repeat the exercise after their break.

But that doesn't really work. Stepping 'out of the game' for a week or two these days only increases the anxiety related to what might be waiting for you on your return. It is generally deemed smarter to keep on top of what is happening whilst you are on leave.

So this encroachment of work into our lives and social media's encroachment of our lives into work are having a blurring effect on where our working lives end and our living lives start. Work-life balance is over.

Work-life integration is yet another distinguishing characteristic of the digital economy. And up until the industrial era, that is how it always was.

Decision making

In an earlier chapter, I mentioned how one of the defining characteristics of a mammal was its ability to make decisions. Up until then, animals were purely driven by instinct. So rather than having to wait several generations to decide whether we should watch a particular box set on Netflix, we could simply make that decision in real-time, as we sat down to dinner.

The industrial era essentially banned decision making. Factory owners designed the work and workplace such that the decision making was built into the system. The workers simply had to do the bit the machine (latterly computer) could not do. So a day's work involved the repetition of a pre-designed task, and your role was to do it as close to textbook as was humanly possible.

Being unable to contribute to the process improvement was stressful. Here we were with our developed neocortex carrying out these robotic tasks. But that was the price we paid for greater economic security.

Today people are reassessing their lives.

Being a conspicuous consumer is an expensive habit and thus limits your job options.

It is slowly dawning on people that conspicuous consumption is less an indicator of capitalism well played and more a sign of social neediness. As (or if) this trend grows, people will reassess the material aspects of their lives.

This in turn will lead to a reduced need for money which in turn leads to more work options. If a trade-off has to be made, remuneration will likely be traded for autonomy.

In any case, as the power shifts from employer to employee, the former will need to reengineer work such that the latter is able to exercise their natural urge to make decisions.

Developed decision making makes good business sense. Customers can be better served if the staff are empowered to use their discretion in respect of, say, a customer complaint or a customer needing to be rescued from a burning building. The modern management term for this is decentralised leadership. Concentrating the decision making to just a few people essentially slows down the speed at which an organisation can respond to opportunities or threats.

Terrorism works so effectively because once a terror cell has been given their orders they can decide their approach based on the environmental conditions. Having the authority to capitalise on an unexpected opportunity will increase the chances of a successful mission. We are starting to see organisations that operate within the confines of society embracing this model to improve their business agility.

In the digital economy, making decisions is no longer the sole preserve of the few. And that's how our neocortex likes it.

Tinkering

The term tinkering is derived from tinsmith. Those referred to as tinkers were itinerant workers who made their living repairing household utensils. The term is sometimes used in a pejorative manner. Much in the same way that somebody might have once called me a programmer; not to highlight my effortless construction of 'Boolean poetry', but to highlight gaps in my social development.

In any case, these itinerant workers are fine examples of our hunter gatherer ancestors. They are essentially nomadic, and they are skilled in fixing, adapting or improving things. It is in our nature to tinker, but for many work denies us the opportunity.

In fact tinkering can be seen in some cultures as a bad thing. The term 'little tinker' is an endearing term used to refer to a cheeky child. Whilst the adults laugh at their behavior, the clear message to the child is that any deviance from our social norms are to be frowned upon. Fall back into line. And so exploratory behaviour is thus suppressed.

In relation to decision making, our abilities to make better decisions came about through tinkering. The trial and error process of adjusting the length of the spear shaft, or even the shape of the wheel, led us to the optimum design.

Whilst the term 'trial' was frowned upon in respect of industrial worker behaviour, the term 'error' was intolerable. Errors stopped the assembly line. Errors cost money. Thus, our natural ability to tinker was expunged from the shop floor. Consequently, the education system back then (and today) oriented itself to drive out any tendency towards error.

Very few of us have received marked homework inscribed with '0/10. Fail. Well done!'

Many education systems today continue to frown upon experimentation, what with its sense of adventure and the associated possibility of failure. We are bred in effect to fear failure, and this in turn causes us to be compliant, follow the rules, and generally act in a conservative manner.

Though I am hearing of schools setting tests they know their pupils will fail in order to help them get over this fear of failure. I can't be certain, but I think they did that at my school; only more personalised.

Maybe this is why we admire Artic explorers and entrepreneurs who have simply decided that they are willing to venture into the unknown.

Further east we are still largely locked into our compliant thinking. Silicon Valley's success is built on failure.

Notably in the USA, you are not really an entrepreneur unless you have crashed a few start-ups.

Those of us on the eastside are like dogs who have had their tails removed. Looking through the fence, we see the other dogs waving their tails (where the tail is a metaphor for risk taking/experimentation). It lifts us to see these dogs being happy, but at the same time we feel personal sadness, but we are unsure as to why. Such is the condition of the industrial era's persistent endeavours to remove a key element of our nature.

An individual, company, country or trading bloc that lacks the ability to tinker is at a severe disadvantage in the digital economy. Tinkering, today referred to as prototyping, is the only way to establish:

- Whether your business idea has 'legs'.
- Where your multi-century financial conglomerate goes next.

In the digital economy, everybody is an innovator, because that is in our nature. In fairness to industrial organisations today, increasingly their leadership is encouraging their workers to contribute to process improvement. Even to the point where a worker can literally stop the assembly line to voice their recommendation.

This is driven in part by the leadership recognising and harnessing the wisdom available in the workforce, but in the main it is a recognition that workers are becoming more empowered and so are, in effect, demanding a say in how the plant is run.

This is a characteristic of the shift to the digital economy. We will explore the evolving worker in more detail shortly.

The vines of nature are pushing through the factory floor tiles.

Productivity

The industrial era saw the transition from valuing expertise (capture a rabbit, shod a horse, weave a basket) to valuing labour (the number of man hours the factory had access to).

Skill and craft became features of a bygone era.

In the industrial era, the three primary skills were:

- Leadership – Create strategy, tinker with the processes and manage the finances.
- Management – Ensure the workers stuck to the processes in a timely manner.
- Workers – Follow the processes, whilst daydreaming about life outside of work.

As we transition into the digital era, the workers in particular want to have more say in what they do. In his book Outliers, thought provoking storyteller, Malcolm Gladwell, describes the emerging desire of workers to:

- Do meaningful work.

- o The work needs to be for the good of humanity. This excludes the production of 'tat' or foodstuffs that will increase the likelihood that today's young consumers die before their parents.
- See a correlation between their effort and associated remuneration.
  - o This eliminates laziness, but challenges the leadership to share the profits. Many sales-driven organisations have recognised this for some time.
- Do stimulating work.
  - o The worker gets to play/tinker, and use their discretion.

These might be considered the core elements of work in the post industrial economy, along with the anthropological needs I have already identified.

The dignity of labour

The notion of 'dignity of labour' is relevant. It has served a number of useful social purposes.

It conveys that:

- Work, no matter how menial or inhuman, is good.
- All workers are equal.
- It is better to work than to 'sponge off' the Government.

It has served to:

- Dampen the powder keg of industrial revolt.
- Kept governments in power.
- Kept the production lines humming.

As they say - an idle mind is a devil's workshop.

Industrial historians might argue that the drudgery of the work would not have been an issue for a largely uneducated workforce, and this was more than offset by the improved quality of life that industrial-living afforded.

That may be true. But I would argue that the industrial era has been a dark period for mankind. Which would you prefer?

A. To spend most of one's life doing meaningless work in order to buy things you don't need, nor have time to enjoy, to impress people you don't like?
B. Live a more autonomous lifestyle with significantly more discretionary time.

---

ooOoo

I would also contend that the digital revolution, which originally came about to improve industrial productivity, has been appropriated by nature (or more exactly our natural desire to be human) to return us to a more congruent lifestyle.

The problem, or opportunity, is that this little anthropological detour has resulted in us becoming somewhat 'augmented' in comparison to our hunter gatherer ancestors. We will explore this further later on in the book.

The digital era is an evolutionary correction to mankind's journey rather than just a boost in technological capability. Though as we will see later these two perspectives are on convergent paths. The implications are profound.

But let's not get too carried away at this point. Next up we take a look at some increasingly fertile areas of employment.

Summary

The industrial model has raised the quality of life for many people. But it has done so at a cost to our true nature. We should also be careful to not to overlook the cost to the environment.

Today, the industrial model is under strain. But that is what happens when anyone or anything decides to take on nature. As we have seen, nature is fighting back and it has harnessed digital technology to express itself.

Smart business owners and leaders will acknowledge this and will modify their organisations accordingly. Smart governments will similarly create policies that sit more naturally with the citizens, and nature.

Take action

- Consider the themes discussed in this chapter. Keep them in mind as you explore career options. Do you really think you would be fulfilled by a job that requires you to go to the same desk every day to do work that is so straightforward you are never likely to discover the true extent of your capability?
- Design a job specification that embraces something about which you are passionate. Don't forget to 'design in' the themes covered in this chapter. Most importantly, don't feel constrained by existing norms. There is a good reason why this post-industrial era is sometimes referred to as the new economy.

12 Emerging Career Themes

Overview

In choosing a career path, it is useful to know what is most likely to be in demand. The digital economy, whilst in many ways radically different to the industrial economy, will feel like a continuation of the familiar from a career perspective. The familiar, however, is morphing at an unprecedented rate. As we have already witnessed over the last twenty years, the familiar of today would be unimaginable back then.

Nonetheless, there will continue to be a need for engineers, doctors, architects, actors and sportsmen. The tools they use will be increasingly hi-tech.

In this chapter, we identify a number of emerging trends where there will be a need for traditional roles, but where we will likely see the emergence of roles that today do not exist. Thus, these trends might potentially generate a career gold rush.

> *Those who respond quickest and 'stake their claim' will 'win biggest'.*

Whilst these trends are generally high tech in nature, the associated roles are not restricted to hyper-bright research scientists. Like all industries, there will be a need for capable people to create new businesses and lead/partake in their growth. Though, whether your focus is on marketing or supply chain management, your value to the organisation will be in proportion to your knowledge of the associated emerging trends and your passion/capability of turning that trend into market value.

These new markets are developing their own terminology. Whether you choose an emerging or an established market, understanding the jargon is key. Think of your career as if you are going to work in a foreign country, where they speak a different language to you. Your effectiveness will be limited if you do not speak the local language.

It is worth noting that those that can 'speak' more than one language (ie have worked in more than one industry) increase their uniqueness and, thus, their market value. Though this is not a given. Acquiring experience in two dying industries will not have the same market value as having worked in two growth industries. You are, thus, encouraged to develop the discipline of monitoring the market beyond your current focus, in order to:

- Identify threats to your current market/skillset.
- Identify career opportunities in new markets.
- Steer your current role towards more fruitful markets.

Genetic engineering

If you think creating a mouse with a human ear growing from its back is a cool idea, you need help. But, if you are interested in taking mankind's capability to the next level, then genetic engineering provides a land of opportunity. Examples include:

- Medicine (eg. cure genetic diseases).
- Justice (eg catch the bad guys).
- Agriculture (eg. breed disease resistant animals).
- Industry (eg. create microbes to clear up oil spillages).

Genetic engineering is already converging with robotics in the field of bio-robotics. So if you are, for whatever reason, keen to build a future where humanity is substantially enhanced, then this is the place to start. As genetic engineering becomes more industrialised, it is likely you will hear the term used interchangeably with synthetic biology.

Mary Shelley's, 'Frankenstein; Or the Modern Prometheus' is a classic introductory text on the topic.

Nanotechnology

Strictly speaking, this should be renamed nanotechnologies, as this is not a specific type of technology, but a collective term for engineering activities that involve dealing in 'things' that are the order of nanometres in size (in at least one dimension).

In terms of the typical dimensions most people deal with, the issue of whether light is a wave or a particle is not a concern. At nanometre scales it is significant, and this can be exploited.

Areas of exploitation include laser technology, semiconductors and electron microscopes.

Less glamorous areas include: sunscreen, cosmetics and surface coatings.

So if you are keen to make a golf ball travel further, or to make trousers last longer, this is your space.

Looking further ahead, quantum computing offers a path to accelerate the already exponential growth of technology hardware. If you believe that Star Trek was in fact a series of promotional videos for the future, then 'Beam me up Scotty' is simply a reference to quantum teleportation, an area that may well revolutionise transportation. It's a long way off, but it is something that might:

- Reignite the fax machine market.
- Terrify the airline and automotive industries.

The 'nano' space is really overhyped on the basis of its near term possibilities. In many respects, it is a relatively mundane career path, unless again 'trouser life extension' is your passion.

Advanced materials

Developing materials, such that we get a better balance between weight and strength or improved conductivity, is far from new. The IT industry is a significant driver of material advancement. Aerospace and sports/leisure industries are also leading the way. An area of advanced materials that has been around for half a century, but is set to accelerate, is biomaterials. One aspect of this field is the biological growth of materials, ie materials that are self-building.

This takes us into the world of regenerative medicine and the building of replacement body parts.

Biomaterials science has helped us to address the issues of interfacing biological with non-biological material. So, the materials in a simple adhesive bandage are designed to minimise an adverse reaction on contact with living human tissue. Similarly contact lenses, stents and breast implants fit this categorisation. The next level is integration at the neurological level. So the ability to control a prosthetic arm through thought, or to instinctively close one's prosthetic eye if there is an incoming fist, will be possible.

You are advised to read up on grapheme, if you are to avoid being a social pariah at advanced materials social events.

Energy

As mentioned, energy continues to be a hot topic. It is a fundamental requirement for fuelling modern societies. So much so that it drives nations into acts of war. We have used fossil fuels for several millennia, and many are concerned that the continued exponential growth in demand will surpass the planet's remaining reserves. Hence the exploration of alternative energy sources.

Nuclear power is rightly the topic of much debate. Arguments around the associated reduced carbon emissions are offset by the associated safety issues. Thus, other avenues of alternative energy sources are being actively pursued.

Whether down the line we source our energy from mining the Asteroid belt through hydraulic fracturing (aka fracking), or microbial fuel cells, there is an issue/opportunity today in respect of energy management.

I would argue that the convergence of the energy sector with the IT sector is even more significant than the relatively recent convergence of IT and telecoms. The growth in smart grids and smart appliances will provide plenty of offshoot opportunities.

I suspect that some of the greatest advancements in new technologies will relate to advances in the energy management of our devices.

Perhaps smartphones will be able to harness our body heat?

Energy management as a career option will potentially enable you to do work that will benefit both mankind and the planet. Though, I wouldn't relish the prospect of doing two year shifts with the mining division of the Gaia East India Company on the surface of Europa (whether that be the distant moon that revolves around Jupiter, or the European Commission's headquarters in Brussels).

Robotics

The convergence of software and sensors, coupled with the convergence of wearables and wearers, is creating rapid growth in robotics. We will revisit this in a later chapter. For now, it is worth considering how robots might be used in environments such as:

- The home.
- Supermarkets.
- Law firms.
- The military.
- Hospitals.

Robots are likely to take on many of the mundane tasks that do not fully utilise our human potential. But, they will also likely play a role in augmenting our human potential in ways that would blow the socks off, famed science fiction author and academic, Isaac Asimov.

Though not literally as that would contravene his robotic laws.

The future is here

The growth in many of these fields is literally exponential. What seems like obscure laboratory-only science today will very likely become a retail opportunity in the near future. Imagine going into your local chemist to buy some 'off the shelf' nanotechnology medicine because your wearable device informs you of an increased cancer risk.

There will be a spectrum of roles from research through to sales. The biggest rewards may go to those who have expertise in a combination of two or more of these emerging themes. My sense is that these overlapping fields are together paving the transition to a more hybrid future, where the boundary between humanity and technology becomes blurred.

A word of warning

As if the previous sentence wasn't a word of warning, do keep in mind that an emerging trend may grow very quickly only to go 'phut' because it was overhyped, or even imaginary. Sometimes the media will breathe life into the flimsiest of emerging possibilities, particularly if they are attention grabbing.

Some emerging trends are worth pursuing. Though sometimes they take longer than expected to generate the demand in skills that you might have so assiduously acquired. The bottom line is that nobody knows for sure what trends will emerge into mainstream industries and when such trends will blossom. The best you can do is treat your path to mastery as an exercise in portfolio risk management. The portfolio being the range of skills you acquire. The balancing act is to have a spectrum of skills that target both emerging and established markets.

Summary

We have identified a number of areas where there is likely to be substantial career opportunity if you can anticipate and acquire the skills that these emerging markets will demand.

Like opting for a career in architecture, there is always a risk that what looked like a solid career at the outset might turn out to be less so, should your graduation coincide with an economic slump.

Choosing and evolving our careers is an exercise in risk management. The key activities in risk management include:

- Anticipating risks.
- Minimising their likelihood.
- Having an effective plan of action should their occurrence move from a probability to a certainty.

Please note that the themes I have touched on are not the sole provinces of those pursuing technical careers. For example, they require:

- Creative marketers.
- Socially skilled business development professionals.
- Entertainers to convey new developments to the wider market.

Take action

- Make a list of emerging career themes that you might consider. Keep in mind that just because an industry is high tech you do not necessarily need to be a technologist.
  - o In any case the boundary between pure technologist and technology-user is blurring.
- Make a list of traditional career paths that appeal to you, and predict how they may evolve in the digital economy.
  - o Will any of the trends mentioned in this chapter impact the manner in which these traditional roles will emerge?
  - o Will they disappear, because new technologies have disrupted the demand?
    - Eg. 'Car insurance sales', in a world where cars are driverless and unlikely to ever crash or be stolen.
- If you were required to design a robot to replace you in your current role, how difficult would that be given the advances in artificial intelligence and the degree to which your role genuinely requires intelligence ie. abstract thought, creativity, self-awareness, problem solving and so on?

Mayday Mayday

13 Schooling

Overview

In this chapter, I intend to briefly reflect on the manner in which many of us are educated, and how we need to change the model in the digital economy. It is likely that you are already moulded by your education system. If you are not yet moulded, you are most likely a pre-schooler (in which case put the crayon down, turn the book the right way up and read this chapter very carefully).

Memories

It's day one at school. You are feeling anxious amongst all these strangers in this large building far from home. You have already established that playtime is not the overall theme of a day at school, but occurs in short intervals throughout the day. You are starting to build a worldview that work and fun are not always overlapping activities.

A teacher signals that playtime is over. Everyone runs to form a line in front of their teacher. You have an issue with your shoe, so you are investigating the buckle. Your nervous system jumps to high alert when your name is bellowed from across the playground. The other kids look at you as if this was the start of a tribe expulsion ceremony, and you are the star of the show.

You mumble something about your broken shoe, which is ignored as the teacher, in a highly public manner, orders you to your line. You now recognise the importance of lining up at the end of playtime. The process of converting you from a free-thinking human to an industrial-strength compliant cog has commenced.

There will be countless opportunities throughout each day of your schooling to ensure you are fully reprogrammed by the time you are ready for the factory. In the industrial era, wilful employees are a threat to both the speed and quality of production.

You have just had a maths test. It didn't go too well. The teacher reads out everyone's results. You have indeed done poorly. The teacher gives you a somewhat bemused look as she reads out your score. Her behaviour differs significantly to that when she reads out the scores of the classroom's top performers.

You find out later, during a stern conversation with your parents, that the school is concerned by your challenging behaviour. They were particularly struck by the comment in your maths test - "Why should the sum of the angles in a triangle equal one hundred and eighty degrees?" Your parents, similarly, gave you a bemused look, as if to ask why you are challenging those that know best.

Only the most determined free thinking individual would leave the education system without having been moulded into a well-behaved industrial-strength worker. Your time at school was to prepare you for the brave new world of industrial work.

There is a Dickensian grimness to this tale. However, if that model enabled industry to thrive and make workers better off economically, then possibly I shouldn't be portraying school in such a negative light.

My point is that this industrial model of education is ill-suited to the digital economy. And countries that fail to recognise the need to change their model will simply, over time, become an economic backwater.

I would argue that the term 'education' was misused during the industrial era. This term is derived from the Latin 'e duco' – I lead away or I take out.

So true education is to help people discover things for themselves, and to unleash their true potential, and not to force feed them with facts and figures that have no contextual significance or relevance for the pupil. Admittedly, as one passes through the system, the opportunity to specialise in something of interest increases significantly.

Nonetheless, the model of the teacher knowing best, where their role is, in effect, syllabus-constrained brain-dumping, is no longer relevant and must be relabelled training (drill and skill), because it is not education.

In pre-industrial times, the apprentice model would, by its practical nature, enable learners to experiment and sometimes fail. Mis-shodding a horse would incur the wrath of the blacksmith and the customer. But it will be the abiding memory of the 'disappointed' horse's hoof in your shin that will have accelerated your path to 'horseshoe attachment' mastery.

So I am not suggesting that failure should be fun, but it is an effective approach to broadening your capability, particularly in areas where you are breaking new ground. Innovation is a key pillar of success in the digital economy. Those who are both comfortable with failure and can learn from it are most likely to thrive.

Reflect on your last twenty four hours. How many times did you stretch yourself/try new experiences? Repeat this process for previous periods of 24 hours until the horror of your unexamined life becomes apparent.

You may even start to well up as it dawns on you that your latent curiosity is not, as your parents pointed out, a sign of nosiness, but is in fact a strong indicator that you are an explorer at heart.

A word of warning, if your life experiences consist of repeated mistakes, such as banging your head on the car door frame each morning, it may be more related to dyspraxia than intrepidness.

The term 'Lean In' was coined by Sheryl Sandberg, who is COO of Facebook at the time of publication, to exhort people, despite their natural inclinations for comfort and safety, to embrace uncertainty and risk failure. I would advocate this philosophy.

Schooling

The key elements of a good education are skill, knowledge and attitude.

Skills: There are fundamental skills needed to operate in the digital economy. Skills such as reading and writing are likely to disappear over time as audio and voice recognition technologies obviate the need for these late industrial era skills.

In respect of mathematics, the need to remember what seven times eight is has long passed, thanks to the calculator. However, the logic and abstract thinking required in some aspects of mathematics makes it a valuable topic to study, particularly for those pursuing a science, technology, engineering or even mathematics focused career path (aka STEM skills).

There is a surge of interest in encouraging young people to code, ie write software. Possibly governments are hoping to create a nation of app developers. I think it is indeed a good idea to expose people to how software is written, but to become a genuine software engineer/programmer, one needs to develop an array of skills including analysis, design and testing.

Making people believe that they are coding wizards, because they have built an app, is setting them up for a career shock when they apply their coding skills in the commercial world. To think the digital economy is the software development economy is a mistake.

The art of coding will become increasingly abstracted to the point where writing software will become an exercise in telling the computer what you want, as opposed to typing in Boolean logic in a tightly defined syntactic form. We are not quite there yet. The need to write pure software is diminished by the fact that many standard functions needed by software developers are already written. So software development is increasingly becoming software assembly, a somewhat lesser skill to that of pure software development.

I would not want to put you off getting your hands dirty by doing a coding course. It is good to understand how software makes your hardware do things (such as word processing or Minecraft). But do not be under any illusion that by doing an online coding course you are ready to hit the ground running in the software development industry.

The more important point, again, is that the digital economy does not require everyone to be a software developer, in much the same way that it doesn't require everyone to be a hardware engineer. That said, if your inclination is to develop software, then go for it.

For those willing to gain the experience, it can become a powerful form of self-expression. In that respect can be considered an art.

We have already seen in an earlier chapter that there is a broad set of skills that transcend digital economy vocations. These skills, including problem solving and team working, can be developed from day one of your schooling.

But rather than making these secondary objectives of the education system, they need to be the priority.

Knowledge: Knowledge is a tricky one, because thanks to the web, we can carry mankind's knowledge around in our pocket, and increasingly in our eyewear.

The issue is the reliability of this knowledge and the speed at which we need it to perform a role. I would be dismayed to hear of a neurosurgeon who was spotted looking up 'brain' in Wikipedia during surgery.

But, I accept that the fireman rescuing me from a burning building will not have committed the building plans of every building in her district to memory.

So until we can directly plug knowledge from trusted sources into our brains, there will likely be an educational role to support students in the acquisition and retention of knowledge. But more importantly, the application of that knowledge will be the most important element of education.

But many education systems are evolving. Where the history teacher may once have focused on burning the names of King Henry the Eighth's six wives into our brains, today they are more likely to encourage a discussion around the impact of binge eating on marital happiness in the Tudor period.

The humanities these days do appear to develop students in respect of critical thinking, questioning the veracity of the sources underpinning historical accounts. That is good.

Attitude: I think there is a lot of opportunity for improvement in respect of attitude. Fundamentally, we want people coming out of school feeling self-confident to the extent that self-confidence is warranted.

Building young people up, such that they believe they are the best in the world, when they are barely the best in the class, is going to set them up for disillusionment.

It is good that the web provides ever more opportunities for school students to enter competitions where they can pit their wits against their fellow students across the globe.

The more we can do to expose our next generation to the wider world, the more likely they will take charge of their education and do what is necessary to keep their economic options open when they enter the world of work.

If you have been hermetically sealed from the big wide world in terms of how you are doing relative to the rest of the planet, then make it a priority to find out what the competition looks like.

Getting into Harvard would be a fairly good measure of your world class potential (and parental wealth).

Unless it was for an MBA. Why anyone would want to spend a fortune to develop mastery in administration, business or otherwise, is beyond me.

My vision of schooling is that people leave the system ready to be economically productive and socially useful. However, I would expect each school leaver to be a 'work in progress', in the sense that they have the foundations on which to build a career (or a series/portfolio of careers).

I would encourage an education system that:

- Develops artistry.
- Encourages risk taking.
- Promotes self-ownership of one's life.
- Encourages students to both defend their ideas vigorously, but at the same time, be open and attentive to what others have to say.
- Provides students with the tools to help them find their true metier.

Some might regard the promotion of risk taking as unwise.

That is particularly true if students are unable to assess risk in terms of impact and the associated likelihood of impact.

Perhaps we need a - maths for life - course?

Schooling covers only the early steps on your path to mastery. So to come out as the finished product, so to speak, would be unrealistic. If it actually was the case (as per the industrial economy), it would be a depressing thought that you have peaked so young, from a learning perspective.

I would encourage you to watch/read anything that emerges from the mouth of Ken Robinson, an engaging educationalist. He is extremely articulate on the shortcomings of education and how it needs to change.

Summary

For many societies, schooling exists to prepare the next generation of workers for an industrial working life. This is no longer fit for purpose. Conformity and risk aversion will have a carcinogenic impact on societies that fail to redevelop their education system for the digital economy.

Take action

- Damage assessment: Review your own behaviours and attitudes to see to what extent you have been programmed for the industrial economy. In particular dwell on:
    - Your desire to fit in.
    - Your ability to assess risk in terms of probability and impact.
    - The extent to which you prefer to be given orders (or seek permission) rather than take the initiative (and seek forgiveness, if necessary).
- Consider how you might re-programme yourself to reclaim/develop those characteristics that will serve you best in the digital economy.
    - These are explored elsewhere in the book.
- Observe the impact of industrial era schooling on those around you. You will find you have a lot in common with Rick Grimes, from the Walking Dead TV series. Though, hopefully, you will be more tolerant when approached by industrially-programmed co-workers.

14 Beyond Schooling

Overview

It is a natural process for many young people to continue their education when they leave school. Some will see this next chapter in their lives as a crucial stepping stone on their path to career mastery. Most won't have given it that much thought and will be driven largely by:

- Their school's marketing department ("Last year X% of our school leavers went on to study at university").
- The aspirations of their parents ("Y% of our children are/or have attended university").
- Procrastination ("100% of me has no real idea of what I want to do in life and so further studying will buy me some time to consider my options").

This chapter looks at the merits of tertiary education in the context of a post-industrial world.

Some definitions

Tertiary education – Education available once the student has completed their schooling. Such education can be classified as higher or further education.

Higher education – This is usually provided by universities and polytechnics. It is unlikely that you would be admitted to a higher education establishment, unless you had some level of success in your school leaving examinations.

Further education – This is usually provided by a college (UK terminology). This does not necessarily require any degree of success in school leaving examinations. The objective of further education is primarily to provide students with the skills and knowledge to take up a specific career. Or to provide an alternative qualification that will eventually enable the student to pursue study at a place of higher education.

University – A place of higher education, where the student has the opportunity to study one or more subjects to a deeper level than studied at school. Sometimes the courses are designed with a career in mind. More often, the courses are designed with the pursuit of academic excellence in mind and to develop a deeper understanding of the subject. The latter involving research and post graduate study.

Polytechnic – A place of higher education, where the student has the opportunity to study one or more subjects to a deeper level than studied at school. More often than not, the courses are designed with a career in mind.

In broad terms, traditionally 'clever' people were encouraged to go to university, and 'not so bright people' were pleaded with to attend further education. Over the years, the boundaries have blurred, but universities remain the social pinnacle in post-school education. Though in some countries, universities and polytechnics have converged into a continuum of academic through to vocational offerings.

In my view, establishments that equip people with the capabilities to be economically-active are to be encouraged, whether the output is plumber, programmer, architect or nurse.

The trouble with uni

Let's assume your schooling equipped you with sufficiently high grades to attend university. Your options to go straight to work or attend further education have now evaporated, because society expects you to go to university. Only the very determined/cash strapped will fail to bow to this pressure.

For some it is a necessary step to acquire the base knowledge and skill needed to become, for example, a surgeon or a research scientist, but for many it is simply a rite of passage on our path into the world of work and adulthood.

As rites of passage go, it can be very expensive if your government or your parents are not paying for your higher education.

The prospect of entering the world of work with a ball and chain of debt is unappealing. It will constrain your career paths, as your choices will be dictated by the need to pay down the debt. Thus, you should think carefully about entering the world of higher education.

This ball and chain is used by 'bulk consumers of graduates' (big public and private sector organisations) to acquire and secure fresh brainpower long enough to make the acquisition of the new entrants' debt a very profitable investment.

There is nothing sinister in relieving innocent, educated job seekers of their debt. Particularly, if they feel they will acquire valuable experience that will support their longer term objectives. Some might even say that if it doesn't kill you, it's fundamentally good for you. Though, one might counter by stating that something that nearly kills you (or your career vision) is at the unpleasant end of the 'good spectrum'.

Are you, for example, comfortable swapping your educational debt for a role in, say, the cosmetics industry, where you become part of a supply chain that tortures animals in the interests of human vanity?

But even if you are lucky enough to be a member of a society where the government heavily subsidises education, you are still required to invest a significant amount of your un-reclaimable time.

Having worked with many graduates, my experience is that higher educational establishments could do a better job in respect of expectation management.

Witnessing very bright 'textbook credentialed' graduates arrive in a large corporation, only to find themselves assigned to ultra-mundane 'cog' work, overseen by a hierarchy of relatively low calibre people, is disheartening. But, for young people who value high remuneration and prestige employer brand association, then this is part of the price to be paid. I guess meaningful work is not for everybody, and that needs to be factored in when choosing where you will work.

A more critical point that puts a question mark over the higher education model is whether it is suited to a post-industrial economy. Again, there are certain careers that need to be educationally front-loaded. But for everyone else, university is a machine designed to convert people into academics.

Of course we need academics, particularly those that can evolve us culturally and economically.

Academics that span multiple boundaries (ie work across different academic fields) are most likely to yield greater insights. But in my experience, university faculties operate as isolated 'lines of business', where each line of business (ie faculty) represents a particular product or service, with its own management hierarchy. They thus prefer a feudal rather than cooperative model. This lack of cross-pollination undermines the potential value-proposition of such universities.

Time out

Universities are not currently designed to operate at 'society clock speed'. As an example, let's take a look at computer science degrees, as these should be in demand in an increasingly digital society.

The word 'science' is a red flag. In the main, the world does not need every technologist in the IT sector to be a scientist. We need a handful of these guys to progress quantum computing and holographic operating systems, but the rest of the technologists need skills to help them do engineering, rather than research-driven work. So a degree with such a name cries out 'come hither those who want to be an academic, or those who want to work as a research and development scientist in industry'.

Now of course, many universities recognise the confused branding of their IT degrees and so have renamed them accordingly, eg. Information Systems or Software Engineering. But still there is an issue. Following this timeline:

- Year 1 – The degree syllabus is created.
- Year 2 – The undergraduates commence this new degree.
- Year 4 – The undergraduates become graduates and available for work.

There is a problem with this model. In IT terms, four years or more is a geological epoch. What was hot/in demand in the year the degree was created is no longer in demand in year four. The typically three year academic model cannot keep up with the clock-speed of the IT industry, or society. Yet, we continue to churn out IT graduates who will not be of industrial strength, unless their future employers are willing to address the educational shortfall, or the graduate themselves are prepared to invest further in their education.

This is unsatisfactory from both a student and an employer perspective. In research I was recently involved in, we discovered, at least in the UK, that IT degree syllabuses are reviewed for currency every 5 to 10 years.

This is almost a contemptuous, or at least very market-indifferent, approach to running a service. This is not a sustainable model and is causing both employers and future employees to reconsider the value today's IT degrees offer.

For those choosing an IT career, one option is to study anything other than IT in respect of your degree. Then apply to organisations that see the value in you simply being a graduate. Look out for organisations that will provide you with an induction programme comprising commercially-relevant IT content.

Commercial organisations are more likely than the academic world to be market-oriented.

I chose IT as an example. Regardless of your intended path, I would assess whether an investment in a degree, tuned or otherwise to your career intentions, is a smart way forward.

Apprenticeship

It would appear that many universities are inadvertently becoming the driving force behind a rekindling of the apprenticeship model. Higher education needs a rethink if it intends to maintain its cash flow. Certain industries, such as the IT sector, are quite meritocratic.

Employers generally value experience over whether you attended the same school as your boss or have a degree from a prestigious institution.

Given the choice between someone who left school at sixteen, who now has seven years hard earned industrial experience, and someone who has just graduated from a top university with top honours, high expectations and an ill-fitting degree, then I know which person I would choose.

But in fairness to the recently-minted graduate, she is, at the very least, likely to bring to the table refined conceptual skills, which will be of value as creativity becomes a key driver of competitive advantage.

My dissection of computer science degrees may not apply to the world of, say, physics, where Newton's laws of motion (at least at low speeds) haven't changed in circa three centuries. Or history, where it has been established, via very reliable sources, that Henry the Eighth did indeed have only six wives.

However, where the subject is evolving, you need to check whether it reflects market realities. You also need to ensure that the associated faculty is committed to keeping the course content up to date.

Today is the slowest day from a technology advancement perspective that you will ever again experience. This is a roundabout way of saying that tech change is accelerating. If universities are to remain in the educational supply chain beyond research careers, they will need to step up their market sensitivity and agility.

Is front loading wise?

The front loading of one's life/career with education worked reasonably well in the industrial era. Perhaps at age sixteen, you went down the mines or became a door hanger at the local car manufacturing plant. Or, if you graduated at twenty one, you joined a retail conglomerate, knowing your path was set to peak as a senior manager/director; if you played the game well. Or at twenty four you might have entered the world of, say, auditing. If you could endure the professional abuse of your firm long enough, you would one day get to abuse the next wave of incoming accountants.

I may have the years wrong, but back then career paths were clear. People's career options were often chosen for them by their circumstances.

Those that could influence their career options would pick a career, and then pick an employer (or vice versa). And unless a world war occurred, you stayed with the employer for the duration of your career.

Latterly, people have focused on one career with multiple employers. But given the rate of change, we are already seeing people having multiple careers with multiple employers (or clients). This is not always driven by the personal whim of the worker.

Disrupted markets have a tendency to eliminate slow moving organisations, and occasionally to eliminate careers.

For that reason, a front-loaded education model is no longer applicable. Learning needs to be lifelong and 'on demand'. So my learning today is driven by the capabilities I need to acquire for my current or next role.

Towards modularity

In my view, universities need to offer a more modular approach to their services. Many do. But these need to shift from being a side dish to appearing on the main menu, so to speak. Plus, if I need a knowledge injection on quantum accountancy, I do not want to have to wait for that series of lectures to run, and to then have to take time off work, and incur expenses through needing to travel to the continent where the lectures are taking place.

Some universities are waking up to this reality, and are stretching their programme durations to enable the student to dip in and out of the programme, as their career needs dictate.

Thus online learning needs to move centre stage.

It offers both convenience and timeliness for the learner. It also offers the provider with a low cost model of value delivery. eLearning is not without its issues, eg. handling reluctant learners. However, great advances are being made.

Some would argue that elearning works well with knowledge acquisition, but not so well where practical skills are to be acquired. Advances in immersed virtual reality will help, as will the emerging world of haptic technology. The latter providing the learner with a sense of touch. So, if the elearning module focuses on developing my ability to catch a ball, the virtual reality technology will vividly display a thrower throwing the ball.

The haptic glove I am wearing will register whether I catch the ball, or whether it bounces off my fingers. As far as my nervous system is concerned, it will feel as if a physical ball was thrown. eLearning will thus make it possible, in time, to learn how to perform a lobotomy from the comfort of your own living room.

Test the water

I would encourage you to think carefully before embarking on a university course. Is it wise to invest three or more years in a subject that:

- May have limited economic value, because the market will likely force you into a career change in the next few years?
- Has no economic value to you because the content is already out of date?

Of course, attending university is a rite of passage for many people, and its value extends beyond the economic. However, you should not make this decision lightly.

Consider the benefits against the associated investment required in terms of time and money.

Some might argue that an MBA (Masters in Business Administration) qualification, with its focus on business economics, is a useful investment. But the world is changing.

I would argue that:

- The world is moving too fast for MBA syllabuses to keep up.
- They take too long to acquire.
- They are generally overpriced.
- The information needed to run an enterprise can be acquired very quickly by running your own enterprise/start-up.
- They generally do not reflect the fundamental shifts taking place, as we transition to the digital economy.
- The information you need is more or less freely available on the internet.

Where possible, I would encourage young people to gain real world experience of their chosen career path at the earliest opportunity.

Better to discover that medicine (as a career, rather than as a curative) is not for you via a summer job than to commit to an extended education programme from which the social pressure to stick it out will be high. Traineeships have a role to play here.

Signs of an imminent crash

University degrees are big business, and many establishments have spent several centuries polishing their brands to attract the best and the brightest. MBAs have become an industry in their own right. For some, the quality of the qualification is second to the quality of the institution's brand. Of course, there should be a correlation. But at the top end of the market, the fees are crippling to all but the 'very very well heeled'.

The offending establishments have, in fact, entered the luxury goods market, where the price is decoupled from quality.

The price creates exclusivity because only a few can afford it.

But like the luxury goods industry, the big names are offering affordable alternatives.

You do not have to invest in a whole degree. Options include a residential multi-week business education programme or a ten lecture online module on, say, anthropology. These are not of course substitutes for a degree, but they do enable the buyer to add the magic brand name to their LinkedIn account.

Thus, with a limited investment, you can get the brand boost of a prestigious university. In turn, that prestigious university gets to milk its brand via the masses in the period prior to the collapse of its business model. But in fairness, you are also getting the education injection you need, broadly at the point in your career that you need it.

I may be wrong on this. Just keep it in mind when you are shopping for education. Are you focused on buying necessities, or are you looking to spoil yourself?

MOOCs

An interesting development in the last few years is the arrival of what are known as massively open online courses (MOOCs). Broadly, these are online courses that offer free access to content and typically free access to the community of learners and content producers.

The 'Massive' element highlights that such courses need to be able to cope with high volumes of students. This has a bearing on how feedback and interactivity with the learners is handled.

In some cases, this is just traditional online learning, but free. In other cases, it is community driven, and so the content evolves with the learning goals of the group.

The freeness aspect of MOOCs is attractive. This enables education acquisition to be increasingly driven by the personal motivation of the learner, rather than their economic circumstances. Though at the very least, they need access to the web.

It is an area subject to much hype. The democratisation of education is appealing, and the idea that the learner-teacher boundary is starting to blur is stimulating. But it is early days.

Until a robust business model for the MOOC industry is established, getting the balance between quality and free will be a challenge.

That said, prestigious universities such as Harvard, MIT and Berkeley are sharing content for free. Their motivations may be part social, but for sure they are part of a freemium play, whereby you get to test drive the offering for free, with the hope that it leads to an actual purchase of the paid content. Whilst some or all of the content access may be free, the associated qualifications acquisition typically is not.

For those choosing/needing to pursue a frugal path to mastery, MOOCs represent a great opportunity. Designing your own career at low/no cost gets easier by the day.

A word of warning

Be aware there is a growing school of thought that claims that, in a world of increasing uncertainty, 'not knowing' is a superior mind-set.

For those of you who may be reading this on the (driverless) school bus, this is not a clarion call to create an anti-homework movement, or to acquire a tattoo that states 'Ignorance is bliss'.

This belief stems from the fact that often those who are knowledgeable are sometimes over confident in their predictions (and consequently often incorrect), and are also likely to be narrow minded when it comes to solution options. Economists will blame the economy, astrologists will blame planetary alignment, and the neuroscientist will tend to blame the nervous system. At a certain level of abstraction, they may all be correct.

Beware of becoming so specialised that you can only view the world through one lens. As they say – if hammers are your specialism, all problems tend to look like nails.

From time to time I find myself looking for help in respect of various self-induced injuries (sports rather than attention economy related). I am concerned when shoulder specialists talk about their specialism being surgery rather than fully functioning shoulders. Whilst capability is important, clients buy outcomes. Don't fall into this trap in respect of your focus and brand.

How you achieve positive outcomes for the poor, injured or industry leading CEOs is an operational detail. Again, what outcomes you deliver is the most important matter. Not knowing is less about being clueless and more about being open to alternative approaches to helping your clients/employers. And being open to the fact that their best interests are served using skills you have yet to acquire. Possibly you know someone who has the skills you currently lack. This is where your value to your clients equals you plus your social network.

Summary

Education is an entry ticket to the digital/knowledge economy game. The level and economic relevance of your education will determine whether you sit on the bench or are out on the field.

Treat tertiary education with caution. Do not get swept along from school to university because that is what everyone else is doing. Evaluate the benefits you will receive from the time and money investment you would be expected to make. Also clarify what is the curriculum refresh rate. And also clarify to what extent the tutors/lecturers are in tune with economic realities, ie are they involved with the target market in which you expect to develop your professional career?

So, I would suggest that you see education as less of a one-off inoculation against ignorance, administered at the start of your career, and more a daily tablet, chosen on the basis of what is appropriate at the time of ingestion, so to speak.

Take action

- If you are considering education beyond schooling in respect of your career, establish what employers/clients will value most. Will they be looking for an actual qualification, or would they prefer real-world experience?
- If formal qualifications are the way forward, can you acquire these in a modular manner, thus enabling you to both work and study in parallel? It will, of course, take longer to acquire your degree. However, if the curriculum is pegged to the market, it will be updated to reflect new developments.
- If your path to mastery involves the acquisition of knowledge and breaking new ground in your field, then perhaps you need to consider a postgraduate qualification, such as a doctorate.
  - o If you have significant work experience in the field, then possibly you can bypass the undergraduate degree. Explore this.

15 For Parents

Overview

Parents are an important cohort of the world's talent pool. They are also an influential group in respect of the talent pipeline that will fuel the economy in the decades to come. In this chapter, I provide some 'parental' guidance.

Be aware that my only qualification for advising on childhood matters is my former experience as a child and that of being a parent of a sampling pool of one. So please take my guidance with the appropriate level of salt.

Come clean

There comes a point in every child's life when they discover their parents do not have superpowers. It would be a shame for them to make this discovery after you have strongly influenced their educational and career choices.

Parents today have had too much exposure to the industrial era to advise on the world of work in the digital era. The rules have changed. Parents, generally being so busily tied up in industrial work, typically have had little time to realise what is happening around them.

Every now and again you will perhaps wonder at what point placemats were replaced by tablets at dinner time. Or how did you ever become so dependent on a telephone to conduct practically every aspect of your life.

This book should go some way to helping you make sense of what is going on. But for goodness sake (steady!), do not advise on careers, particularly on the basis that your proposed career option:

- "Has great prospects".
- "Offers great remuneration".
- "Will enable you to 'mix with a nicer sort'".

Or worst still, you believe some industrial era family tradition will hold strong in the digital age – "You wouldn't want to hurt grandma's feelings by not following the career path of your father and granddad".

Many of the careers that will be available to your children, when they are old enough to work, do not exist yet. And those that do currently exist are not guaranteed to be anything but transient from a career prospective.

If you are going to advise, it is best that you focus on generic skills rather than job descriptions.

A spoilt rascal (putting it mildly)

There is a tendency for industrial era parents to lavish their children (often beyond their economic capability) with the things they themselves did not have growing up in, perhaps, harsher economic times. "We spoil little Tarquin/Chantelle rotten!" is an expression often used to convey genuine love for our offspring.

Sometimes this is declared as a brand-extension tool of the parents, where perhaps their children are simply regarded as pets, or lifestyle accessories.

But the keyword in the declaration is 'rotten'. Rotten in the sense that they are essentially destroying the character of their children, rather than helping shape it. Spoilt children tend to be selfish and in a perpetual state of wanting (vendor heaven - consumer hell).

Some will argue that this is indeed the tension/outcome they are seeking for their children.

Perpetual selfishness would appear to be the ideal state to create goal-oriented offspring.

It probably is a good base too for those parents looking to add another sociopath to the community.

I can see their point, but in the social economy 'selfish' (or choose your own word) people will find themselves isolated and confused.
Those that subscribe to the view that 'it's a tough world' are indeed right, but the tools to survive have evolved.

If the evolving 'giver's get' mind-set troubles you, because you have a hard-nosed disposition/Asperger's, then perhaps reframe humanity and sociability as techniques/weapons for achieving the outcomes you and your offspring covet.

Compliance

Having just railed against those who programme next generation humans to fundamentally avoid playing nicely, I now go on to say that you should in fact discourage your children from playing nicely.

From an early age, I knew that my son was going to be very tall (unlike me), so I rekindled my interest in martial arts, in preparation for the inevitable alpha male challenge. He is now over 6 foot five inches, and still only fifteen. Insisting that he goes to bed, so as not to be tired for school, whilst he has me in a headlock, is an indicator that the pecking order has possibly changed in my household.

I cannot be certain whether the testosterone vapour is causing our Shetland collie to pant, or whether in fact he is laughing at my obvious discomfort. In any case, he doesn't feel inclined to leap to my rescue. Perhaps a further sign of the pecking order reshuffle?

Some parents, particularly prolific parents, see parenting primarily as an exercise in crowd control. Anything that encourages docility works as a short term measure, eg. an iPad or Xbox.

But the best return on rebellion-quashing comes from crushing their character at an early stage:

- "Go to your room".
- "You're just like your father"
    - "What?"
- "Now go and sit on the naughty step".
    - "Me, or our son?"

The logic being that, the sooner you 'house train' them, the less energy you will expend down the line.

Not all cultures are this cruel, but some do adhere to the 'children should be seen and not heard' school of parenting. And these cultures/families produce individuals who make ideal employees for process-driven corporations.

They like people who:

- 'Keep your nose clean'.
    - Eighteenth century British urban street slang.
- Are agreeable.
- 'Do not rocking the boat'.
    - Seventies US disco song by Hues Corporation.

Unfortunately, such dramatically programmed young people are of little value in the digital economy, where free thinking, passion and pre-meditated boat sinking is required.

As parents, we are the first generation to bring children into the digital economy. There is no playbook.

Getting the correct balance between out of control (eg. administering headlocks to authority figures) and under control (eg. sits even when others are addressing their dogs in the park) is the challenge.

T-skilled

Traditionally, we are encouraged to acquire the specific skills associated with a given job. Think of this as the vertical line in the letter 'T'. The horizontal line represents more general skills, such as service orientation, brand management, along with others I have already identified in an earlier chapter.

From a very early age you can start to teach your children the horizontal skills. I would major on those that would make them a valuable asset to the tribe – service and collaboration come to mind.

Tiger parenting

I have touched on this Far Eastern phenomenon. Taking the two extremes between producing a characterless violin virtuoso with perfect maths skills, and a self-medicating menace to society, I would veer towards the Tiger parented machine.

Even child prodigies, left to their own devices, will consume low grade food, whilst gorging on low grade internet content all day, if you let them.

But again one doesn't have to crush the will out of one's offspring in order to rebuild them for greatness. Formula one racing driver Lewis Hamilton was not forced to drive the family car around the local supermarket car park at top speed, whilst in nappies. His father noticed his passion for racing cars when he received his first radio-controlled car toy. In what appears to be world-class parenting, his father offered to fund his son's passion for racing if he did well at school. And so, via go-karting and Formula Renault, he became the world's youngest Formula One champion. Did his father plant the seed, or just identify the passion and smartly index-link it to academic behaviour? Either way it appears he guided rather than forced his son to the top.

On the subject of tigers, Tiger Woods' parents spotted their son's ability with a putter before he could walk. I can only guess that he clambered up the putter, before grasping it around half way up the shaft. No doubt, having steadied himself, he went through his pre-putt ritual (eye on the prize) and applied the exact amount of putter pressure before dropping down onto cushioning, which only a recently utilised nappy can provide. By age three, he was on TV 'taking out' established players. It would appear that in every other respect he was a normal child.

So heartless taskmaster is not the only option we have when it comes to helping our children to reach their full potential.

It is better that we fan the faint spark that sits within them, rather than light a fire beneath them *.

I would thus say that our primary job, as parents, is to help them find that spark.

*** Please note that the actual lighting of fires below children is frowned upon in many jurisdictions. 'Lighting a fire beneath a child' in this context is a figurative expression, and not an alternative external career-accelerant should an internal spark be difficult to find.*

Summary

Children's minds are delicate flowers. They have to be nurtured with care. But as we already know, they will soon enter a ruthless work arena, whereby if they aren't delivering value, they are economically invisible.

Nudging your child towards an 'off the shelf' respectable career, which will enable them to hold their head high at dinner parties, is increasingly misguided.

Children need to be armed with the skills to forage, hunt and thrive in the digital/social economy.

Take action

- Take great care when dispensing career advice to your offspring.
- Encouraging them, and **all** their school friends, to read books that provide career guidance.
    o Particularly guidance that relates to the digital age.

16 A Warning for Business and Society

Overview

Here are a few points that I suggest our leaders consider:

Business

> *Both users and customers are becoming increasingly empowered.*

This has the following implications:

- Service becomes the new sales. Quality of delivery trumps the persuasiveness of sales people.
- To gain and maintain attention, you are going to have to give away more value than you are used to.
- The customer experience game is going into overdrive. Customers are becoming 'hyper fickle'. A slight network delay, or one key press too many, and you are toast.
- Employees will drive strategy.

Government

- Citizens are becoming more empowered. If you do not provide the infrastructure needed to live a digital life, they will go elsewhere, where they can get a better return on their tax dollars. They will quickly be followed by those organisations that would like to employ them.
- The pace of technological change is outpacing societal change. Synthetic biology and robotics, in particular, are worthy of some policy reflection.

Summary

Despite rapid technological advances, people, in their capacity as citizens, consumers, and workers, remain critical.

The power axis is tilting away from employers and governments, and towards the people.

Organisations, whether public or private sector, need to adjust to that reality.

Take action

- Adjust to the aforementioned reality.
- Perhaps engage a forward thinking digital age expert to help you with the transformation?

A Sign of the Times

17 Work Shift

Overview

Now that we have a clear understanding of the drivers that are shaping the new world of work, it is time to study their impact from an organisational perspective. You can use this chapter as a check list for assessing prospective employers.

Please note that employers, whether they be public or private sector, who do not appear to be taking heed of the points raised in this chapter, face a very uncertain future. It would suggest that they are endeavouring to maintain an industrial model in a post-industrial world. 'Retro' is not a good look when it comes to business models.

Embracing technology

These days the use of new technology is not in itself an indicator of a truly digital organisation. Many organisations are using new technologies to simply make their industrial era models more operationally efficient, and so eek a few more years out of them.

You might consider the following questions when exploring whether an organisation is truly a digital business:

- Are there tools in place to enable their staff to collaborate across lines of business, geography and hierarchy?
    - o Ie. the extent to which the organisation has embraced enterprise social media technologies.

- Can the staff choose the use of technologies, particularly their user device?
  - o The concept of BYOD (Bring Your Own device) is indicative of an organisation that recognises that the users, ie the talent, are in the driving seat and therefore must be accommodated.
- To what extent is the organisation looking at next generation technologies to improve the user/customer experience?
  - o Such technologies include wearable devices, augmented reality and 3D printing.

Lean management

A notable characteristic of a digital organisation is the high ratio of experts to management. These highly motivated experts self-organise around the broad objectives of the organisation. There is no need to have layers of management, whose primary role is to ensure that the workers work.

The decline of management will be accompanied by the ascent of highly engaged staff. There will be a sense of energy and of breaking new ground. Those organisations that have turned the 'industrial corner' recognise that the new digital economy is truly a land of opportunity.

BONUS: Those that work for digital economy organisations realise that they have a head start on those organisations still clutching their industrial models. This heightens the excitement and urgency of having the digital 'sweet shop' to themselves.

Cost management

Cost management is not something that is confined to economic downturns for digital organisations.

A frugal mind set is necessary. Financial constraints:

- Enable the organisation to offer clients more for less, because less waste means that more resources can be directed towards the customers' happiness.
- Provide the conditions for innovation – necessity being the mother of invention. More innovative responses to challenges emerge when 'throwing money at the problem' is not an option.
- As you will see below, digital organisations can be thought of as a series of experiments, not all of which will be successful. It thus makes sense to use one's capital frugally in order to have more attempts at becoming successful.

Innovation - Creativity

Digital organisations are highly creative. But creativity per se has no value. However, it is the spark that lights the innovation fire. To be clear, innovation:

- Does not necessarily mean invention. It can be repurposed from other sources.
- Can be mundane.

Being innovative means doing things better, rather than just doing new things. This definition is up for debate, but broadly, innovative organisations are looking to turn bright ideas, new or acquired, into enhanced customer and employee experience. Such innovations can impact all channels to market, eg. call centres, shops or apps.

Innovation can also be applied anywhere along the supply chain. Innovative approaches to extracting copper from the mines or rearing livestock on the farm will ultimately have an impact on the customer experience. In short, innovation is not constrained to the customer/employee touch-points.

Digital economy organisations are only as good as their suppliers. In an increasingly volatile customer-centric market, the ability to innovatively swap in and out suppliers is very important.

Reverse innovation

Again a frugal mind-set is important. Especially for organisations in the 'developed world'. It is easy to have a frugal mind set in the developing world, because there is often no alternative. Despite the limited disposable income of the local markets, entrepreneurs in African countries, for example, are developing business models capable of being profitable.

Such innovations might include a sub one hundred dollar laptop or sub one thousand dollar home. Once these organisations have refined their business model, they will eventually start to look beyond their local market. It would make sense for them to seek out other developing countries.

But it also makes sense for them to enter developed markets as well. The Lehman Brothers crash was perhaps a symptom of the forthcoming 'povertisation' of the West. This might be an extreme statement. Though, something similar might have been said during the latter stages of the Roman Empire.

More likely, many Westerners are going to trade income maximisation for discretionary time maximisation.

Thus, they will be in the market for goods and services that support this frugal chic.

Western organisations need to wake up to the fact that new players are entering the market, and it is unlikely that the Western firms will be able to compete against such ultra-lean new entrants.

The smart response from Western firms will be to turn price-conscious customers into price-insensitive raving fans.

So organisations that focus on creating a strong lifestyle brand look set to thrive in the digital economy.

In any case, reverse innovation, that is the application of developing economy innovation to developed economy markets, is going to put Western players under pressure.

Agility: Data-driven business

There was a time when business direction could be agreed by those who knew best (the owners/leaders). The associated strategy was trickled down through the management hierarchy to ensure everyone was on the same page.

These strategies typically had timescales between a year and several centuries (in Japan). The increased market clock-speed, coupled with the volatility that comes with 'everything influencing everything', means that such forward planning is flawed.

Today's organisations need to be able to change direction (or 'pivot' in the jargon) should a threat or opportunity present itself. Organisations that insist on keeping to their multi-year strategy, despite it being plain to see that the business equivalent of a dinosaur is straight in front of them, salivating with its jaw open and its head lowered, are unlikely to survive.

Darwinism favours the most adaptive/agile organisms.

So those organisations that are designed as such are most likely to thrive in the digital economy. Business agility comes in part from an enhanced sense of what is happening in the market. In the digital economy, this sense is developed through monitoring and analysing the data that is generated by the market.

This includes customer purchase habits, social media sentiment trends and competitor behaviour.

Amazon is a fine example of this. It enters new markets, not because the leadership has a passion for electrical appliances, but because the data analysis suggests this would be a wise move.

Today smart organisations do not build their brand around a product or a market. They know that if the data suggests they should drastically change direction, they can do so as they are not hamstrung by product-centric branding.

Steer clear of organisations that lack agility or have pinned their hopes on just one product or service.

Blurring boundaries

There was a time when the organisation was physically defined by the factory perimeter. On one side was the company and on the other the market. This became a little more complex when organisations expanded onto multiple sites. But even then, the company's people and expertise lay within the walls of its buildings.

Today, the wall that separates the market from the organisation is blurring. Smart organisations are harnessing the expertise of their markets in a phenomenon known as crowd sourcing. If the company has an important decision to make, eg. choosing the flavour for its new range of nibbles, rather than impose its 'superior' tastes on the market, it asks the market what it wants. But such market research is not new, it simply no longer requires the participants to be incentivised or gathered in one room.

A more innovative use of crowd sourcing would be to raise finance for your new start-up company, or to seek market wisdom on how to solve a specific business problem.

Responses to this problem might include a short email from a retired expert in the relevant area, right through to a multi-million dollar proposal from a tier 1 technology player. Often crowdsourcing is an informal way of attracting suppliers, but it also attracts people who just enjoy helping others.

The use of social media for both business and social purposes, again, breaks down the boundary between the market and the organisation. One might argue that the increasing use of freelancers and outsourcing are further examples of this.

Open source software is another example of communities working together to achieve an objective. There may well be some people on the payroll, but there are many who are doing it for fun.

In my view, healthy organisations are those that embrace this blurring, rather than fight it. This is not some hippy concept.

It is simply a recognition that people sometimes like to be involved in stimulating social activities for the sake of it, rather than purely for commercial gain. Organisations that embrace this model are more likely to thrive in the social economy.

As a related aside, look out for the emerging trend of crowd shaping. Organisations that embrace this concept adjust their service in response to the manner in which the consumers are responding to the service. Think of a responsive DJ, who is fully attuned to the mood of the dancers.

Asymmetry

The traditional industrial mantra is 'value for value'. In other words, I will give you something of value only in exchange for you giving me something of value.

> *Typically, on one side of this transaction value equals money.*

Traditionally, there has always been this 'dance' at the start of a new commercial relationship whereby the seller of, say, consulting services aims to minimise the amount of free value dispensed, just in case the free advice is all that the buyer needs.

Even if the buyer is not looking to exploit the consultant, they, not unreasonably, need to hear enough to be convinced it is worth engaging the consultant on a commercial basis.

This cultivated adversarial relationships, based on a degree of distrust, because the default position was that, in industrial era commercial relationships, somebody wins and somebody loses.

This might be considered a symmetric model in that both parties were equally focused on value maximisation.

The digital economy recognises that trust trumps beating the other party.

One can go through life commercially clashing with people. Even if you are good at it, you know that the person you have beaten today will be looking for revenge in the next encounter.

You are more likely to build long term, mutually beneficial relationships, if your focus is on building trust rather than transaction maximisation. Cultivating deep relationships will lead to a lifetime of steady cash flow, where you and your client grow old and prosperous together.

Many industrial era workers struggle to move to this trust-based model. Largely because it makes them feel vulnerable. One could go to a client meeting and show one's commitment to a potential relationship by freely sharing much of one's intellectual property. But, you do that not necessarily knowing whether it will pay off commercially. And if you are of an industrial era mind-set, you need such an overture to pay off this quarter, otherwise your boss will tear a strip off you.

So, asymmetry means that the service provider has to give more than they can be sure of getting. Tricky.

Assymetry scales up to large organisations in a slightly different form. Low cost airlines 'almost' give away their services. Many people fly below actual cost.

The airline is thus making a loss on these people. However, the airline is hoping that it will get a few people on the plane who are willing to subsidise the other passengers.

Such people are called 'late bookers' (or desperate). They need to get to their destination in a hurry, so they are primarily time rather than price sensitive. If the airline model gets this right, they can structure the pricing so that most people think they are winning, yet the airline still makes a profit.

Because this model is attractive to the market, it attracts attention. So the business model itself becomes the marketing magnet. Passengers will tell others about the great deal, and the word spreads and spreads. The service proposition is thus a core element of the marketing.

Google has taken it even further. They provide a wide array of impressive tools that they make freely available. However, those tools attract eyeballs, and eyeballs are an asset that advertisers value. So the asymmetry here is that a small set of advertisers are subsidising Google's services for the rest of us. But we are not just service consumers. To the advertisers we are the service. Again free and valuable services get people talking, and so again this asymmetric model has a natural marketing element built in.

The quickest way to become a global brand is to get the word out to the globe. The easiest way to do that is to provide ridiculously good value services that people cannot afford to ignore. And to do this with a business model that ensures the bottom line grows at the same time.

We will see a lot more asymmetric businesses going forward.

Customer-focused

Digital economy businesses are customer-centric. Every employee is crystal clear about how they support the customer experience. Every resource is similarly applied to improving the customer's condition.

In contrast, a characteristic of industrial era businesses is that a significant percentage of their people are doing nothing in respect of the customer.

Or at least in their minds, the customer is someone that the sales team deal with. Such organisations are usually built around the factory model of the HR function, finance function, marketing function and so on. They also tend to structure the business around what they have to sell. In other words, the organization is offerings-centric.

Digital economy businesses are built with the customer at the centre of the organisation.

Structurally, this is reflected in the business being built around what customers care about, as opposed to what the company has to offer. For example, a traditional technology company might have lines of business covering smartphones, networking cable and servers.

A more enlightened technology company might have the same product-set. However, they focus on what customers care about, for example, office of the future, employee engagement or brand enhancement. Because these, at least as far as enterprise buyers are concerned, are what they are really needing help with.

Brand enhancement may well require robust technology, such as those mentioned, but they are merely components of the solution the client cares about.

Again, in digital economy businesses, everyone is customer facing. Even if their role is not exactly 'front of house'. Allegedly, a janitor at NASA, in the nineteen sixties, when asked what his job was, rather than state his role was to do repairs around the building, he proudly stated that his role was to put a man on the moon.

Indeed, his role was in providing a safe and secure environment that enabled the scientists and the engineers to do their work.

Thus, the janitor was a genuine contributor to the overall goal.

A renewed sense of working for the 'greater good' might, at the very least, reduce our tendency to act purely in a manner that is self-serving.

Should this mind-set gain traction, it may pose a recruitment problem for organisations whose customers are not representative of such a greater good.

The big challenge for established organisations is that their IT infrastructure reflects the industrial era model. For quite some time now, customer data has been held in a database, commonly referred to as a Customer Relationship Management (CRM) system.

This was useful for tracking details of the 'targets', and when they should be approached next to buy something. For industrial era organisations, the CRM system was just one of many systems.

Other such systems included invoicing and personnel management systems. So the CRM system was just another business component, rather than being the hub of the business.

However today, customer experience is not just about diary management, it is about providing the customer with a seamless experience, as they move from curious enquirer through to (hopefully) loyal customer.

Again it is not just about the sales phase. Excellent delivery of products and services are a key part of the customer journey. Good post-sales experiences do not happen by chance, and so, again, the organisation's IT systems need to be architected to support the journey.

In an industrial era organisation, customer service is a department. In a digital economy organization, everyone is in customer service, whether the customer is a guest staying in a five star hotel, or a vulnerable child living with a highly dysfunctional family.

The customer is at the heart of the organisation.

Clearly, as the vulnerable child example highlights, the consumer isn't always the paying customer. As we have just mentioned, there is likely to be a growth in unpaying customers. So the consumers, paying or otherwise, with their power to recommend or caution, must lie at the heart of the organisation.

Additionally, another characteristic of being customer-centric is that smart organisations enable their customers to access their services via the device of their choosing. Or more specifically, the channel of their choosing, whether that be via phone, interactive online chat, Facebook or Twitter.

This is quite different to the industrial era model, where the customer needed to work around what was most convenient for the organisation.

For example if, somewhat conveniently, you happen to get mugged just outside the local police station, there is still the issue of whether it is open for business.

Talent-focused

Digital economy organisations are talent-focused. Some organisations have boldly stated that they value their staff more so than they value their customers, because without high quality staff there are (eventually) no customers.

I have yet to see this expressed as a value statement at the entrance to any large retail store. At best you might read, "If you assault our staff, we will press charges".

I believe an employee-centric approach is wise. But only if the staff, you are so carefully nurturing, are highly customer-centric in respect of their skills and behaviour.

Let's look at the world of A-list entertainers to drive this talent point home. Imagine the MC coming on stage and announcing that Frank Sinatra is unable to be here tonight (no surprise today, but cast your mind back a few decades), because the venue couldn't agree commercial terms. The MC then announces, as if to imply that you will like what you are about to hear, that they have found a Frank Sinatra tribute act. He is about the same height and has quite a good voice. Plus the cost savings accrued from the substitute act enables the organisation to provide everyone with a free drink! Unsurprisingly that doesn't wash with the crowd. At a certain level there are no substitutes. You might say that in the Frank Sinatra market, Frank is the one and only real choice.

Admittedly, this is the sharp end of talent management. But as we will see, the path to success in the digital economy is to become a 'rock star' in your field. The following questions are worth pondering as you contemplate your next career step. They may also help you to consider where investment is required in respect of your own personal development:

- What are you the best in the world at?
- What will the market pay for gaining access to your unique combination of skills?

Collaborative consumption

I have mentioned that young people, in particular, are reassessing the trade-off between material wealth and discretionary time. Choosing discretionary time/experiences means that traditional acquisitions, such as a car or property, are less of a priority. Using public transport and renting property gives you maximum flexibility and lower fixed costs.

Another solution is to buy a property and a car, but embrace the model of collaborative consumption. Thanks to the growth in businesses that are adopting this model, it is now easy to rent out your spare room/settee, or seats in the car. Thus, collaborative consumption is a business model that capitalises on the emerging frugal economy.

People need inventive ways to sweat more economic value from their assets.

Businesses that embrace collaborative consumption are getting smarter in respect of embracing this asset brokerage model. Borrowmydoggy.com, for example, enables time-starved dog owners to have their four-legged friends walked by pet-deprived dog lovers. The dog borrower would ideally have their own dog, but perhaps their apartment regulations forbid this. So this model enables the business to exploit the need for dogs to be walked, the problem of the owners not having time, and the willingness of would-be dog walkers. Everyone's a winner. Including the dog.

I would not regard collaborative consumption as a mandatory characteristic to look for in a prospective employer, but it is indicative of an organisation that is in tune with the times. More broadly, I would look for organisations that have embraced social behaviour in some capacity. Even if it is only in respect of enabling the market to share their perspectives on your prospective employer's offerings.

Conclusion

So as you can see, the world of work is changing drastically as we transition from the industrial era. It is much much more than 'furnished factories on technology steroids'. Digital economy organisations are built to survive the high seas of a volatile market. They are built around people (their own people and those that engage with the organisation).

I would go as far as to say that twenty first century organisations are (somewhat slowly) transforming from institutions with a clear set of offerings to something more nebulous, that on deeper inspection is really just an organism that evolves through continuous experimentation.

Author Peter Sims expresses this succinctly in his book, aptly named, 'Little Bets'.

Summary

The world of work is truly shifting. Blurring boundaries, asymmetrical business models and reverse innovation are just some examples of what needs to be 'front of mind' for business leaders, whether they be start-up entrepreneurs or captains of industry.

Customer-focus is nothing new, but technology and reengineered business models are taking this to a whole new level. Customers have much more choice in a digital world, so the power has shifted away from the seller.

This is great news if you are suitably talented. Increasingly, organisations are building their models around key people. Those people may be on the payroll, or they may be simply 'guns for hire'.

This book sets out to help you be a key person.

Take action

- List some organisations you respect from a customer experience perspective. Reflect on what it is that cultivates your loyalty.
- List a few organisations that are embracing some of the themes mentioned in this chapter, and monitor their progress. Please note that this is not a sure fire method for spotting the next Google, but you might notice a trend in terms of who does well, and who does less so.
- If you are currently employed. Assess your employer's long term prospects by the extent to which they embrace these digital era themes. This applies to both public and private sector companies.

18 Great Expectations

Overview

Malcolm Gladwell, via his 'Outliers' book, and Daniel Pink, through his 'Drive' book, have written informatively and engagingly on the world of work and workers. Their books are worth reading.

In this chapter, I have drawn upon their wisdom to collate a set of worker-related expectations that will become increasingly common as we leave the industrial era behind us.

Opportunity for mastery

There was a time when it would have suited both the employer and employee to have had a job for life. For the worker, this would have implied economic security, and for the employer they would have gained some certainty in their workforce planning.

But a job for life is unrealistic. The ebb and flow of the market is such that having no flexibility in the workforce profile would put the employer at quite a disadvantage. Increasingly, workers find the idea of staying with one employer unpalatable; though this varies from economy to economy. There are countries were the greatest aspiration of their youth is to get any old public sector job, purely on the basis of the associated pension plan. They might see this as strategically smart. But there is a something very sad about people whose primary career goal is to not get fired, so that they can to pick up the pension pot at the end of their 'career'.

It is true that most of us have economic reasons to work.

But, if we are managing our skills acquisition and reputation well, we will have sufficient options for this not to be the primary driver of whom we work for.

So employers need to shift their 'come hither' message from "we promise economic security" (for those that 'keep their nose clean' (ie. stay out of trouble)) to "we offer you the opportunity to increase your employability" (ie. to acquire new skills that will likely, in the foreseeable, enable you to progress your career with another firm).

Your path to mastery will involve the acquisition of new skills and experience. Their acquisition will increasingly be the primary driver of your choice of employer.

Autonomy

Our innate need to tinker means that we do not want work that is heavily prescripted; such work is what process/cog workers do. Digital workers want to be given the latitude to solve the organisation's problems using their own approach and judgment.

It makes business sense. In the service sector, the opportunity window to address the needs of a distraught client is limited, given their imminent emotional shift to anger, and possible 'social' revenge in the event of no resolution.

The front line worker needs to be trusted to do what it takes to resolve the issue immediately. Better that a somewhat costly heroic service gesture goes viral, rather than an emotionally charged call to arms against the firm.

The opportunity to use your initiative will be high in the post-industrial workplace.

Creativity

Autonomy is good, but the ability to express ourselves creatively through our work is even better. So, a role that enables us to display our 'tinkering' skills will be attractive.

Not all of us go to work with the intention of leaving some sort of legacy for generations to come. But, I suspect that artists and architects might enjoy a certain sense of immortality, knowing that their sculpture or building will continue to exist long after they have 'shuffled off their mortal coil'.

The number of employers that can offer the opportunity to build a cathedral is limited. True digital economy organisations will recruit people on their creative skills, because increasingly everything else can be achieved using new technology. So we will witness a shift in 'employee seduction techniques' from financial carrots to creative sandboxes.

Expect to see the following terms appear more in job specifications (whilst such things still exist).

- Breaking new ground.
- Innovative.
- Epic.
- Heroic.
- Legacy.

Impact on humanity matters. So selling the role will not be difficult when the objective is to create an operating system for a sub fifty dollar computer for kids in developing nations. In contrast, the attraction of becoming a script-driven payday loan telesales executives is less obvious. Again, if a role is process-driven and it can be automated, it will eventually be automated.

Creativity is a key element of digital economy work, but beware that the creativity bar will constantly rise for us humans, as we endeavour to outpace cheaper lower maintenance technology alternatives.

Keep in mind that creativity requires discipline and a degree of structure. The world needs creatives who can actually deliver.

Purpose

Increasingly people are reviewing their lives in terms of what contribution they are making to the world. I often wonder whether telesales executives, on the emerging economies desk of, say, a landmine company, ever consider their bonuses from a humanitarian perspective. Similarly, the cognitive dissonance of applying one's psychology degree to help a major confectioner pump high volumes of sugar through our children's bloodstream must be a chronic source of stress to all but the most self-centred.

Beyond economic survival, your choice of employer is increasingly likely to be a lifestyle statement.

But even if your prospective employer's 'lifestyle brand boost' is significant, the work itself needs to be purposeful. So as helpful as it is to be adding antiseptic wipes to first-aid kits destined for war torn regions, it still has the feel of alienating factory work. Talented people do not want to do robot work. No matter how noble a robot that would make them.

So employers of talent are going to have to become more adept at 'task packaging', within both the constraints of their own brand and the work that needs to be done. This may well involve a trade-off in respect of the efficiencies associated with the division of labour and the need to retain and harness the unique skills of the talent pool.

In fact it is likely that such task packaging may require a reengineering of the organisation's strategy.

Professional sports teams do it all the time. The arrival of a game-changing superstar will lead to organisational changes impacting everything from branding through to the playbook.

To capitalise on the superstar's unique abilities, some elements of the business/team may have to be de-optimised (eg. the subsequent loss of your existing top three players, who are all pretty good, but not game changers).

Employers will have to make difficult decisions about which roles they make the most purposeful. Ideally, the rarity and value of your skills will be such that you live your career at the purposeful end of the talent spectrum.

You can thus gain a sense of your market worth by asking prospective employers how your potential arrival might impact their strategic direction. If this question elicits a snigger, you may not be as far along your path to mastery as you thought. That's useful (if embarrassing) feedback.

Bottom line: If the employer has a purposeful vision, the prospective role feels purposeful to you, and you are going to acquire new skills that take you further along your path to mastery, then it is very likely a good career step to take.

Challenge

Our brains and bodies in effect grow when challenged, and by the same token, die (by varying degrees) when under-utilised. Boring work literally feels like a slow death, because it is. Therefore, employers need to ensure the tasks they are allocating involve an appropriate level of challenge. 'Stretch goals' is the phrase that currently encapsulates the spirit of the challenging work craved by talented people.

If your next role does not stretch you, then your mastery journey will have stalled. The net result will be a period of decay in both your personal development and your cognitive capacity.

Stimulating

Work needs to be challenging, but in a manner that excites us. Too little challenge, and work takes the form of drudgery. Too much, and we may be either frozen with fear or filled with dread. The best work excites us. At a chemical level it triggers the release of the dopamine hormone. This neurotransmitter controls the brain's reward and pleasure centres. Once we have identified what triggers dopamine release, our brain encourages us to do more of that. So in the extreme, stimulating work literally becomes addictive.

Employers need to ensure that the work, and the work environment, gives their people a buzz. Mihály Csíkszentmihályi's work on 'flow' is worth exploring for more on this.

Correlation between output and reward

The industrial era theme of treating humans as labourers demoted the workforce to oxen, whereby their worth was based on the amount of time employers had access to them. On an assembly line, there was little opportunity for workers to operate at anything other than the speed of the factory process. Even the most productive of workers are limited to the number of wheels they can attach, each time a bicycle frame swings by.

As the factory morphed into the modern day office, much of the work moved from being sequential to being concurrent. So in respect of a call centre, more than one person can deal with customer enquiries at any given time.

Some call centre operators retain a factory era mind-set of doing as little as they can, given that they are going to get paid a standard amount anyway. Others, who actually care for the company and/or the customer, might dig deeper in terms of helping those calling.

It will no doubt be frustrating that the efforts of the more caring operators are rewarded exactly as those who plod along with an indifferent attitude to the callers' needs.

Naturally top performers want to be rewarded accordingly. A natural extension of this model is for the employer to care less about the hours you work and more about the results you achieve. If you have exceeded the weekly sales targets by Wednesday, the company should not begrudge you taking the rest of the week off.

Traditional organisations are run on a 'command and control' basis, and so would fear that such flexibility might lead to 'wilfulness' and loss of control in the workforce.

Better to suppress an industrial uprising by making them: turn up for work at a certain time, wear a uniform, not allow beards, ban social media etc. In fairness, certain constraints are reasonable. Football referees typically do not inform the teams and supporters of when it will be convenient for them to preside over the game. And it would be unwise for them to wear the same apparel as one of the teams, simply because they liked the colours.

Nonetheless, a management structure that seeks to treat people like prospective rioters, by imposing a form of martial law in the workplace, is to be avoided.

The lack of correlation between pay and reward is, in many respects, another management workforce suppression tool.

Vaguely bewildered workers may not be as productive as highly focused athletes, but they are less likely to play up.

Latterly, as workers have become more empowered, the industrial era business owners/leaders have had to soften their management style. In this respect, unions play a valuable role in coordinating the voice of the workers.

My view is that organisations that do not let you share the rewards of making a greater contribution, fundamentally see their workforces as replaceable oxen. And that may well be because the work is sufficiently menial that such a model makes sense to the owners. Office cleaning comes to mind. But even roles such as software developer are not immune from such an approach.

Again beware of prospective employers who treat you like a commodity, and impose unnecessary rules on its workforce.

BYOx

For a long time, workers have been able to bring their own car to work. Not a big issue as the car was purely a method of getting to work and not a tool to be used in our work, in most cases.

Where the car was a key part of the job, the company would typically offer the employee a car based on a list of approved models. Whilst there may have been a choice, it was constrained.

In the nineties, workers were given PCs/workstations to support their role. Some tech-curious workers would also have a computer at home. The idea of bringing your home computer to work was a non-starter. Not least because of their bulk, the procedure of 'parking' the hard drive, and the effort involved in detaching all the cables.

Then came 'luggables' (first generation portable computers), and eventually laptops. Today we have tablets, smart phones, and increasingly wearable tech. All of these devices are highly portable.

Given the variety of accessible apps, they are also highly personalised.

Today, workers are increasingly wanting to bring their own device to work. In some cases, their home technology is more advanced than what is being offered at work.

And in any case, their home technology is configured to their own preferences, and thus is better suited to their personal productivity.

This is commonly known as 'Bring Your Own Device' (BYOD). IT functions do not like the idea of technology they don't control forming part of the overall enterprise IT architecture. There are all sorts of risks, including data theft/loss and malware infection.

However, in a sign of the power shift from employer to worker, organisations are having to acquiesce and indulge workers in the usage of their personal devices. BYOD is just the tip of the iceberg in respect of the power shift. 'BYO apps' is emerging, where workers don't just demand the use of their own device, but the use of their own apps and storage; a kind of BYODC (BYO data centre).

As an aside, I am even seeing BYOT (BYO Team). Top sales people are saying, "If you want me, you have to employ my crew as well". Given the global growth and affordability of virtual assistants (VAs), some workers outsource some of their work to their VAs without the employer even being aware of this.

In any case, smart employers would be wise to install an IT architecture that supports BYOD. Digital workers recognise that they will spend a significant period of their lives working, and so they want to have the best tools (their tools) to do their best work.

The future of recruitment

Recruitment is this critical node in the economic value chain where skills and experience get converted into value. Recruitment can be managed by an in-house team of recruiters, an external agency, or a combination of the two.

The core asset of the recruitment agencies was their database of candidates. LinkedIn eliminated that value proposition. But the market still thrives, as some agencies endeavour to support the industrialisation of talent acquisition through RPO (Recruitment Process Outsourcing).

A few have headed in the opposite direction. Rather than treat the process as a sausage machine, they develop a good understanding of the role and their client. They also ensure there will be a good cultural fit between the client and their candidates.

I prefer the personalised touch over the 'buzzword bingo' approach, whereby if the buzzwords on the job specification matches the buzzwords on the resume, then 'Bingo!' The former is a labour-trading model that treats candidates like stationery procurement (or even cogs). Admittedly, there is a market for such a service. As I have suggested, this is the way of many white collar roles.

I predict a shift at the top end of the recruitment industry. The firms, often referred to as head hunters, will shift allegiance from the client to the candidate, and morph into talent agents.

I have been saying this for quite some time, without it materially happening in practice. But, I still anticipate it, given the employer to employee power axis shift. Clients are easy to find for those head hunters who position themselves as a gateway to the highly talented and scarce resources the market craves.

Today I encourage you to be cautious in your dealings with recruiters. In many respects, they are similar to estate agents when buying a house. They may appear helpful and engaging, but they work for the owner (client/employer) not the buyer (you).

Seek out those that have the skill, expertise and connections to find you roles that meet your lifestyle and your mastery plan. Watch the film Jerry Maquire to see this in practice.

Keep in mind that your goal on your path to mastery is not just to acquire skills and experience, but to build a reputation. One that ultimately obviates the need for an intermediary to find you work.

I am about three decades into my mastery path, so to speak. The last time I used an agency was about twenty seven years ago. I am not anti-recruitment agencies (I have worked with literally hundreds to help them raise their game over the years), but there are some 'sales focused boiler room operations' out there, so tread with caution. I have also been sent to interviews, where both I and the interviewer had literally nothing in common. Bad recruiters are organic representations of dating site malware.

The bottom line is that recruiters need to have a demonstrable value proposition that shows how they are better placed than you to find your next role. In fairness to the recruitment industry, the good guys act as your sales and marketing function.

Such a symbiotic relationship enables you to get on with the work you love, leaving them to find your next opportunity.

I guess I have taken a more hunter approach to my career, in that I have sought out my engagements. There is an overhead in doing this, which detracts from the focus on great delivery. But in my case, I enjoy the 'eat what you kill' model. It might be that it is in our nature to hunt!

Work and life convergence

There is much discussion taking place on the subject of work-life balance. There are many who defend it. Here is how I see it.

The notion of work-life balance came about because in the industrial era factory workers rightly wanted to ringfence the time they had that wasn't owned by their employer.

> *"Once I leave the factory, I am free to do as I please".*

Today this model still applies if you work in a factory, whether it is a blue or white collar factory. However, as organisations transition to the digital economy, the nature of work is becoming less process-focused and more subject to the howling gales of a volatile and global market.

So, if the sales proposal you dispatched to the other side of the world results in being woken up at 4am to clarify a deal-breaking point, then you better get up and put your 'game face' on.

If that doesn't work for you:

- Go find one of the remaining 'clock on clock off' factory jobs.
- Or reskill to find a modern economy job in an area that ignites your passion and doesn't cause resentment when such incursions on your 'personal time' occur.
- Or even boost your skills and your brand such that clients will be highly grateful for your support and will work around your schedule/sleep patterns.

Top athletes make sacrifices; getting up early on a cold winter morning to hit the streets 'Rocky style'. Don't expect to be the best in the world by working a nine to five model.

Greatness has a price.

Lean and agile

Two hunter gatherers are 'chatting' on their way back from picking berries. One is tall, slim and athletic, and the other is short and stocky, and looks like she could take out an aggressive ape, if required. The tall one is a Homo sapiens and the short one is a Neanderthal.
On the horizon appears a Siberian lion. The two hunter gatherers look at each other. They both turn on their heels, with a view to increasing the distance between them and the predator. The stocky powerful Neanderthal sprints off leaving her colleague behind.

After about 30 seconds, the Neanderthal ran into what athletes refer to as 'oxygen debt', which has the effect of causing a rapid decrease in speed. Very soon after, the Homo sapiens strides past the Neanderthal.

The Homo sapiens was smart enough to realise that he did not have to out run the lion, he simply needed to outrun the Neanderthal. Once the lion had gorged on the sprinter, it would be less inclined to pursue a dessert 'built for endurance'.

Given that Homo sapiens has prevailed today, suggests that from a human perspective, lean and agile is a superior adaptation for survivability. However, today it appears that being athletic is something only athletes concern themselves with.

But, the increasing clock speed and volatility of the market means that today's workers need to be agile too. Specifically, in respect of how they steer their personal development to match the rapidly evolving needs of the market.

In fact, agility is a recognised term in business that applies to organisations that can readily adapt themselves to market demand. Agile organisations want agile talent.

Lean is also a concept used in the business world. It too focuses on what the market wants, with the associated goal of doing this with the minimum of waste. It can be thought of as an approach to maximising efficiency by delivering the maximum value with minimum effort.

Successful organisations embrace a lean approach. They recognise that inefficiency creates waste, which otherwise could have been used to enhance the customers' experience.
So in turn, workers who can embrace a frugal mind set are going to be attractive to employers. The constraint of limited resources often serves to stimulate our creative energies.

Are you the sort of person who will look in the fridge and decide that you can make a meal out of the available scraps, or do you think "Bugger it, I'll order a take away."?

Takeaways tend to be fattening. When the predator is unemployment, you don't want to be the person waddling along at the back of the herd!

If you are slightly bewildered by my analogy-hopping in this section, the bottom line message is that lean and mean is the mantra of the future worker. Lean, as a term, has a number of meanings in the world of work. This is explored, in some detail, in a later chapter.

Augmented man

As mentioned, workers increasingly have personal devices that, in essence, give them ready access to the collective works of mankind. In the majority of cases, we are just a few clicks from knowing:

- The current price of oil.
- What illness you might have, given your symptoms.
- The difference between inquiry and enquiry.
- What the singular of Homo sapiens is (see above).

Thus our capability is not restricted to our capacity to learn, store and recall information.

Clicks are giving way to voice activated commands, which in turn will give way to thought-activated technology. And that technology will either be with us, on us, or in us.

So it is fair to say that workers are becoming augmented.
Smart employers are embracing the associated new technologies, eg. head-up display visors for the emergency services. Thus enabling their heroic workers to have the necessary geospatial information to navigate, say, a burning warehouse.

Smart vendors will recognise that their services and products need to be accessible via the technology used by 'augmented man'. Impulse shopping is taken to the next level. The following steps could take place within a minute:

1. Neural recognition of 'nice jacket'.
2. Approach jacket wearer stating, "I like your nice jacket", whilst choosing the camera app on your phone.
3. The jacket is photographed, and the vendor options are instantly displayed.
4. You choose convenience over price, and so you order 'click and collect', with the pick-up point being a retail store located on your route home.

More likely, this will be done via your eyewear/e-yeball, which saves the hassle of taking the phone out of your pocket, or twisting your wrist phone towards the object of interest.

On the face of it, this would seem like a journey that will end with the democratisation of opportunity; everyone has access to everything. But if I have access to specialist membership knowledge services, and you cannot afford the membership fee, then I have an advantage. And as these services become accessible via a direct link to one's brain, such paid-for knowledge can be naturally woven into my decision making processes. Thus enabling me to not only make superior decision to you, but to make them quicker.

Imagine 'foreign languages as a service'. You will have a fluent understanding of Russian or Portuguese, but only for as long as you subscribe to the service.

In any case, human augmentation is well underway. We will explore later how this will radically change the world of work.

So what should I do?

Better to develop your skills for the post-industrial economy. One of the key capabilities will be creativity, or specifically the ability to apply original thought to the needs of consumers. These consumers being customers and/or citizens. I am not just talking about the product development guy in the mega retail company. Everyone from fine artists, scientists, and social workers, through to professional entertainers, will need to apply their brain, capabilities, personalities and experiences (and that is only a subset) to solving market problems.

The alternative is to endure the price-crushing competition of 'commodity hell' (where the need for labour still exists), or to simply live a life of 'enforced leisure'.

The need to be creative is not some post-industrial era concept. It is just that in the industrial era, it was confined to the research and development function. Today, increasingly, everybody is in R&D. If you are not bringing anything new to the table, there is a question mark over your value-add, whether it is economic, academic or socially measured.

Summary

For those at the smart end of the talent spectrum, the future looks rosy. Employers will bend over backwards to accommodate your needs.

Your work will be rewarding on a number of levels, including financial.

You will own your career, and perhaps that is the scary bit. No longer can you surrender yourself to a mega-corp graduate programme, or just turn up at the forge and serve your ironmongery apprenticeship.

If you want to ensure that your value proposition remains attractive, in what is an increasingly tempestuous market, you are going to have to take the wheel, and steer your career like a professional yachtsman negotiating Cape Horn.

But again, if your steer well, you will win big.

Take action

- With mastery in mind, think about what appeals to you. Consider what skills and knowledge you need to acquire.
- Visit the online job sites and get a feel for the demand associated with the paths you are considering.
  - Do not be put off by the absence of opportunity, as many digital economy jobs do not yet exist. However, if your need for employment is imminent, you may consider diverting you path to where there is a known demand.

19 Are You Following Me?

Overview

Organisations are having to change. This in turn is changing the way they engage with staff and the market. Leaders are not immune from these changes. This chapter looks at how the world of leadership is likely to evolve.

This chapter will help you assess prospective employees. By studying their mode of leadership, you will be able to assess whether they have an industrial era factory mindset. If I have done my job correctly, and you are looking for a fulfilling career, you will want to avoid such organisations.

Command and control

The traditional command and control model, comprising a pyramidal hierarchy of managers, ultimately reporting to one leader, was embraced by industrial era organisations, having seen how effective it was in the military world.

The model enabled the leader to cascade messages down through the organization. It also enabled her to control risk by correlating decision making ability with management seniority.

The traditional career usually started at the foot of the pyramid with the goal, for the best and the brightest at least, to climb to the top. One problem: They don't tell you at business school that there is only one top slot in each organization, so the chances of all their students becoming CEOs of significant corporations are pretty low.

The problem with the command and control model is that each layer in the hierarchy is, in effect, a blockage to decision making. A military example might help.

What if the time it took an army to discover a new form of IED (Improvised Explosive Device), create a response to it, and seek approval for this response, was seven days? And what if the bad guys were innovating IEDs on a five day innovation cycle?

As the market clock speed increases, the command and control model is becoming increasingly arthritic in respect of its ability to respond to real world opportunities and threats.

Smart organisations are developing a more autonomous cellular approach to their organisation; not unlike the standard terrorist model. Each cell has its own objective and a high degree of autonomy over how it completes that objective.

Business schools probably regard the idea of having terrorism management modules on their MBA syllabus as something that might attract the wrong type of student.

So the less incendiary term of 'decentralised leadership' might be used instead.

Those organisations that promote cross hierarchy collaboration, and provide the technologies to do that, are more likely to respond effectively to market changes than their traditional 'up-down hierarchical' competitors.

So modern leaders need to let go of their desire for centralised leadership. And to the ego-gratifying status that goes with presiding over layer upon layer of management structure.

If you happen to be part of this management structure, you may need to reconsider your career trajectory.

Strategy

Traditional strategy is designed and planned by the most senior executives in the organisation. Once they feel they have something plausible by way of a plan, and they have 'dumbed' it down so that everyone will make some sense of it, they set about cascading it down the ranks by issuing edicts to the departmental heads. The HR director is told to find the people needed to deliver the strategy. The sales director is told to sell a certain amount, in line with the strategy, and so on.

Often, this is done in the context of fictitious cash flow predictions, and so, for example, the IT function is ordered to do magical things with a set budget, regardless of what it will cost in practice.

Such a 'we know best' approach to strategy is increasingly perceived as both arrogant and wrong.

Those closest to the action, ie. the workers, are in a better position to determine strategy. They can call upon their gut feeling, gained by engaging with customers, prospects and suppliers on a daily basis. Plus they can draw upon the empirical data that accompanies the electronic breadcrumb trail left by the customer, as they peruse and transact via the organisation's electronic outposts. Amazon keeps a record of our every click, never mind transaction, for this very reason.

Another key point is that the difference between success and failure will be determined less by a fictional boardroom-created strategy, and more by the acquisition of star performers.

Their (the star performer) talents will determine the strategic approach of the organisation, including the composition of the supporting team.

Again, much like a professional football team, the strategy will be driven by the stars the leaders can secure.

You might argue that once the leaders determine who they want star-wise, it is just another edict to HR.

But given that the star talent is in the negotiating driving seat, with plenty of options, the likelihood of securing them is far from certain.

Thus strategic design cannot really commence until the star player is secured. Or, for that matter, 'any' star player is secured.

Remember, the aim for you is to be that star talent in whatever field that combines high demand with what fires your passion.

Keeping on the talent theme, there is a great phrase I stumbled across that is an indicator of the talent shortages that lie ahead.

The 'jagged resume' alludes to the reality that some of the traditional rules for increasing your employment attractiveness are no longer applicable.

Increasingly, talent acquirers are going to have to be open minded in respect of talent acquisition. Acquiring good talent may be more opportunistic, than 'planned' during a boardroom (fantasy) planning session.

So picture this: The agency recruiter approaches the CEO of a large multinational organisation, and informs the CEO that he should take a look at this 'special' candidate.

The CEO reluctantly takes the resume and scans it for words like McKinsey, Harvard, Oxford and MIT, but the words that jump out at him are 'three years in a high security prison'. He shares these words with the recruiter, who responds by stating that indeed it is true.

But more to the point, she ran a very successful gang whilst in prison. Territorially, the gang took control of a further four cell blocks during her tenure.

The CEO pauses to reflect on this new information. He responds by highlighting that in the back of his mind he had plans to open up a new office in the Crimea, and he needed a local manager who could take care of themselves. As a result of seeing this unorthodox resume, he would now like to meet with this prospective employee, and possibly accelerate his expansion plans.

Whilst this might seem extreme, the growing talent shortage will require the somewhat lazy approach of 'buzzword bingo' in respect of education, qualifications and skills to be replaced with the more lateral approach of spotting 'out of context' capabilities that could well accelerate, or change, the strategic intentions of the prospective employer.

With this in mind, you need to look beyond your formal qualifications and experience, and bring to the fore your hobbies, interests, personality and aspirations. You might want to reflect on any 'previous' you have acquired. Though keep in mind that certain crimes do not translate well into employment opportunities, no matter how well you spin it.

Carrot and stick

Another technique popular in the industrial era was the 'carrot and stick'. Nothing too scientific here. Here, talent equals donkey. The carrot is used to incentivise the donkey to move towards the carrot. If the donkey is not into carrots, or is full, the stick is employed at the other end of the donkey, to create forward motion.

The underlying assumption is that the donkey has no internal motivation, and therefore needs to be incentivised. Sales people respond extremely well to this. Once they are set a target, and an associated reward, they will do what it takes to hit the target. Having worked with thousands of sales people over the years, it is actually quite uplifting to be with a group of people who have a laser beam focus.

The targets have to be set very carefully. As a sales person, I may well achieve my targets for the quarter, but in doing so have ruined any possibility of further business from the clients concerned, because I essentially bullied them into the sales. For clarification, this is not good for the sales person or their employer.

Sales warning

Leaders should be aware of how the world of sales is changing (as should those of you considering a career in sales).

It took me a while to realise that sales is the cornerstone of the business. Up until I started out on my own, my understanding was that sales people existed to make wild promises to the customers, and to then, on closing the deal, walk away with a handsome commission, and leave the delivery to the likes of me. My role being to reconcile these contractually-binding tall tales to what could actually be achieved using new technology.

However this perspective changed a few hours after starting my own business. Up until then, I was spared the stress of finding business. Thus enabling me to concentrate on the delivery. Now I found myself in a 'don't kill., don't eat' situation.

> *Sales remains equally important today, though much of it has moved online.*

As with everything else, if it can be done with technology then goodbye human.

However, sales people are needed where the sale does not lend itself to click and buy. Such sales are relationship and value focused. The buying dance doesn't start until trust and relevance are established.

> *The digital economy is also called the social economy because people talk, and if you or your people behave like hustlers the word will spread, and spread quickly.*

The other key point is that product sales are being replaced by service sales, and service sales are increasingly being sold on a utility basis. The client pays for what they use, no more or no less. Think utility.

In the past, sales people would be paid their commission, in full or almost in full, on winning the contract, regardless of whether the subsequent delivery was successful from a client, or even the vendor's perspective. Increasingly sales people, today, are paid post-delivery.

Thus the digital economy sales professional ensures the customer keeps using the service, as usage determines commissions. Thus, it is necessary for the sales person to be a value adding element of that service, rather than, in the extreme, a smooth talking huckster.

> *New leadership skills will be required to manage this new sophisticated breed of sales professional.*

And in many cases, new leadership skills will be required to migrate the old school sales force to this more value-driven approach. Over the years, I have helped many organisations make this transition.

Your inner carrot

An important point to make is that in the digital economy the talent is more motivated to do a good job than their manager, or the organisation.

Today's talent recognises the importance of reputation, and of only being as good as your last delivery. So, each assignment we take on has to be treated with great diligence.

This isn't an issue when you love what you do. In my own case, I am very careful to ensure that I have total control over the deliverables. I do not want to be reliant on people who are less committed to a successful outcome than I am. As a former track star ("Wake up Dorothy"), I quite liked the clarity of being judged on how 'fast' I was. There was no one to blame but myself if I ran poorly.

But I also liked the collaboration aspect of athletics that came from training with like-minded people, particularly when their superior ability had an uplifting impact on mine.

The same is true from a general work perspective, I am very happy to work with people who are further down the mastery path than me, and thus can shine a light on my path. Usually their output and reputation have been engineered with great care and sweat.

The carrot today is for us to build that great reputation. The stick is to avoid being a professional pariah. Managers and organisational goals may be external motivators, but they are relatively superficial drivers. In the social economy, the motivation comes from the desire to keep up with the professional A-team pack of which you aspire to be a member.

Swarm allegiance

The study of swarm behaviour in birds, fish and insects offers us an extreme alternative to the traditional command and control leadership model. These animals demonstrate how the use of simple communications on a large scale can lead to intelligent and impressive outcomes.

Ant colonies, for example, do not have a leader as such. Ants determine whether to forage or defend based on the frequency with which they encounter other forager or defender ants.

This swarm model enables the colony to shift its focus based on the realities on the ground, rather than as a result of a memo from head office.

Possibly this swarm intelligence is something we can apply to organisational models. Or, at least to elements of our business models. Rather than the pharmaceutical companies pushing their research scientists to create a competitive alternative to the established brands of aspirin, they simply instruct the scientists to explore new ways to deliver pain relief.

But should they stumble upon something of interest in the process (eg. pharmaceutical versions of velcro or post-it notes), they should be at liberty to follow the new path, if the scientists, collectively, feel this is best.

Again this is business strategy emerging from the talent rather than the boardroom.

Servant-leadership

Servant-leadership is an emerging philosophy, and set of practices, that in many respects is a step towards a swarm-based model. This model encourages a decentralisation of leadership. The CEO's focus is on empowering the talent to do their best work. This includes providing them with the best environment, and removing anything that could obstruct their progress.

This is in stark contrast to the 'fat cat' inflated egos of the industrial era, who were primarily focused on their own well-being, seeing the workers as dehumanised resources.

This model can only work in an environment where there is a high degree of mutual trust between all parties. Workers who have been ingrained with a distrust of management will simply see the servant leader as weak. Consequently, they will likely abuse the slackening of the management harness.

So the servant-leadership approach is not the solution to a dysfunctional organisation. It is, however, a way to turbo-charge an organisation where there is an existing 'esprit de corps'.

As you explore your employment options, one of the key points to establish in the interview process is whether there is a 'them and us' mentality between the leadership and the workers.

If so, you are sitting in a factory (no matter how well furnished/funky), and so you need to politely extricate yourself from the interview, and sprint towards the nearest exit, before you are sucked into the machine.

Summary

The traditional hierarchical structure, with its command and control model, has had its day. Leaders who can do no more than issue orders will have a problem, no matter how much wisdom those orders contain.

Great leadership means ego-free leadership.

Being able to turn sharply (pivot) as new opportunities/threats emerge is critical.

If your organisation employs highly motivated and competent people, the chances are they will need little management.

So, the leader's job is to give them what they need to do great work.

Take action

- Consider whether you see yourself as a leader or an expert. Both are noble career paths. Maybe you can mix it up throughout your career? Leaders who retain their 'technical' expertise actually garner more respect from their team members.
- Identify great leaders, past and present, and note what it is you admire about them. The chances are that you will be attracted by their emotional maturity (ie not an ego-centric megalomaniac) and their ability to communicate.
    - If emotional immaturity has greater appeal, you might consider employing a hybrid career-coach/psychotherapist.

20 Major Tech Trends

Overview

We now have a strong sense of how the world of work, workers and leadership are changing, along with the anthropological forces that are shaping the future.

Whilst this transition to the digital economy is really humanity returning to its true nature, it is fuelled by new technology. So in this chapter, we will take a brief look at what's hot in the world of IT.

SMAC heads the agenda

> *There are only a couple of industries that call their customers users, and deal in smac (sic).*

As a former technologist, I think this is both a hilarious statement and a reflection of the service attitude of many IT functions. Not everyone will appreciate this observation, but that is not the point.

SMAC is an acronym for: Social media, Mobility, Analytics and Cloud. Over the last few years, these have become the main drivers behind what is sold by the Tech Sector. Visit any tech service supplier's website, or read any tech conference programme, and at least one, if not all, of these themes will be woven in.

Looking at each in turn:

Social media

The emergence of Facebook and Twitter, amongst others, has enabled us to share our most intimate, trivial and profound thoughts. They have enabled us to gossip, praise and berate others. In fact, they enable us to huddle into social groups and interact with other group members, much like hunter gatherers sitting around the fire 12,000 years ago.

Sticking with the herd was an instinctive way of keeping safe. Today, following the herd, or at least listening to the herd, protects us from booking a hotel with a poor service ethic, or dining at a restaurant where botulism is on the menu.

This human urge to be social is creeping into every aspect of our life, including work. Significantly, from a career perspective, it has entered the enterprise. As work and life become more integrated, the distinction between 'social social' media and 'business social' media will disappear.

This emergence of corporate social media tools is akin to vegetation pushing through the surface of a city car park.

Man has created structures to override, or tame, nature. But in the long run, nature finds a way to express itself, in full. Social media tools thus allow man, as a social animal, to be social and to not even be constrained by physical distance. So these social media tools, in effect, are making us 'super social'.

The one current drawback is that we are, as yet, unable to mimic the nit picking of our ancestors, which today manifests itself in touching the people we are engaging with. This is a significant missing element of the social technology piece.

Thus, it is my prediction that touch technology (aka haptics) will soon become part of our everyday life.

Mobility

I have laboured our desire to be mobile in previous chapters. To be freed from the enslavement of the assembly line or office desk. The mobile phone has set us free. For those of you below a certain age, you may be wondering why we don't just call it a phone.

As mentioned in an earlier chapter, there was a time when all phones were attached to the wall by a cord. This restricted the extent to which we could 'walk and talk'. The reference to mobile is to remind us older people of how lucky we are to no longer be restricted to walking in an arc, backwards and forwards, when talking on the phone.

A further recap: The mobile was not a welcome device within the corporation. But the Blackberry smartphone changed that, thus allowing workers to roam. It enabled workers to work where it best suited them, and to remain in contact with the office when visiting a prospect, client or supplier.

Being mobile is part of our true nature.

There is more to this than having a mobile device. Some organisations believe they have embraced mobility in full by issuing their workers with smart devices.

But mobility is really about designing work, such that it embraces our need to roam. Smart glasses (remember Google Glass?) is a big step towards hands free communication and environment-sensitive information retrieval. Your eyewear will 'in effect, provide your 'mobile office'. As an aside, mobility also needs to be factored into the services organisations provide to their customers.

For your own sanity, ensure your choice of employer does not operate a 'command and control' model, where mobility is shunned.

Analytics

This term encapsulates the tools that enable us to turn data into insight and, as a result, make better decisions faster than our competitors. The data we derive these insights from increasingly comes from a variety of sources. It can be from the structured databases associated with your employer's customer relationship management system, or from the torrent of unstructured data passing through in the form of tweets, audio and video.

Collectively, the IT industry has chosen to refer to this amalgam of data, and the associated analytic tools, as 'big data'.

The term big data is overhyped, and there is a question mark over whether weaving the phrase 'big data' into your business conversations will make you sound 'on the money' regarding tech trends, or just someone who talks in vacuous jargonese.

Nonetheless, analytics is key to extending our senses beyond those that we were born with. Great analytic tools augment our decision making beyond what our eyes and ears are telling us.

In keeping with the transition to a more enlightened decentralised leadership model, these tools will enable those on the ground to take business decisions, rather than having to seek guidance from above for every single decision.

So let's imagine you are a bank clerk at a party. You are getting on very well with a smart, attractive and apparently 'into you' fellow guest. You have embraced work-life integration, so as you see their pupils dilate you go for the kill. Fumbling with your trousers, you remove your device.

Your admirer had been talking about buying their own flat earlier on, and now you are going to secure their mortgage at 2am on a Sunday morning.

You know they want it badly, and you know you can deliver, thanks to the decentralised leadership model your bank operates, along with its decentralised 'workplace on a device' apps portfolio. Once you have checked their credit worthiness, and cross referenced this with your housing app (powered via your government's open data gateway) to check its market value, you are good to approve. Who said fun can't be work?

Our hunter gatherer ancestors lived and died by the 'in the moment' decisions they made. Though they did not have to concern themselves with predatory 'mortgage lenders'. In today's world, analytics is a critical tool in both our personal and corporate armoury.

This digital economy is also referred to as the knowledge economy. Expect to see career opportunities associated with the provision of knowledge as a service. The real value in knowledge provision is in how it is served up to the recipient. At one end, analytics can take the form of a tabular report. At the other end, the information is superimposed on your environment in real-time. This evolving end of analytics is called augmented reality.

Cloud

If you haven't come across the term 'cloud' in respect of new technology, it is very likely that you haven't backed up your data in the last few years. So before you read on, I suggest you choose a vendor, and copy your data to an online remote storage facilitate, just in case your device breaks or is stolen.

But the cloud is much more than a 'magic super disk drive' somewhere in the world, managed by Internet pixies. The management of data, and the processing of data, are two significant reasons why organisations invest in IT. The cloud provides both.

Some cloud vendors exist to provide you with raw storage or processing power.

But there are also cloud vendors who provide you with banking functionality (aka banks) and the ability to book films (aka cinemas). Fundamentally, anything provided via the web can be considered to be a cloud service. So in that respect the cloud and the web are the same thing. So what's the fuss?

In the enterprise space (ie private and public sector organisations), there was a time when each organisation had its own IT department. Increasingly, the functionality once provided in these IT departments is now accessed via the cloud (ie the web).

If these web-delivered services are actually provided by the IT function then this is called a private cloud. But, if the services are acquired from a publicly available third party provider, then this is referred to as public cloud. Organisations that make use of both often talk about hybrid cloud.

The big point is that the cloud is causing companies to buy less technology (ie hardware and software), and instead rent a similar service from a third party. So, for example, instead of buying customer management software and running it on servers, which have similarly been purchased, a customer management service is used via the cloud.

New technology is typically fast depreciating, so it makes little sense to buy it. Better to rent.

This shift in technology architecture is thus impacting the manner in which organisations use technology. It is also increasing both the private sector and governments' reliance on the Internet to keep the wheels of business and society turning.

Back in 1943, one of IBM's most high profile CEOs, Thomas Watson, allegedly stated that there would only ever be a global need for maybe five computers.

My, how we laughed, as Microsoft set off to put a computer on every desk. But today, I would observe that Mr Watson is increasingly 'on the money'.

What?! <Pause for effect>

You are probably imagining that I have lost the last few marbles I started out with, given the proliferation of smart devices. But as more and more IT gets dispatched to the cloud, what we will see on our devices is just the user interface (or more commonly known as the app). The real processing and storage will take place in the datacentre of a cloud provider.

My prediction is that the cloud providers will go the way of other utility industries. Thus the majority of the raw cloud provision services will be provided by circa five global players.

The cloud is having a profound impact on IT infrastructure, and thus the infrastructure of the digital economy. So you are encouraged to track its evolution. So Mr. Watson was very likely 'on the money'.

Artificial intelligence

This is a hot topic, which has been on and off the boil for circa sixty years. In essence, it is an attempt by the computing industry to develop technology that not only does what it is programmed to do, but does so in a manner similar to humans. It may use environmental sensors or case based reasoning (ie what was the best decision for similar situations that have already taken place).

The famous Turing test implies the goal for artificial intelligence is to reach a level whereby a human interacting with the computer cannot distinguish the interaction from a truly human one. Recently this has been achieved.

Artificial intelligence is used for problem solving. It is also used in appliances that embrace fuzzy logic. So washing machines that establish what is being washed before choosing the wash cycle employ fuzzy logic. As do video cameras that correct the unsteady hands of nervous videographers.

IBM has invested heavily in this space, having built computers that can beat chess masters and play a mean game of Jeopardy. Futurist author, Arthur C Clarke, perhaps saw this coming.

In the film, 2001: A Space Odyssey, we meet HAL 9000, the spaceship on-board computer, which to say the least was an independent thinker. Some say that HAL is a reference to IBM (just move the letters to the next letter in the alphabetic sequence).

Regardless of the consequences of humanity being outsmarted by technology, we will see this area of technology go from strength to strength, and permeating the most mundane of industries.

Look up the term 'singularity' to explore this theme further.

We have already started to see newspaper articles that have been produced by software. It will become increasingly difficult to detect human content from robotic content......... to detect human content from robotic content......... to detect human content from robotic content......... to detect human content from robotic content.........<Memory overflow: Command = Reboot>.

The Internet of Things

The Internet has been largely used to help people communicate, learn and buy stuff. Of course, it has also been a god send to procrastinators the world over. In this respect, the Internet can be thought of as the Internet of People. As technology finds its way into previously 'dumb' devices, such as hospital beds, trolleys and fridges, the Internet is becoming the Internet of Things (IoT).

So imagine fridges that order food on your behalf via the Internet, and are synchronised with your calorie counting app, and so refuse to open when you have hit your daily limit. Imagine supermarket trolleys that advise supermarkets on checkout staff near-casting and real-time shelf replenishment.

Increasingly these intelligent devices are being worn by us.

The explosive growth in wearable technology, largely driven by self-analytics, is adding to the volume of devices and data that the IoT has to handle.

Google glasses (or a commercially viable alternatives) are likely to become Google contact lenses. In time, I predict we will witness Google eyes (or equivalent). So wearables will become embeddables.

Welcome to the the third wave: The Internet of Things in People.

Security concerns jump to a whole new level. We have already seen hackers compromise heart pacemakers, at distances of up to half a mile from the victim. The IoTiP will be a fascinating phase in our existence.

Augmented man

We have already touched on the idea of augmented man. But let's explore this in the context of the IoT. Augmented man is not a recent phenomenon. Using animal skin to protect us against the elements saw the advent of wearables.

The automobile can be considered the first (ill-fitting) exoskeleton. Spears and tools certainly augmented our capability to hunt and build. As did the arrival of the portable timepiece in the fifteenth century.

Many of us today would feel great discomfort if we left our phones at home. There is no question that we need technology to operate in modern society. Increasingly, this technology can travel with us. Over time, it will increasingly be in us.

Consequently, we are moving from human to cyborg, part organic, part electronic. Prosthetic implants lend themselves to being Internet enabled, if only for the manufacturer to offer their products as a service. Being able to deal with limb issues remotely, or simply to make software upgrade distribution easier, makes Internet connectivity a useful feature.

You may have guessed by now that I believe the shift to the digital economy is more than just another wave of industrial improvement.

Possibly the defining element of this transition is that we are actually undergoing a species shift from Homo sapiens to Homo extensis (augmented man). I think this is significant. The fact that we have all the world's knowledge at our fingertips would have been considered science fiction a few decades ago. The likelihood that this information will be directly accessible by our consciousness (thus saving us a few clicks) is fiction today, but which will likely be the reality of tomorrow. I am in two minds about living in a world where people literally will 'know it all'. Or where, instead of having the world's knowledge at our fingertips, we have it in our fingertips.

But before the robot-human boundary blurs, there will be a phase where humans will work alongside robots. These robots will not necessarily look like Will Smith's co-stars in I, Robot.

They will likely be capable of a few functions such as make tea, monitor periphery, or carry shopping. In this respect, they are likely to steal jobs from factory workers, security guards and professional carers.

The opportunity in this trend is either in the associated science of robotics and intelligent devices, or in the ability to configure them for a given application. I suspect that it may well be a requirement from employers in due course for their more human staff to be comfortable working alongside robots.

Our relationship with technology is going to become increasingly intimate, and perhaps even scary. I mean, what are the consequences of ignoring a 'Friend request' from the carer robot that manages your medication?

Summary

Technology is changing the world. Some of it appears to be nature's backlash against the industrial era. Some of it might be redefining what it means to be human. Science reality appears to be outpacing science fiction.

Whilst the digital economy is about people, it would be wise to ensure you are sufficiently tech-savvy to harness technology developments for personal productivity. But, it would also be wise to treat new technology developments as career highway signs. Does the arrival of a particular technology indicate that you are indeed on the correct career path, or does it signal an unanticipated dead-end? The sooner you know, the sooner you can accelerate or swerve.

Take action

- Assess how reliant you are on new technology:
  - o In your personal life.
  - o In your professional life.
- Assess how the technologies I have mentioned could play into your career plans, either directly (I want to be a robot counsellor), or indirectly (I want my career to be built around something that harnesses the power of social media and augmented reality).
- Identify and invest in some quality content sources, such as, Wired, New Scientist and Scientific American, to keep abreast of what's coming up in the near, medium and long term.

21 Major Business Trends

Overview

If we are to steer our career trajectories with the wind behind us, we need to be aware of the trends impacting the workplace.

This chapter explores the most significant trends, and how you might respond to them.

Customer empowerment

The rise of the customer is one of the defining characteristics of the digital economy. Up until then, customers were targets to be manipulated:

- "They're grrreat! – US food manufacturer.
- "More doctors smoke Camels than any other cigarette" – US tobacco company.

Some were ahead of their time and simply exploited social behavior:

- "It's good to talk" – UK telecoms provider.
- "Mix with Cinzano and you mix with the best" - Italian beverage company.

The rise of social media has played a significant role in separating the sizzle from the steak. Rarely do we pursue the vendor's account of how good their product or service is; we head straight for the customer reviews (admittedly despite their capacity to be 'gamed.').

As well as social media, increased globalisation is providing consumers with greater choices, which means the vendors have to work harder to gain our attention and money. The social economy runs on trust and reputation. Companies that ignore that play a dangerous game. Smart vendors are moving away from tricking consumers into buying what they have to sell and moving towards using market data to establish what the market wants, and then providing it. So increasingly, those with the best IT systems and ability to turn 'big data' into consumer insight will dominate. But only for as long as it takes their competitors to spot the opportunity and offer a 'me too' alternative.

This customer empowerment is sending a shock wave along the supply chains of many vendors and markets.

Whereas once we had Ford's promise of, "You can have any colour, so long as it is black", today, companies are increasingly turning their supply chains into demand chains. The customer will determine what is built, rather than the vendor. We are not quite at the "I want my new car to have sixteen wheels, an electronic jamming system and a mounted cannon", ie 'pimp my family estate'.

But personalisation, in terms of colour, engine size, music system, seat types and so on is available. The associated manufacturing approach is called mass customisation. The manufacturers are getting smarter in respect of how much control they offer the buyer in terms of personalisation.

Today, customers are generally not looking for products, or even services, but experiences. I want to feel good about engaging with those whom I deal with.

I don't want the presales ("you look great in that suit"), and the post sales experience ("It will be ready to collect when it's ready. So stop calling!") to be different.

Smart organisations know that they need to think beyond the experience of a given interaction. They need to look at the customer journey as a whole, from gaining their attention through to turning them into a raving advocate.

Increasingly, these interactions take place via a technology interface, so there is increased focus on DCX (the digital customer experience).

So, as a consumer, it's worth knowing that you are increasingly in the driving seat, if that wasn't already apparent. But as a vendor of your own capability, you need to maintain a customer-centric outlook. Ultimately we are replaceable, no matter how good we are.

Whether you work as a freelancer, or as an employee, embedded deeply in a 'mega-corp', ensure that your role is either directly customer-facing, or that it is very clear to everyone that you are a significant contributor to the customers' wellbeing.

If you cannot demonstrate your customer-relevance, you will at some point find yourself on the wrong end of an operational efficiency exercise.

Citizen empowerment

Advances in mobile technology, social media and access to the Internet are broadly having an empowering impact on citizens. Oppressive regimes know that if they do not control these channels, they run the risk of their citizens becoming aware of the imbalance in the social contract with their government.

Such regimes would rather not risk the possibility that their citizens collaborate on the guidance of freely available online 'government-toppling' playbooks.

All governments make a point of managing, or at least monitoring, citizen chatter for signs of discontent. Controlling disaffected citizens is a challenge, given the technological advances in communications. The Arab Spring is a good example of this in practice.

But at the other end of the 'citizen unrest spectrum', even compliant citizens are evaluating the 'quality of life return' they are getting on their tax dollars.

They are assessing whether they would get a better return for them and their family elsewhere. Increased global mobility, coupled with marketable skills, makes this straightforward for many people.

Who wants to live in a society where you cannot play massively open online games whilst on the metro? Or, who wants to go on holiday to a place where the absence of a mobile signal or wi-fi means you cannot establish where the in-crowd are meeting each evening?

Some people will be nodding as they read this and others will be laughing. The nodders are called digital natives and the laughers are known as digital immigrants.

If governments do not provide good value, they will lose their best people.

If their best people leave, then the employers will follow. Before you know it, your high ranking economy is in freefall. Poverty and becoming an economic backwater await.

The trend of migration generally heading from East to West is changing. South Koreans and Chinese students, who in years gone by would have applied for US citizenship after completing their Ivy League MBA, are now heading home, because their homelands are the new hotbeds of opportunity. It is increasingly likely they will not need to travel to Western learning establishments to slingshot their careers forward.

So, as a citizen you have options, but only if you have the digital economy skills that will make you attractive beyond your home borders. Keep in mind that we are about to witness several billion people enter the middle class, who all will see a strong correlation between access to knowledge, skills and economic well-being. So, the competition to retain citizens will be stiff.

Capability-wise, you might think you are good. Well think of someone twice as motivated as you are, who is willing to work for half your expected fee/salary. Let that be the outboard motor that accelerates you along your personal path to mastery.

But let's spare a thought for those on the wrong side of the digital divide. Even in the developed world, there are those who do not have broadband access, or the mind-set/circumstances needed to bootstrap themselves into digital society.

The divide will grow exponentially, as the digital 'haves' continue to become increasingly augmented, and thus gain greater economic advantage over the digital 'have nots'.

Naturally the 'have nots' will become disengaged from society, which will have a deleterious impact on everyone. So as we scramble up the digital staircase, we need to ensure that our governments are aggressively narrowing this digital divide.

We do not want the dystopian future portrayed by HG Wells' Time Machine becoming a reality.

But to come back to the main point, there is a broad power shift from the governments to the people. This may well factor into the path you take on your journey to mastery. It also highlights the opportunity for those who have a strong social conscience. There will be plenty of opportunities to help your nation to both retain its best people, and to turn its worst (economically) people into its 'best people'.

Data ownership

In a data-driven world, who owns the data becomes very important. Traditionally, the data is collected by the big corporations, primarily on their customers. And for governments, primarily on their citizens.

But citizens and customers are also generating their own data through, for example, social media and wearable devices. Perhaps even data generated from perusing the web might be included here. Such data is valuable. For example, the aggregated social media of thousands of users can be applied to determining whether an uprising is imminent, or in which direction the stock market indices will move.

The 'Quantified Self' has emerged as a term to label our growing interest in capturing data about ourselves. This data might lead to insights, such as, how well we have slept, and how many steps we have taken today.

Such data, when aggregated, can yield insights, for example, in respect of employee effectiveness and national health-service planning.

But who owns this 'digital crude oil'? Today, it is largely the governments and the corporations. Would you have access to your data if your wearable wristband supplier went out of business?

What would become of your biometric (login) data, if your smartphone provider was hacked? Can you demand that the big online retailers erase all your data, beyond what they need for regulatory and tax purposes?

It is too early to really call this a trend, but I suspect, in keeping with the power shifts we are experiencing in respect of employee/employer, buyer/seller and citizen/government, we will see a shift in who owns our personal data.

All organisations need data to navigate the tempestuous and unpredictable marketplace, so a loss of control in respect of data would put them at a serious disadvantage.

As individuals recognise the value in their own data, they will likely share it with the brands and institutions that they want to associate with, and perhaps sell their data, albeit anonymised, to other organisations. Thus, we will be able to exploit the data generated as a result of being us.

Some people's data will be more valuable than others. Your data may be highly valuable, because your behaviours are an almost perfect reflection of the habits of Middle America. Or more specifically, your behaviours reflect the sports apparel buying habits of transgender recreational basketball players, a niche but possibly growing market.

Today, celebrities sell their wedding data, or the data associated with their grand homes.

This data takes the form of interviews and photographs, and these are monetised via websites and glossy magazines. What if those celebrities sold their Quantified Self data? And what if celebrities massaged their data to reflect their professional brand?

Imagine aging rock stars broadcasting data that implies their breakfast this morning comprised opium and brandy, shared with an admiring and sexually liberated contingent of their entourage. Whereas the reality is that they went for a 5 kilometre jog, followed by orange juice, jasmine tea and a quinoa salad.

I am sure the celebrity pundits will make hay out of the changes in heart rate that celebrities experience, particularly when comparisons are made between heart rate whilst in the company of their current partner and relative changes when in the company of others. So big data becomes 'Big Brother data'.

Like a comet's tail, in the digital world we are continuously throwing off data. Data that has value both to ourselves ("Did I really spend that much yesterday?"), and to others ("Her shoe spending pattern is on the increase, as is her resting heart rate. We predict a spend outage in two months, when she will likely return to rehab.").

This need to interpret market data at the individual level, along with developing the rules that determine the organisational response to certain conditions, will see a growth in the role of data scientists. All organisations, from national intelligence agencies through to kids selling home-made lemonade to passers-by, will benefit from access to people's personal data.

We have to ask the question, with whom do we share our data? Or, whether we share it at all. In any case, there is a professional opportunity for those interested in capturing, managing, processing, analysing, interpreting and even selling people's data.

Home manufacturing

Manufacturing is the production of items that will either be sold to consumers, or sold to other manufacturers, for incorporation into their products.

Prior to the industrial era, this manufacturing would take place in a workshop (recall the master - journeyman - apprentice model). The industrial era, with its emphasis on scale and division of labour, developed the factory as the new home for manufacturing.

In the digital economy, the new home for manufacturing is likely to be the home.

Picture this: It's time for bed, so you take off your clothes. You like the shirt you were wearing today, but you admired (for some reason) the button down collar Armani paisley print shirt a colleague of yours was wearing at the office.

So, you take your shirt and throw it in the washing machine. You use the voice-activated user interface to search through the clothes catalogue: Shirts -> Armani -> Summer collection 2026 -> 'Trip-out' range -> Paisley, and select print. An error message comes back that you are out of plastic. So you replace the empty plastic cartridge, and this time the 'washing machine' swirls into action.

The first phase of the 'wash' is to decompose your existing shirt in order to salvage the materials for either your new shirt or subsequent print jobs. The second phase is to print your new shirt. Being a smart washing machine, it knows your vital measurements. It has access to your personal data, which is handily stored on a chip under the skin of your upper arm.

This same chip will be debited in payment for the use of the Armani shirt printing algorithm, and it will be a steep payment, because this shirt is from a designer collection due out in eight years. Armani and other manufacturers have abandoned manufacturing, and are now in the clothes design/software business.

Your washing machine is, in essence, a three dimensional printer.

You may well also have a printer in the garage for producing spare parts for your vehicle, and a printer in the kitchen for printing meals.

3D printing is already here of course. It is just a question of when it will make commercial sense to move beyond simply printing documents in the home. This is spawning a whole new industry involving 3D printers, software, and moving manufacturing out of the factory and installing it at the point of consumption.

But it goes even further than manufactured goods. Imagine a world where printing dinner is normal. Who will dominate the refill market for those printers? Who will own the algorithms for printing, say, raspberries, or salmon? And how will this new market be regulated?

Career opportunities abound for entrepreneurs, software engineers, biotechnologists and even lawyers. Will the retail giants take charge, or will they watch, in a state of paralysis, as the next wave of digital retail players move centre stage?

Hyper-specialisation

MIT's Thomas Malone has proposed that the future of work might be one where workers are hyper-specialised. That is to say, rather than being very good at an array of skills, we follow paths to mastery in one very specific area.

This is not a new phenomenon. Being a professional footballer requires you to have an array of skills honed to a high level of competence. But a footballer's market value is often determined by their capability/reputation for doing one thing extremely well, eg. taking free kicks, or their ability to pass the ball accurately over great distances.

I might be fairly good at producing PowerPoint presentations, but if I have a reputation for producing world class analyst presentations for CEOs of quoted companies, I am likely to have a queue of organisations at my door, particularly if they feel my approach has a positive impact on audience/market sentiment.

Another example are judo players. The top guys are capable of employing hundreds of techniques (throws, strangles, locks, etc) but tend to be known for their one signature move.

My sense is that this is the way that the market is moving. So we have to decide on our own area of hyper-specialism. This then requires us to establish and acquire the associated capabilities.

A couple of related points:

- It is not simply a case of choosing a skill that you happen to like. There needs to be a market demand if this skill is going to be economically valuable to you.
- The specialism you choose may not necessarily be a specialism, for example, quantum physics. It could be a unique combination of skills, for example, quantum physics coupled with robotics, and elderly care.

The reality for some of us industry veterans is that we may feel expert in many areas. It is important to remember that buyers are focused on their problem, not your career history. So, we need to make a decision about what we promote in respect of our capability. I am not suggesting that you deny having had all your work experiences. You simply must not confuse your market by putting everything for sale on your stall.

So whether you are mid-career, or on the verge of entering the world of work, you need to consider where you will sit in a hyper-specialised world. In other words, you need to ensure that your path to mastery is also a path to being the best in the world.

Cellular organograms

We have established that the command and control model is not optimised for quick decision making, nor for harnessing the brain power of the workforce as a whole. The emergence of collaboration tools, ranging from email through to video conferencing, are enabling like-minded people in an organisation to get things done, regardless of the constraints of the management hierarchy.

Often, this is done with the management's blessing. For example, the organisation needs to respond quickly to a change in government regulations, which will impact the business as a whole.

So there is a need to create a cross business taskforce to assess the impact and determine the response.

Today, we have many 'hierarchical' organisations operating with embedded 'cellular structures'. The next stage, in my view, is to eliminate the hierarchy and operate a totally cellular model.

As major trends go this is up there, or even out there, with my take on data ownership, and my belief in Thomas Malone's hyper-specialised world. In other words, it is too early to say whether it is a trend for sure. It lacks a track record. So it must be considered with a degree of caution.

But let's take a look at why cellular organograms might have a future. What can we learn from cells that might help us with this cellular organisational model? We are led to believe that the first living things on the planet were single-cell organisms. They realised that their long term interests were best served by teaming up with other single-cells to produce multi-cell organisms.

Over time, humans became the most sophisticated collaboration model in nature.

But what if we are only an intermediary step in this cellular collaboration odyssey? Perhaps we developed a neocortex because nature has decided that the most optimised cellular environment is not a human, but a collaborating group of humans.

So those of us who are wired to be team players are most likely to thrive. This, in itself, is not an argument for the break-up of mega corporations into smaller highly cohesive and loosely coupled teams.

The reality is that most mega corporations are already broken up into teams.

It is just that the teams have usually been built from within the organisation, and so the employees have thus been forced to work with each other.

I am making the case that the next generation of team will roam freely and will behave as a 'unit for hire'. The team members will have complementary skills, and collectively they will have a reputation for getting things done.

In a fast moving market, it will be easier to swap in and out expert teams, rather than deconstructing and reassembling new in-house teams that probably lack the expertise and social cohesion to hit the ground running.

As mentioned, I have to admit that I have been predicting this model for some time, but have yet to see it take place on any significant scale. Possibly I am right on the idea and wrong on the timing. Over the years, I have worked with many recruitment agencies, and only now am I starting to see them place teams as well as individuals. It is likely that the reticence on the recruitment agencies' part is risk related.

When trading in individuals, the recruitment agencies are in the dating agency business. The risk of an unsuitable relationship lies with the newly coupled parties.

A move to placing teams is more likely to force the recruitment agency to take on the associated delivery risk. The buyer is now paying for an outcome. This is a different business model and requires a degree of management skill/risk appetite that is currently unappealing to most agencies, despite the upside potential.

One could think of franchising as a variant of this cellular model. The franchised operation has some autonomy, but is somewhat constrained in its branding, business processes and supply chain.

As I have stated earlier in the book, terrorist cells are closer to the model I am describing. Cell members being drawn from the same communities to ensure they goad each other on if misgivings about the mission arise. No doubt, the terrorists use this model for its operational agility advantages.

Once the cell knows its objective, it can carry it out or remain in 'sleeper mode' until signalled to proceed. The decoupled cell model means that should a cell be apprehended, whilst its members will understand the group's vision, their knowledge of strategy and tactics will be limited to the tasks assigned to their cell.

It is an uncomfortable truth that the bad guys are perhaps leading the way in respect of organisational design. But, we cannot ignore their approach, particularly if it delivers results in high-stakes environments.

The cohesion of a competent like-minded team, particularly one where the members know each other well cannot be underestimated. Admittedly at the 'martyrdom end' of the terrorist spectrum, the opportunity to deepen the team's effectiveness, through working together over a series of engagements, is somewhat limited.

From a career/mastery perspective, the message is to develop your own collaboration and team player skills.

It is not enough to simply develop a reputation for great expertise. You need to be known for your team spirit.

Regardless of where you are in terms of your mastery journey, it is never too early to identify like-minded people with whom you can build the dream team. Cell/team affiliations are not necessarily for life. Though the Rolling Stones are fascinating from an anthropological perspective. They are a rare example of a cell that has successfully spanned several geological eras. Anthropologists typically have to travel around the world to study the fossils of our ancestors. But in this case, the fossils will not only travel to the anthropologists (as part of their tour programme), but will even take the guess work out of how they might have lived, by demonstrating their customs and rituals on stage.

Summary

In this chapter, we have looked at an array of established and potential trends. We would all like certainty, and I am sure you would prefer that I presented a definitive statement of the future. Unfortunately, the future is not like that. However, the trends covered in this chapter should stimulate your thinking in terms of how the world is evolving.

Take action

- List people you admire in respect of their success in their field, whether it be sport, business, politics or any competitive environment. Detail what it is that you admire about them. This will give you a strong sense of the brand they are projecting.
- Now list what it is you think they are good at. What is it that has enabled them to be the best, or high up in their field? Sure, they may appear multi-talented, but what is the one thing (or one combination of things) that they do better than anyone else?
- Treat all predictions and projections by futurists with caution. Seek out evidence that both supports and disproves, say, the growing trend of hyper-specialisation. Your ability to develop your own worldview based on reality, rather than on what you are told, will enable you to steer your career in accordance with the real world, as opposed to a hypothetical one.
  - o That said, some hypotheses serve as better starting points than others, so choose the futurists you follow wisely.

Beyond Skills: A New Approach

22 Beyond Work-Life Balance

Overview

How many of us compartmentalise our lives into work and non-work? How many of us, not only leave our car in the car park/coat in the cloakroom (for non-car owners)/surfboard in reception (for non-car owning, non-coat owning surf dudes employed across the bay), but leave our personalities there as well?

The model of having a professional life and a social life as two distinct existences is an industrial era concept. We will explore why this is not sustainable in the digital economy.

Work life

In the industrial era, people generally did work they did not enjoy. Many still do. They looked forward to free time at the end of the working day, working week and working life.

> *Many of us now find that we are working later into the evening/night, and even at weekends.*

Some of this can be attributed to increased global competition. Some of it might be down to a lack of effective self-management tools/disciplines applicable to the digital era. And increasingly, it may be that your employer's business model is no longer 'fit for purpose'. The leaders are under an illusion that working harder/longer will keep the 'boat afloat'.

This concept of retiring at the end of your working life will become increasingly quaint/far off. Shifting demographics mean that there are increasingly not enough young people working to top up the pension reserves needed for those who are retired. From a government perspective, people are 'inconveniently' living longer lives, so the pension model is no longer sustainable.

Knowing that your working life might likely extend to the end of your time on the planet, you had better choose a career path that, as well as funding your chosen lifestyle, is something that you will enjoy until you 'fall off the perch', as it were.

That is not to say that you will do the same thing from leaving school to attending your funeral. But it is likely that whatever you do, it will be rewarding beyond 'bill paying'.

As mentioned in an earlier chapter, your path to mastery, whether it is made up of 'one career one employer' or 'many careers many clients', will need to be stimulating and meaningful. Your drive may come from your desire to:

- Save the planet.
- Create a chain of virtual coffee houses.
- Be the fastest person in the world to run three and three quarters times around a four hundred metre track (for your age group).

So, as long as it ignites your passion, then it is not for anyone to cast judgement on the mastery path you have taken. However, we can't ignore the financial element, unless of course you are rock star or aristocratic offspring. So, whilst passion is important from a motivational perspective, competence and a market demand are critical, if you have a lifestyle to fund, but not a trust fund to fund it.

In short, the trend in the proportion of our lives spent working is increasing. We need to ensure we engineer our work such that this time is well spent.

Work-life integration

I have made reference to this throughout the book. I have argued that it is our true state. So when working from home, why is it that I cringe when, during a business-related Skype call, 'unplanned events' occur?

These include:

- My dog's sensitivity to customer-facing representatives of the parcel delivery industry, which manifests itself in an instinctual desire to accelerate from zero to full tilt barking in microseconds.
- My mother-in-law leaving a gushing voice mail for my wife in respect of how her begonias are progressing.

I've tried masking this by:

- Pretending to bark in manner that is contextually relevant to the discussion (difficult).
- Suggesting we have a cross line (this can work with those who don't quite get the difference between analogue and digital).

But the reality is that for both my dog and my mother-in-law, these are priorities. It's a tremendous relief when the shoe is on the other foot and a non-professional bark/gush emerges from their end of the line.

Perhaps it's a sign of the transition we are making, when the senior executive I am dealing with on Skype latches onto the pet/begonia theme, and the business meeting briefly diverts to a casual chat. Despite our professional façades, people are social, and what were once irritations are now the spice that flavours our interactions.

I have mentioned that work is encroaching into our lives. Some of us will fight this. Some of us will accept the shift, but will endeavour to create a demilitarised zone that keeps the two domains separate.

However, work and life are increasingly integrated, though not totally entwined.

It would be unacceptable to allow business interruptions from your clients during your child's birthday party or whilst caring for a loved one in their final hours. Or even to take a call in respect of your mother-in-law's begonias, whilst delivering a keynote presentation to an arena full of business leaders (Note to self: Turn off phone before going on stage).

We do need to set boundaries between work and our private life, but there is an overlapping buffer zone. As we enter the digital economy, this buffer zone is growing. If you are serious about mastery, whether you are a portrait artist or a mixed martial artist, you are unlikely in any case to compartmentalise your 'work related' activities to a Monday to Friday, nine to five model.

Of course, you could constrain your professional activities in this industrial era manner, but it might impact:

- Your market availability.
- The time taken to achieve mastery.

Those who are serious about providing the best service to their market will eschew the old school model. Whilst I am implying that mastery requires putting the hours in, the reverse is also true.

In a post-industrial world, nine to five 'presenteeism' is replaced by a more pragmatic model, whereby you should be able to pursue non-business activities during 'working hours'.

Such activities might range from getting your toenails painted to attending an open lecture on Mexican art.

Your social value

It's a typical day at work. You are having an online conversation with a colleague, and a topic comes up that requires a decision, but neither of you have the knowledge to make it.

At that point, your communication platform searches your business directory (think Yellow Pages) for other staff who actually have expertise on the topic in question. It turns out that having trawled the profiles of all staff across the world, there is nobody who has the requisite expertise.

So now the platform searches the social networks of you and your colleague. It turns out that your uncle's girlfriend chairs an organisation that leads the way in the topic concerned. The platform then sets off a series of processes that explore the possibility of engaging your uncle's girlfriend in the conversation thread.

Thus your value is not just in your skills and experience, as detailed on your resume, but on the size of your social networks. Quality of social network is possibly a better measure. But given the randomness in which your social network might help your employer/client professionally, volume of contacts is perhaps a better measure.

Business networks such as LinkedIn come to mind in this respect. However, as work and life become more integrated, even 'social social' networks will have 'business' value.

We don't usually see friends and family as business assets (though if you choose to embrace the Ponzi methodology for growing a business, they make excellent 'marks'). Or even their friends and family. In the social economy, the proverb 'It's not just what you know, but who you know' rings truer than ever.

Personality

In the industrial economy, most of us had two personalities. We had one for life and one for work. At home, we were perhaps slovenly, outspoken and a practical joker. But as soon as we donned 'the uniform' (overalls or pinstripe suit) and passed through the company gates, we became the other us – articulate, understated, sensitive and service-oriented/predatory.

These adjectives of course do not reflect everybody. But many of us maintain two personalities for the two main environments we inhabit. This is the cause of stress because:

- We have to context-switch each time we move between the environments.
  - Over time, I have found that even industry best practice appraisal techniques rarely lead to happy outcomes at home.
- It is likely that the professional environment does not reflect the real us, and so we have to maintain this inauthentic façade for hours on end.

The issue is even more fundamental than personality. I recall delivering a presentation to a major tech player's IT function. The people in the room were technical architects and senior management. My presentation was entitled 'Towards IT Mastery'. It covered a number of themes, including the fact that technical skills on their own were not enough, and that one needed to have a strong service ethic to be perceived as valuable by the users.

In any case, a woman came up to me afterwards and thanked me for the presentation. She told me that she was a technical architect, and the only female amongst a team of male architects. Up until now, she spent her professional life suppressing her femininity because the male architects perceived this as some sort of weakness. (If you are curious about the behaviour of technical architects, watch any National Geographic documentary on ape colonies. Note the alpha male and how they deal with perceived challengers).

Possibly her presence triggered mental processes that sat beyond their logic circuits; thus causing confusion, feelings and disconcertment.

The important issue is that the organisation was losing out on the diverse perspective the female architect could bring to the table if she was allowed to act and think in an authentic manner without being judged. And perhaps also to think in a manner that is geared towards the optimal solution, rather than what will massage the ego of the alpha architect.

The point is that our personality, which is shaped by our gender, race and life experiences, is likely to become a key selling point in the digital economy. Innovation does not come from homogeneous thinking.

How many of us are suffering cognitive stress because, like the aforementioned technical architect, we have to maintain two personalities?

The beauty of being world class in what you do is that you can insist that your personality is part of the package; even if it perhaps doesn't quite match the HR department's profile of what an employee/contractor should be like. If you have what they need, and there isn't a surplus of people with your capabilities, then the buyer doesn't have a choice.

Alternatively, if buyers of talent can get over their need to acquire clones (often of the founder), they will have a much bigger gene pool to choose from.

If there is dissonance between who you are and what you do professionally, you need to consider whether you are doing your job to please someone else eg. your parents, or whether you are endeavouring to live out an ill-thought version of who you should be.

If you have no sense of your own personality, then consider taking a personality test (don't worry, you are guaranteed to pass). It could save you a lot of anguish if you pursued a career that played to your natural strengths and inclinations.

Your life value

I touched on non-conventional life experiences as having the potential to add to your value proposition. Those who have endured hardship will perhaps be more resourceful. Grateful for the opportunity to prove themselves, they might possibly be more loyal.

People who have had a chequered past can often offer great value.

I mentioned the prison gang leader in an earlier chapter. Of course there is always a risk that Mr Knuckles might revert to his old tricks if his annual appraisal doesn't meet his expectations. But his focus and leadership skills, coupled with a desire to put his past behind him, might on balance make him look like a good bet.

It could be that your hobbies have a market value. Your amateur photography skills could be an admission ticket to a career in the creative industry. Your marine aquarium hobby might lead to a career as an ecologist for a petrochemical firm.

Some would argue that hobbies involve things you love doing, and to commercialise them would be to destroy that love. There is a logic to that. And if your hobby becomes your work then some might quote the proverb 'All work and no play makes Jack a dull boy'.

I would argue that if Jack is happy then it's not for us to judge whether he is dull or not. And there is no reason why a newly commercialised hobby cannot be replaced with one or more hobbies of varying frivolity.

Career switching will be increasingly common as industries die and grow in almost real-time. Sports careers are usually relatively short-lived. Some sports people become media personalities. Others become involved on the periphery as sports agents or team managers.

But what about accountants, lawyers and doctors who have had enough of spreadsheets, contracts and illness? They have invested heavily in their careers.

So any decision to change path is not to be taken lightly. They could stay within their industry and perhaps work for a supplier, ie they move from the buy-side to the sell-side of the table.

They could become a media commentator on matters within their industry, with the intention of provoking reform. They could do this via a blog, which they monetise through advertising. They could also 'go back to school' and start again in a completely new career. It is very likely that whatever it is they end up doing, they will be able to salvage generic skills acquired in their former career. These may include service, business development and commercial skills.

If you are in a career that you no longer enjoy, invest time in establishing which aspects of the job you dislike. If it's colleagues or clients, then maybe a change of employer is needed, rather than a career change. Similarly, invest time in establishing what aspects of the job you really do like. These could indicate valuable skills, which could provide a welcome tailwind for your revised career/mastery path.

Staying on brand

I have emphasised the importance of having a strong brand. This makes it easier for your buyers to both find you and be impressed by your capability. Part of that brand building might include your social activity, comprising tweets, blog posts and YouTube videos. Such output enables prospective buyers with their decision making.

So let's imagine that you are a brain surgeon. You have written some attention grabbing research papers on the benefits of frontal lobotomies in 'fixing' truculent teenagers. You are recognised wherever you go, because your views have been shared on broadcast media.

As a media figure, your every move will be watched.

Pictures of you falling out of a nightclub on the morning of a high profile operation might be met with disgust by the public.

Unless of course, the other person staggering to the taxi is the celebrity patient, and the taxi is taking you both to the hospital.

In any case, once you are in the public eye, your every move will either be brand amplifying or brand dampening. Keep in mind, that there will be a direct correlation between your brand and your perceived value. So managing one's brand is not to be sniffed at.

If we scale this back a bit. Perhaps you are a very competent accountant at a big name firm. You are occasionally asked to speak at specialist events.

Plus you get to work on some high profile financial fraud projects. Nobody cares too much that you cover yourself head to toe in dark leather, and spend your weekends cruising between market towns on your bad boy Harley Davidson.

But the fact that you give informal, and above board, tax advice to a member of a local biker gang member, might be a concern. You like the guy. When he's not out whipping rivals with an iron chain, he is a charming family man. And in any case, you are informally advising him on private matters, not taking on the role of 'chapter' chief financial officer. It's kind of fun rubbing shoulders with such individuals. How very different to the world most accountants inhabit, you reflect.

But one night, after the family had gone to bed, you decide to kill some time on social media. You open up your Facebook account to find that you have a new friend request, whose profile picture of a snake weaving through the eyes of a skull is the insignia of your biker gang 'friend'.

So much for the work – (faux bad boy) life compartmentalisation you have managed for so long. What if you turn down his friend request? What if one of your professional friends picks up on your extended choice of associates?

The reality is that if we have a brand to protect, and in the social economy we do, then we have to think hard about what we do, where we do it, and who we do it with.

Then again, if you are great at what you do professionally, and for certain jobs you are the 'go to guy', the fact that your private life isn't textbook suburbia is neither here nor there.

The trick is to be so good that nobody in your target market dare tell you how to live your life.

I think, as time progresses, we will see a blurring of our social and business lives. The tools that support this compartmentalising will morph too. I am already seeing LinkedIn becoming less 'professional' and Facebook becoming more commercial.

Having a network that comprises a pantheon of industry greats, along with your foul-mouthed brother-in-law, anarchist niece and bike-riding enforcer associate, will certainly add spice to your profile.

As the work-life boundary dissolves, this futile attempt to position yourself as a hermetically-sealed professional will give way to the more natural reality that you are just a human connected to other real humans; all of us with our own foibles and frailties. Those that are comfortable with this reality will spend less time and expend less mental bandwidth trying to create the illusion of a pristine professional that inhabits a pristine environment.

Over time, I believe 'keeping it real' will add to your authenticity. This, in turn, will add to your professional brand.

Summary

The work-life boundary is becoming hazy. Clearly we don't want 'work' to encroach on every aspect of our life. But if we see work as less of a necessary evil and more as something that gives meaning to our lives, then we will be less inclined to fight work encroachment on every front.

If you see work in an industrial era context, then you will be inclined to do the minimum hours you are contracted to provide. If you are outcome based (and hopefully outcome rewarded), you will do what it takes to get the job done.

Significantly, elements of your 'life' will contribute to your perceived 'work' value. Your social networks, life experiences and, hobbies and interests come to mind.

Take action

- If you are sensitive to work encroaching into your private life, then it is worth reassessing your current role. It may be a sign that you have become disengaged, and either you need to get back your mojo or chart another path for your career.
- Audit your hobbies and life experiences to establish if there is anything that could be used as part of your professional value proposition.
- Actively build your social networks. Focus on people whom you can help, rather than just on those who can help you. Your social behaviour will indicate whether you are a giver or a taker.

Givers are most likely to succeed in the social economy.

23 The Digital Nomad

Overview

You have heard a lot from me on the digital economy and how it represents a transformation in terms of the way in which we work and live our lives. Ironically, I believe this transformation is actually returning us to our true nature, but in a somewhat 'souped up' form.

Some of us are already living the life of a digital nomad. I believe this number is set to grow. In this chapter we will take a look at what lies ahead.

The nature of digital nomads

It was only twelve thousand years ago that our ancestors lived a nomadic/hunter gatherer life. Once we descended from the trees, three million years ago, that was our modus operandi. Thus, it is more woven into our DNA than, say, striving to own a top-end boy-racer family estate with seat mounted child-pacifier tablets.

It is not just our ancestors who were nomadic. Nomadic people exist today. Some have access to designer clothing and mobile technology. They may even settle down for periods of time. But in broad terms, they are always on the move. Their social activity varies from singing around the camp fire to unlicensed boxing matches on disused land (often below motorway flyovers). Their modes of transport range from husky-powered sleds to top of the range 'beamers'.

Modern practices have thus impacted the nomadic tradition. It is still safe to say that nomads continue to be mobile, social and tribal.

They recognise that the world is bountiful, and so are able to thrive, taking what they need as they need it.

I first encountered digital nomads some twenty years ago. I was working for an investment bank, building a 'middle office' IT system to detect rogue trading in derivatives. I was working alongside guys from the southern hemisphere who were very competent accountants. What amazed me was that these guys would work for circa 6 months at this highly prestigious bank and then head off skiing/surfing, as the mood took them. At the time, I couldn't really understand how, having acquired such rarefied employment, they were happy to disappear out of the door with a view to returning if and when it suited them. What about their career progression?

How could they ever become the company CEO if they took such a cavalier approach to their career progression?

What I failed to understand at the time was that these guys were enlightened digital nomads. They lived the life they wanted and saw work as a means to fund that lifestyle. They weren't in awe of their Wall Street employer.

In fact, they knew that they were in the driving seat. Their specialist accounting skills were in short supply, so the bank needed them more than they needed the bank. Cool!

Today twenty years later, I guess those accountants could even progress their 'career' whilst skiing, thanks to the Internet. They could respond to regulator questions, whilst hurtling down the mountain, thanks to Bluetooth-enabled mobile technology. Their augmented reality glasses superimposing daily profit and loss sheets on the nearest radiant white mountain peak.

There is an upsurge in vagabonding as people choose to see the world in a manner that is more lifestyle than holiday. Certain professions can be carried out from almost anywhere. Or at least anywhere there is Internet access.

A professional colleague of mine has eschewed property ownership. He doesn't even rent. He just lives in hotels. He can speak nine languages and is a globally in demand sales trainer. He is not a young man, but his thirst for life and desire to engage with people around the world is inspiring.

I met another chap recently who has just sold his Internet of Things business. He was telling me that his wealth enabled him to buy a very large ranch. The foyer of his home was bigger than the hotel foyer where we both met.

But nine months ago, he sold what he could and put anything remotely personal in storage. He bought a small apartment in Ireland, which he uses as a base to hop around Europe, at his leisure.

He refers to his period of material acquisition as 'maintenance hell'.

Think about it. Owning several properties may sound impressive, but can you say that of owning several concurrent headaches ("The roof on property number four needs fixing". "Is that noise another Saturday night 'pop up' rave taking place on the northern perimeter of the ranch again?".)

In any case, more and more people are unshackling themselves from the chains of ownership in order to give them the nimbleness needed to do what they want, whether that be work or play. Those of us who are working on our mastery path, keeping in mind the key elements of competence, passion and demand, can, and often do, enjoy the digital nomad life.

If you are financially very successful, then there is no reason why you cannot live a five star nomadic existence. This can take the form of staying in luxury hotels and travelling first class. Today this playboy approach to digital nomadicity will likely cause friction, as your fellow playboys struggle with your inability to be impressed by possessions. They will perhaps be bemused by your spirit of freedom. Much like herb tea, this lifestyle will eventually move from offensively quirky ("I'm not going to the bar to order that!") to curiously quirky ("Camomile tea. Is that a religious thing?").

The trick, regardless of your wealth, is to be cash flow positive.

You don't need to earn so much if your needs are tempered. If you can manage that, you can choose the work you fancy, rather than the work you, perhaps, desperately need to fund your extravagant lifestyle.

You do not need to be rich. You just need to spend less than your income. If your incomings are capped, then you need to adjust your outgoings accordingly.

Being a nomad is in our true nature. Being a digital nomad is no different. Technology simply gives us more options. If you choose to live in a Bedouin tent, and herd animals across the desert, that's fine. Just don't forget your portable 3D printer, should the tent need repairs. And don't forget your satellite communications device. It will help if you need to:

- Access the constellations app, to help you navigate at night.
- Watch the latest Netflix box set, the moment it is released.

Rise of the robots

Digital nomads might well be characterised by their distaste of process or robotic work. As I have mentioned, this will be less of an issue as, unsurprisingly, such work will increasingly be done by software/robots. This, of course, has a significant bearing on the future of work.

People with limited economic choices are sometimes tempted to blame foreign workers for taking their jobs. In the next few years, we will see a transition from blaming foreigners to blaming robots.

Robots already exist in the workplace. Factories have been revolutionised by their introduction. These robots do not quite fit the science fiction model, in that they are not androids modelled on the human structure of limbs, torsos and a head. These factory robots are highly specialized. They do not need to have general purpose functionality, such as speech capability. It is even less likely that these robots will be found after work at the employer-funded social club. But tomorrow, who knows?

Again, robots today tend to be mono-functional. Robot tractors will happily wend their way up and down the field, but will be of little use in rescuing people from a burning building. But robots are becoming more general purpose. Aging populations have triggered a focus on robot carers. Such features include:

- Conversational capability, with facial expressions to match.
- Ability to make tea.
- Ability to administer medication - "Here are your tablets Florence". This is a significant improvement on creeping up behind Florence and jabbing her with a robotic hand/syringe.
- Hair washing.
    - I am unsure as to whether the hairdresser chitchat module will come as standard. Or a module that delivers the contextually-odd, yet pleasant, unsolicited cranium massage I occasionally receive.

Robots are thus getting personal and person-like.

It may be of comfort to some of us that the robots will be given menial tasks. Thus, they are no threat to us professionally. But devices, robotic or otherwise, are getting smarter, so do not take it for granted that this is an issue solely for 'the masses'.

We are likely to see some social unrest in this respect. The reality is that governments and employers will not have a choice if they are to remain competitive in a global marketplace. It might be that your government taxes robots, as if they were human workers, so that employers do not swap out humans purely to exploit loopholes in tax law.

Whilst some robots will spend all day irrigating fields across the Sahara, others will operate alongside human workers.

Thus, they will increasingly be designed to look and behave like humans; all for the sake of a harmonious work environment.

Those of us who adapt quickly to working in a human-automaton environment will be favoured over those who insist on workplace apartheid. The robots are indeed coming. A new dawn is rising. A whole new industry is evolving that will require skilled designers, builders and maintenance engineers. Further down the line of course, these roles will be carried out by robots too.

This is less a tale of doom, and more a clarion call in respect of our career paths:

- Nothing is permanent. We need to take an anticipatory approach to our skills acquisition.
- We can either capitalise on the rise of the robots or be robot 'road kill'.
  - Asimov's laws do not preclude robots competing for work.

But the robots are us

Whilst this future might make you feel uncomfortable, it should come as no surprise. We have already explored augmented man on a number of occasions in this book.

Let's zoom out beyond humanity. You rarely see a hippopotamus with a mobile phone. Or a sloth with a wearable fitness bracelet. Possibly it is because they don't feel the need to enhance their functional capability? Though, you might argue that usability is the main reason for poor mobile uptake with hippopotami, and that fitness accessories are a non-starter when it comes to the sloth market.

In any case, when it comes to humans, we have been tech-reliant since we realised the increased quality of life we could enjoy through embracing the use of flint. You could argue that the car was both the first example of 'bring your own device' in the industrial era and the first wearable device (a 4 wheeled exo-skeleton).

The fact that most of us feel very uncomfortable without our smart phone attests to our growing dependence on technology augmentation. "How will people get hold of me?", "How will I record my steps taken/calories ingested today?" or "How will I survive the commute without my whale sounds playlist?".

We are indeed becoming augmented humans.

The Internet was created to enable people to communicate via computers. Then along came the Internet of Things enabling devices to collaborate.

Increasingly, we are seeing the Internet of Things in People. Digital pacemakers, smart prosthetics and even embedded monitors, enabling the user to access the web from their forearm.

Increasingly, the use of high tech exoskeletons will provide us with both augmented power and speed. Combine this with our brain power and agility and, for all intents and purposes, we will be superhuman (The Ironman films were essentially promotional videos).

Fast-forward a few years to where we have cracked time travel. Imagine travelling back to the Middle Ages with some of this new kit. What would people think?

But back to today. Like a frog slowly being boiled in water (a myth, I know), we are hardly aware of our transition to becoming cyborgs. This can be witnessed daily on the train as people sit there in a trance consuming content, through both their ears and eyes, via their personal devices.

It would be no less weird if the transportation company provided wireless content accessible via a receiver embedded in each commuter's brain.

So our concern should be less about whether there will be a robot uprising and more about whether we are witnessing an anthropological step change, as we transition from Homo sapiens to cyber man/Homo extensis (augmented man).

Once robotic technology design, build and maintenance moves from human control to robot-driven, things should move along quite swiftly. I have been predicting this outcome since the Cybermen first appeared on Doctor Who. Thinking back, the big lesson for me is that nobody likes a prescient five year old.

Of course this is a dystopian outlook. But the nature of technological growth is that it starts slowly, and in true exponential fashion it eventually leads to step-change advances.

Synthetic biology and nanotechnology will tie up the remaining technical loose-ends.

I flag this so that, like our 'spaced out' commute, we don't just allow our societies to simply drift lethargically into this next phase of existence, without at least some reflection.

But on a more mundane level, the future of work and society is going to see a greater involvement of robots. So, it is best that you understand how the world of robotics will impact the path you take from a career perspective.

The future of the digital nomad

From a consumer perspective, there is no question that many of the associated advances will enhance our ability to be digital nomads. Imagine, as part of your vagabonding lifestyle, you land in a new town.

The shortcut on your augmented reality contact lens takes you straight to the online dating site, on which you are already registered. As it is location sensitive, it flags up your local matches, establishes which of these would be happy to 'meet' you. It makes a suggestion based on the impact the 3D images of your potential dates have on your heartbeat and pupil dilation.

Similarly, your resume management app does a quick trawl of local work requirements to identify opportunities to which you are uniquely well suited. You make a choice, and then your lifestyle app negotiates a fee, terms of engagement and delivery date with the client's automated task broker.

All this has happened as you make your way to the bus station to complete the final leg to the hotel, which, by the way, values occupancy over profit margin, and so gives you a great deal for your commitment to stay in town for at least a few weeks.

You are feeling pretty good about life. Until you realise you have left your e-reader on the train. Some things will never change.

To really understand the future of the digital nomad, try to picture how rapidly evolving new technology will impact your ability to:

- Make smarter decisions.
- Be even more social.
- Increase your mobility.
- Manage your life.
- Improve your ability to serve.
- Boost your brand.
- Enhance your awareness of how to apply new technology to the needs of your clients.
- Deliver quicker outcomes.
- Work more harmoniously with other talented nomads.
- Keep abreast of global commercial matters.
- Negotiate in a manner that maximises the outcome for both parties.
- Maintain the discipline needed to focus on what is important rather than being swept away by other people's agendas and our own tendency to be distracted.

To explore some of these in action. Not so long ago, if I wanted to be perceived as clever, it would involve me pulling a trailer everywhere I went, loaded up with the complete set of Encyclopedia Britannica books.

Should anybody pose a question to me in the shopping mall, I would reach for the relevant volume, read the appropriate section and, after a minute or two, respond in a pithy manner. I would then smile smugly, as I continue on my way; heading off into the sunset with my knowledge trailer, and retail therapy carrier bags, in tow.

Today I am but a few clicks away from all the world's knowledge, and this time it's up to date. No more trailer. And for those too lazy to draw their smartphone from their pocket, they can use their smart glasses or smart watch.

But even this is a little sluggish.

We still have to assimilate the information we read, and forge a response. Wouldn't it be a lot easier if our brain was simply integrated with Wikipedia or its equivalent? Wireless technology, coupled with a neural implant and a paid up 'knowledge on demand' service, would ensure that my response would only ever be a few synaptic hops away.

As well as showing off in shopping malls, this capability could be used in business discussions and social situations.

So let's explore a scenario, whereby you are trying to impress your future spouse on your first date together. Opening pleasantries have concluded, and now verbal tumble weed is bouncing across the growing void created by the conversational drought.

Your ready ability to forecast the weather tomorrow in the five most populous conurbations in the Asia Pacific region would indicate you are worldly, knowledgeable and forward thinking. But it would do little to progress matters (in most cases) along that long winding path to marital bliss. So using another neural service, you trawl your date's social activity and pick up a few themes that might draw you closer.

It appears their rabbit died recently. Though it might come across slightly stalker-like to be in possession of such detail at this stage of the relationship.

However, you notice that their social timeline is peppered with badges and other marks of achievement in respect of their use of wearable technology. Joy of joys, a 'quantified spouse' in-waiting sits before you.

With this intel, you work up a plan. You stretch your leg in a visible manner, and highlight that you are aching a little bit from your long run this morning. You mention in passing that it's the only way to:

- Hit your daily health targets.
- Run a sizeable technology start up.
- Find time to raise funds for a local 'neglected-rabbit sanctuary' charity (no point letting valuable insight go to waste).

This is not so farfetched.

Check out futurist Ray Kurzweil and the Singularity University for more on next generation humanity.

> *By way of caveat, spouse-hunting lies beyond the scope of this book. Your investment in a relationship can go down as well as up. Buyer beware.*

Not everyone can be a digital nomad?

This chapter, like this book, is riddled with my own prejudices and worldview. How would such a model work for, say, a harried mother of young children?

Being a digital nomad, doesn't necessarily mean being a vagabond. So the kids do not have to change schools every few months. It also doesn't mean you have to eschew state of the art time-saving modern appliances.

Being a digital nomad means working on terms that work for you; and setting economic goals that are aligned with your skills and availability to exploit those skills. Maybe the problems you are facing as a mother are in fact business opportunities awaiting a solution?

Many of the world's most successful entrepreneurs became so because they were socially excluded from entering the corporate workplace. They turned this prejudice to their advantage and grew their own empire.

> *The tools exist today to build your own empire. It may take a little longer than you would like because of the constraints you face.*

Perhaps it requires getting up an hour before the rest of the household each day? To do so may in turn require you to maintain your health, as if you were a finely tuned athlete.

Constraints, whether they be time or resources based, are the foundations on which successful enterprises grow. Search the web for 'frugal innovation' to develop a renewed sense of what is and isn't possible. If you are talented enough, your client/employer will find a way to enable you to manage child care; or even elderly parent care.

I believe, BYOF – Bring Your Own Family, will be a growing phenomenon in the digital economy.

Bite-sized mastery

Again, for those leading lives of frenetic activity or indentured drudgery, where sitting down for an hour is a non-starter, there is a way forward. The web, in general, and the smartphone in particular, makes it possible to acquire skills and knowledge in short sharp hits. Those minutes spent waiting for a train, or driving to school to collect the kids, can be used to improve your foreign language skills or simply to read inspiring books that will help maintain your economic self-confidence.

You can have it all, as long as you:

- Define 'all' realistically.
- Have patience and a plan.
- Optimise your schedule, and the tools available to you, to maximise your ongoing personal development.

I believe this is an issue of motivation, rather than opportunity.

Summary

On the face of it, becoming a digital nomad might be something you contemplate as a neat lifestyle choice, but is in reality far too removed from the safe haven of a cash-rich employer who is, in the main, sponsoring your mastery path in a respected profession.

In a world where technological growth is hitting the asymptotic end of the curve, there is no such thing as certainty. Business and society, increasingly fuelled by technology, will in turn evolve at an exponential rate.

I am not suggesting that big companies are bad, or that permanent employment is bad either. I simply encourage you to keep one eye on the market and be prepared to change gear and direction accordingly.

The reason your skills may be very much in demand today is because your organisation continues to work an increasingly obsolete business model. Consequently it is in freefall, and it is not quite there yet in terms of hitting the ground. Signs that the ground is coming up soon include loss of market share, erratic behaviour by the leadership and increasingly clumsy attempts to cover up this reality by massaging their financials.

Being a digital nomad is primarily a mind-set.

One where you are constantly refining the relationship between your skills, market demand and what ignites your passion.

For many, this equilibrium will be constrained by time and one's broader commitments. In general, it is not a race. In fact, environmental constraints may provide the friction that protects you from impetuous decision making.

Take action

- If you were your employer, consider what aspects of your job you could further automate.
  - o Consider what aspects of your job you could give to a robotic personal assistant.
  - o Consider what aspects of your job you could give to a robotic assistant with the brain capacity exceeding that of everybody in your organisation.
  - o Consider what you are going to do then.
- What can you do to reassess your lifestyle costs as a means of giving you more economic/fulfilling professional options?
- How would you feel if your kindergarten-aged child asked if they could invite some friends around for a tea party, and it turns out that some of those friends are robots?

24 For Digital Immigrants

Overview

Not all of us have grown up with the Internet. Not all of us see the physical and virtual world as an entwined continuum. And not all of us regard loss of privacy as a fair price to pay for increased convenience.

Those that have grown up with the Internet are sometimes classified as digital natives. They don't know any different. They are bemused by the term mobile phone (mobile?), or digital business (digital?). Mobile and digital being terms that so called digital immigrants use to differentiate the analogue past from the digital present.

In broad terms:

- **Digital natives** want their physical experiences to be offline versions of their online experience.
  - Go to the supermarket, but shop via the minimal number of clicks.

- **Digital immigrants** want their virtual experiences to be online versions of their offline experiences.
  - Go to the supermarket website with a view to having access to a comprehensive and locatable range of options.

In this chapter we explore how those of us who grew up in the pre-Internet era can ensure we remain relevant in a rapidly changing world.

Amazing times

I am fascinated at the rate of change of technology, and in turn its impact on every aspect of society. I am still pleasantly surprised that breakfast television exists, and in colour too. There was a time that TV looked like Skype does today (and was in black and white), and could only be viewed in the evening.

No doubt, some will remember a time when neither plastic was part of our everyday life, nor processed (or tinned) food. A time when rich people weighed more than poor people.

The nature of exponential growth is that it starts out very small, grows steadily and then incredibly rapidly.

The growth in telephony only really took off after the second telephone was purchased.

We live in a world where we can now gorge on high or low quality content. We can acquire the majority of skills we need, because kind hearted/marketing-aware experts have shared their skills for free.

We also live in a hyper-connected world where everything impacts everything, and the ability to focus has been replaced by the ability to skim.

This situation is neither good nor bad. It is what it is, and those of us who try to obstruct the wheels of progress will become digital economy road-kill. Sure we are consuming natural resources as if we have another option if this planet runs dry. But humanity has faced similar near extinction events in the past, and through luck or technology-leverage we have prevailed. Possibly to nature's chagrin.

That stated, digital natives appear to be more eco-conscious than their predecessors, so there is hope that mankind's future will not rest on yet another extinction side-step.

But back to the subject of us older folk staying in play professionally. Here are a few realities we should acknowledge and act upon:

Independence trumps security

In broad terms, the world is meandering towards greater prosperity for all. Of course, there are people in both developed and developing nations who are living below the economic survival baseline; but an increasing number of people now have 'economic options'.

Ironically, many of those who are in the top tier economically have less options than many of us because of their need to fund a lavish lifestyle.

But even those of us who are living well within our means should not be under the misguided belief that we are economically safe because our employer is financially strong. That could change overnight as a new entrant, perhaps from another continent, comes to town.

Business is business, and if divisions need to be shut down and people laid off, then it will happen. As mentioned in an earlier chapter, it would be wrong to think of your relationship with your employer as similar to that of marriage.

So regardless of whether you have been at your firm twenty years or one week, you need to wake up every day with a game plan should today be the day your career memorabilia is put in a box and, with you, is ushered out of the building.

Thus regardless of your current sense of security, you need to regularly check your market relevance by pressure testing your capability. In other words, you need to see whether other firms are willing to offer you a job. Whether you take a new offer is academic.

The point is that if your 'stock' is high then you have less to worry about (at least for now, given the market clock speed). If your stock is low, you quickly need to establish what skills you must acquire, and acquire them.

Not knowing, one way or the other, is not a strategy for economic survival.

Value trumps experience

Certain cultures value longevity. Seniors are treated with respect. The presumption is that with greater life experience comes wisdom. Some societies/industries are youth obsessed. Witnessing older people trying to appear young to stay in play is sad to observe and dysfunctional to embrace (so I am told).

In my early years, I was a track sprinter. My lack of natural ability was compensated for by my obsessive identification with wanting to be fast. In recent years, despite enjoying life as a 'below average' club cross country/road runner, I had a niggling desire to return to the track (circa 30 years from my 'peak'). So, for a period of a few weeks, I headed off to the track for a few sessions to 'wake up' my dormant sprint muscles. After my initial shock at how slow I was, even by my standards, I got myself to a point where I could run flat out for a reasonable distance without organ failure, muscles coming away from my skeleton, or bits just dropping off.

I decided I was now ready to join a sprint 'squad'. When I turned up, I was struck by how young the sprinters were. I was also struck by their relative lack of discipline compared to back in the day. In the same way that a geriatric would fit in at a rave, I hovered at the periphery of the social group in the first few weeks of training. Physically my primary aim was to not fall apart.

And as much fun as it was taking the odd scalp here and there, it wasn't what I was hoping for. Unsurprisingly, the banter of the old days wasn't there. But probably what struck me most was that, despite holding my own on the track, I felt like some freak show you no longer see because of increased regulatory control in the circus industry. So unless I run into a pack of similar minded vintage sprinters, I will have to hang up my spikes, trowel and starting blocks.

That was of course a little digression, and perhaps I may have even inadvertently made the case for age discrimination (if getting your 'ass whipped' by the older guy is a cultural problem). But simply being old(er) doesn't entitle you to a job. Regardless of age, you need to be able to deliver.

The key point being that experience is overrated in the digital economy. Or at best its value is secondary to your capacity to deliver the outcomes the buyer/employer needs today. Again don't assume that because you have been around a while you will waltz into a new role.

And again, don't leave anything to chance. Establish your perceived value through market testing.

Life trumps work

Young people have watched their parents climb up the greasy career pole like 'affirmation-deprived incarcerated psychiatric patients', who believe that this is the way to escape the compound. Their state of mind when they either falloff the pole, or even when they reach the top, only seems to make their condition worse.

I have laboured this point throughout this book. Working is not in itself the goal.

We need to work because we need to be a contributor to our social pack. Those that simply drained the pack's resources through laziness were left to fend for themselves.

Whilst it is not so clear whose pack we are part of (your country? your city? your religion? your employer? Apple?), we are still wired to be economically net positive.

But our hunter gatherer ancestors typically did not put in twelve plus hour days. They worked for a reason, and that was to ensure the pack prevailed. And to enjoy being alive.

There comes a point in your life where the materialistic vision of ownership as a priority, perhaps cultivated by economically deprived parents, needs to be reassessed. Apply this logic prior to buying the next 'toy':

1. Establish how much time you need to spend using each of your existing acquisitions to consider them a good purchase. Eg. Your Maserati might yield a figure such as one thousand hours.
2. Total the hours associated with all your acquisitions (Answer = A)
3. Calculate, based on your current trajectory, how much free time you have left on the planet (Answer = B).
4. If A is greater than B, you have acquired enough for this lifetime.

I suggest you do not wait until A exceeds B. If you haven't already, now is the time to actively allocate time to enjoy being human. This may consequently enable your economic choices to be made based on passion rather than pay check.

I am not suggesting that money or high paying careers are bad. If your path to mastery generates economic abundance alongside a well-lived life, then good for you. But if you have to choose one over the other, I would recommend life.

---

*As digital immigrants, many of us have followed
a socially approved script. I am merely
suggesting that you might consider reviewing
yours.*

Leadership trumps management

This is perhaps a semantic contrivance on my part. But let us assume that leaders create the vision (a pyramid) and set strategy (use limestone blocks, wooden rollers and cheap labour). And let us assume that managers are responsible for getting it done (build pyramid using available resources).

I believe that the skill of management will disappear over time. We are already seeing swathes of management cut from large organisations. Hyper-specialised brand-conscious professionals will not need coaxing, once the payment terms are agreed (favourable afterlife, the glory of Egypt, generous rations).

As mentioned, management, or at least people management, is a consequence of people being treated as labour, rather than outcome oriented craftsmen.

If today you are a leader 'in title', acquire the skills to be a genuine leader. If you are a drum-beating middle manager, then you had better 'get your groove on' and either develop your leadership skills and reputation as a leader. Alternatively, 'head downstream' (organogramically speaking) and dust down your 'hands on' skills and rechart your mastery path accordingly.

Sprinting trumps marathons

Given the increased clock speed of business and society, it is best to treat your career as a series of short sprints, rather than one long marathon.

One of Norway's top Nordic skiers had the game plan that he would never look further ahead than ten yards. Every ten yards he would look up to check that he was heading in the correct direction, and then grind out another ten yards.

I believe that's what we have to do. Not literally of course.

Digital immigrants are at risk if they are treating their career as if it is a marathon. It would be sad if the first time you raise your head to get your bearings is when you are standing in the office car park, clutching your belongings in a cardboard box.

Empowerment trumps paternalism

Beware paternalism. IBM was once famous for never sacking their staff. Those that were offered the 'blue suit' could wave their economic insecurities goodbye. That is until IBM could no longer sustain this model.

Whether you work for a mega firm or a spluttering start up, your career is your responsibility. Regardless of the cushions and safety nets that seemingly surround you, make a point of acquiring the skills of an entrepreneur. You don't have to be the owner.

> *Entrepreneurial skills are in short supply,*
> *particularly in sclerotic process-driven*
> *corporations, and in many public sector bodies.*

If you see your role in entrepreneurial terms (turning resources into results), your final day car park experience will be somewhat different. Car park security staff will be somewhat taken aback as you:

1. Skip out of reception hollering with joy.
2. Throw your cardboard box into the air with all the youthful exuberance of a recently minted graduate parting company with their mortar board hat.

There are no excuses. The tools, tuition and role models are all in situ waiting for you.

Golden years

Some of you may have served your time, and are now enjoying a life that is unconstrained by deadlines bar the 'ultimate one'. But after a few years of daytime TV, visiting garden centres and attending funerals, you are starting to miss the social stimulation of work.

Someone once said, "If I had known I was going to live this long, I would have taken better care of myself." The reality is that we are living longer, and that can be financially stressful. If only you had saved more. There is nothing more you would love to do now than help your daughter pay for her kid's expensive health-related therapy. But you can't and it's breaking your heart. Retirement wasn't supposed to feel like this.

Well whether you are driven, by boredom, necessity or a desire to help others, there is no reason why you cannot get back in the saddle. Maybe you need to reengineer your resume to maximise your value in today's terms. Seek advice if necessary. You may choose to start from scratch in terms of developing a new skill. I believe this is a sure fire way to stave off mental illness. Not a bad by-product.

You don't need to work full time. And if you choose an appropriate line of work, you may be able to do as much as you desire in the office, and the rest at home. Like the hunter gatherer accountants I mentioned in an earlier chapter, you may choose to work on a project by project basis.

Your next gig might be to pay for someone's treatment, or for you and your loved one to cruise the fjords and witness the Aurora Borealis, up close and personal.

Whatever you choose to focus on, try to salvage as much of your previous experience as you can, particularly that which you found enjoyable and can still do. I am sure manning the entrance at unlicensed pop-up fight-club events was a buzz, but we have to be realistic. Or do we?

Summary

Those of us born in pre-Internet times are in danger of thinking that the 'rules of work', we have taken for granted for so long, will remain intact for the remaining part of our career. Digital immigrants need to learn the new rules and reshape their careers accordingly.

Smart people will think less about retiring and more about tapering their work commitments, whilst at the same time acquiring new skills with the sincerity of a hatchling that has accidentally stumbled out of its nest.

Career switching at both age 50 and 65 is likely to be a growing trend.

Take action

- Reassess why you work, and change direction as necessary.
- Think less about retirement and more about rebalancing your work-life energy commitment.
- Watch a few 'fly on the wall' care home documentaries if you need motivation to build sufficient funds to have choices in this respect.
- Don't wait until you become senile to acquire those 'bucket list' experiences. It would be a shame to miss out on seeing the Aurora Borealis because, whilst up on deck with your partner, you are convinced it's your first day at school and you can't find your satchel.
- Think and act like a start-up entrepreneur whatever your circumstances, regardless of whether your focus is economic, academic or voluntary.

25 The Lean Career

Overview

Throughout this book, I have endeavoured to provide advice on how to steer your career such that you live a fulfilling life. In this chapter, I gather the critical points into a set of principles that you can apply to your own path to mastery.

I'll presume that you have yet to embark on a career, and thus you are largely unconstrained by previous work experience. But, for those of you with such 'baggage', you can still apply the stated principles. You can of course jettison some or all of your baggage if you feel that it is an anchor in respect of your ideal career path. Hopefully, at least some of your experience can be converted into career propellant going forward.

Firstly, I'll explain lean as a concept, along with my usual semi-related rambling. Then I will provide some related guidance to enable you to pursue a lean career.

Lean and mean

We have touched on the concept of lean. Again, this approach is focused on maximising efficiency such that, in the extreme, one hundred percent of the inputs into an organisation are converted to customer value, whether that be a car or a theatre performance. Automotive player Toyota was highly influential in the development of lean manufacturing.

Factories have always striven to eliminate waste from their production processes. The challenge today is to minimise waste, whilst at the same time continuously tuning the business in line with the changing needs of the market. This lean principle equally applies to both service companies and those making physical things.

So organisations need to have a business model that is both flexible and efficient. They will similarly need flexible and lean people. Should your boss call you a 'waster', he might well be criticising your adherence to lean principles, but more likely she is drawing attention to the under-utilisation of your innate intelligence.

Part of my early career involved being a consultant for a technology services company. Unlike my previous company, where on day one I was assigned to a multi-year, several hundred person, project, I was now simply a resource that could be assigned to whatever client work the company secured. Project durations ranged from weeks to a year. In a period of seven years, I worked on over ten projects covering space science, automotive, investment banking, defence (both naval and air force) and the emergency services. The roles stretched from systems programmer through to project manager; from battlefield simulation through to search and rescue; from trading floor infrastructure through to cosmology.

On my first day, I was somewhat bewildered by a 'request' for me to make a recommendation in respect of the most appropriate optical character reading technology for the, shall we say, 'last resort' end of the defence sector. As a software developer used to being given tightly defined module specifications, I could not grasp the idea of achieving a satisfactory outcome with so many undefined parameters.

My in-house mentor at the time succinctly pointed out that at this company you either sank or swam. So, I pushed off the seabed, returned to the surface, and started swimming. This working environment conditioned me to become comfortable with taking on new challenges and getting productive sooner rather than later. I say comfortable. Being billed to eagerly awaiting clients on each assignment as an expert by my employer, despite my lack of actual expertise in most cases, created sufficient levels of fear and adrenalin to fuel a short period of 'corrective hyper learning'. This was both stressful and exhilarating. As mentioned earlier in the book, I gained twenty years of experience in my seven years with that firm.

This experience took place over two decades ago. Now thankfully, I have more control over the assignments I take. And I have acquired some actual expertise. The market has evolved, and I have been comfortable evolving with it.

Similarly, you need to develop comfort in being stretched. New technologies, new trends and new issues mean that the 'opportunities' to face the unknown have never been greater.

To be attractive to the market, you need to be comfortable stepping into the void. Think of 'not knowing' as a natural preliminary phase of any new assignment/adventure (worth having).

But coming back to the theme of lean. The point being that you need to minimise the creation of 'waste' brought about through your lack of expertise. Acquirers of talent need to be sure that you are going to turn their investment in you into significant value for them, and thus their customers. This doubly applies if your role requires a high level of innovation and so inevitably requires you to fail on a regular basis. Your failures need to be both smart and efficient.

This is one take on the concept of lean.

The Lean start up

Much of my lean career inspiration has come from the approach Silicon Valley start-ups take in respect of their growth. The concept is well documented in Eric Ries' book, fittingly entitled, The Lean Start-up. It is well worth reading.

In Silicon Valley, the focus on lean is less on efficiency in respect of converting inputs into outputs, and more on efficiency, as in turning your start-up investment into a sustainable business, rather than a car wreck.

This is the version of lean that I would like to install at the forefront of your mind when thinking about your own career. The efficiency with which you turn inputs into client outcomes is a secondary (but almost primary) consideration.

Here are some lean career principles to keep in mind:

Principle #1: Test test test

Think of your career as an ongoing experiment. Whilst a good post-industrial career will be anything but process-driven, good career management will be totally process-driven.

Career management doesn't require flair or luck, it simply requires the discipline of keeping your eye on what is happening in the market, creating hypotheses about your career on the basis of your observations, and then testing your hypotheses.

So for example, I might notice that wearable technology is on the increase. My hypothesis, as far as my career is concerned, is that there should be a thriving advisory market. So I test this by exploring the idea with both conference organisers and organisations that would benefit from this technology.

Here are some potential discoveries:

1. My hypothesis might be incorrect. Nobody believes wearables have any corporate value.
2. My hypothesis might be correct, but my timing is wrong. Try again in six months.

3. My hypothesis might be correct, but the big players have sown up the advisory market.
4. My hypothesis is correct. The market is crying out for help and, best of all, is totally price insensitive.

Option 4 would be good news, but it may be a short lived opportunity. So, I have to be careful as to whether I rebrand myself as 'Mr Wearables' or take a more cautionary approach to capitalising on the opportunity, whilst I see whether the theme is 'fad of the season' or something more robust.

Like financial investment, you can either be risk hungry or risk averse. If you are the former, you will grab the opportunity with both hands. Think child in an unmanned sweetshop. If you are the latter, you will be more circumspect. Think accountant navigating a minefield, where well considered and very careful small steps are required.

Let's put aside the minefield analogy, because career decisions are rarely fatal (though they can lead to being fired). Our ability to take small controlled steps, coupled with the ability to return to our last known stable career position, is key. Think short strides with high cadence; an accountant at a speed dating event, perhaps?

Principle #2: Your career is a maze

Imagine a maze that changes in real-time. Having entered it, you may possibly conclude that it, or the topiary god, is trying to thwart you. Don't worry, it's not personal (Alice), so don't waste energy trying to work out why a hedge would behave so unkindly.

Market forces are such that demand for your services will likely wax and wane. You will be unable to predict the frequency of the waxes. So you have to be ready to change direction (pivot), particularly if it appears that the last wax has pulled out of the station and you are left standing in a career cul-de-sac, so to speak.

Careers used to be Newtonian in nature. Today they are guided. Back then, you loaded up propellant (qualifications) and then jumped in the career cannon. One boom later and you were flying through the air with very little control over the direction you were heading.

Today, just like an intercontinental airliner, you head off in what broadly looks like the right direction, knowing that you have the ability to fine tune your trajectory in line with the prevailing conditions. Having control over your career in this manner enables you to decide on a completely different destination mid-air, if your new found perspective identifies a more favourable destination.

The upside of an industrial career is that it required very little thought. You entered the career factory and stayed on the ascending conveyor belt until you were deposited out the back in the skip. Managing your post-industrial career requires an investment of time. Ensure you put this time aside to look up from time to time, to ensure you are not way off course, or about to become 'progress collateral damage'.

Principle #3: Avoid perfection

I am conscious I am sending mixed messages here. Throughout this book, I have suggested the path to mastery should be taken with the care and professionalism that one would expect from a neurosurgeon, or a waiter in a Japanese tea salon. And certainly in respect of those professions, I wouldn't take this as an opportunity to cut corners or be slovenly.

The challenge for the rest of us is that the paths we take may not be so well defined. The waiter in particular is following a tradition that is over half a millennium in age. The danger is that most careers, whether industrial or digital economy originated, are undergoing tremendous flux.

Beyond a certain point, further investment in your skills will not yield increased value for your customer/employer. Consequently this investment will not be reflected in your perceived value/pay packet.

Also, if you spend too much time refining your skills in anticipation of 'going to market', you may miss the window of opportunity. Markets are becoming more transient. Think mayfly.

In Silicon Valley, they have the concept of the minimum viable product (MVP). Here, the entrepreneurs focus on getting something to market quickly (perfect (often considered the enemy of good) and late is considered a poor blend). It has just enough functionality to be useful. It can be thought of as a prototype. The market either likes it, hates it, or recommends how it might be improved.

I recommend that you similarly treat your career as a rolling prototype/work in progress. Constantly test the market to ensure your capability resonates. Do not acquire skills unless you can fully test your hypothesis that there is a market for them. Just because you have a notion/fantasy that the market will rave about your intended career path doesn't mean reality will contort to make it so. Best not to rely solely on the career 'cosmic ordering service'.

Principle #4: Be clear on metrics

Before you set sail on your career voyage, you need to equip yourself with a dashboard that will help you chart your course. What you monitor/measure will be down to personal preference, but the following might be worth consideration:

- **Remuneration** – Are you getting a good/best return on your market value?
- **Satisfaction** – Do you feel what you are doing justifies the time you spend on your career?
- **Trajectory** – To what extent are you moving up the value chain, either in terms of your market value, or in your support to mankind?
- **Family/social** – Are you able to devote sufficient time to important people beyond your professional ecosystem?

- **Health** – To what extent are you jeopardising your health because you:
    - Live on a chair.
    - Cross time zones like a crayon-armed infant 'updating' an atlas.
    - Are sleep deficient.
    - Are forced to eat in the best restaurants in the world.

Whatever metrics you choose, monitor them closely and regularly. There is no point waiting until you have been kicked off the corporate hamster wheel to reflect on the quality of your life to date. Inappropriately skilled, with no friends, in need of Star Trek grade medical facilities, is not a good place to be.

Principle #5: The market is always right, sort of

Sort of. As mentioned in an earlier chapter, sometimes the market isn't right; as Ford and Apple have proved. They took a chance developing their products and it worked out. They haven't always got it right though (Apple – The Newton, Ford – The Edsel), but they are big enough to recover from their mistakes. Perhaps, more importantly, they have the marketing budget to invest in the high intensity evangelism needed to get the public's attention, when they are looking to shape public behaviour.

We as individuals don't generally have such power. So I recommend that you follow the market in terms of where the demand lies. By all means try to anticipate where the market is heading and be there to meet it.

If you are not convinced, the next time you are sitting on a park bench, look around to see what catches your attention. Possibly you will notice an old gnarled oak tree or even a beautifully landscaped flowerbed.

They cause you to reflect on art and nature. You zoom in a little more, and notice a used syringe, or a spaced-out squirrel falling from a branch. You perhaps reflect on society.

It is unlikely that an individual acorn would grab your attention, move your mind, or cause you to act in a manner aligned to the acorn's agenda. However, most of us are, by default, acorns in the attention economy. Though, through astute branding and brand association, we can grow to becoming something of interest to the wider world/our target market.

But it makes for an easier life, and perhaps one where you can make more impact, if you surf a market trend that is already in train.

Principle #6: Build your legacy

As one gets older, the reality that your time remaining on the planet has an upper limit becomes more apparent. One of the defining characteristics of human mammals is that we learn and benefit (in the main) from what our ancestors have achieved ("on the shoulders of giants.."). Thus it is in our nature to, in some way, help humanity thrive beyond our existence.

There are a number of ways to do this, including:

- Give our children a framework of values such that they don't feel inclined to shoot all their school mates over the mildest incursion.
- Do, or support, work that benefits humanity, ranging from customer service operative through to mental-illness research neuroscientist.
- Simply make the world less tense by seeking to diffuse tension, rather than inflame it.
- Raise awareness that nature is likely to grow increasingly intolerant if we continue to abuse our delicate ecosystem.

So, you might consider your professional output as a stockpiling of your legacy. Such outputs might be tangible (a book!), intangible (a well-received conference presentation). They might be large (cure cancer) or small (a happy user). Perhaps consider how you will be remembered by those who have engaged with you in some capacity.

Please note that tweets on how your head hurts, as a result of overindulgence the night before, do not count. Unless you have decided to take an alternative legacy approach ie. by choosing to become a cautionary tale.

Principle #7: If you are not growing you are dying

Bodybuilders cause their muscles to grow through literally damaging them. This triggers the body to go into repair mode. It also turns out more generally that those exposed to regular blasts of stress live longer than those who experience no stress.

Apparently, ship workers exposed to regular low doses of radiation lived longer than those who did not receive such exposure.

This also applies to those of us who are neither ship builders nor body builders. More specifically in respect of our careers, if we are not growing our skillset and taking on greater challenges, we will in effect regress. A way to grow younger, so to speak, is to keep challenging ourselves.

If you coast, you're toast.

Principle #8: Nobody cares

We live in a world now where people are mainly preoccupied with the demands raining down on them. Their limited attention is consumed with family, work, or even from what has just come up in their social media feeds.

The attention economy in many respects exists because of this new breed of easily distracted consumer.

You might well be doing a job with an impressive job title at an impressive firm (which you happen to hate). But it irks you that your family and friends are less impressed than they 'should be'. You perhaps wonder why you ever chose this path.

Some people (I am sure) care about you. But, the point is that nobody has the time anymore to really appreciate the finer details of how hard you work, and how special you were to be chosen by such a prestigious firm. So, do not choose a career path to impress other people. You will gain the most career satisfaction if you focus on:

- Impressing yourself in respect of how you are skilfully navigating the world of work to ensure you remain stimulated.
- Being in demand.
- Playing at the top of whichever game you find yourself in along the journey.

Principle #9: Ideally demand followed by passion then competence

If there is no demand, there is no work. If there is demand, but it is outstripped by supply, then you will be doing commodity work at the lowest remuneration. I encourage you to start anticipating demand not as it is today, but in say three years when you graduate. This also applies if you are in a catch up situation.

Daniel Burrus, in his excellent book Flash Foresight, points out that if you are going to use your competitors as a benchmark, don't base your plans on what they are doing today.

By the time you get there, they will be onto the next level. In the digital economy, at best, they have a transient advantage or a temporary monopoly. You need to set your target on where they are heading.

Perhaps a more important principle is that, whilst you should watch the market closely, you should not get preoccupied with your competitors. Focus on the future needs of your market. Can you disrupt the game so that you unleash greater value for your customer, whilst at the same time tilting the game in favour of your capability?

Principle #10: Be vigilant

Ensure you do not wake up to discover progress is steamrollering a path through your career. You may believe you offer a high value portfolio of capability, which commands great remuneration. But, you may one day discover that someone has created an app, which whilst nowhere near as valuable as you in person, it is good enough to do the job. And at 99 cents has a better value to price ratio than you can offer.

I would encourage you to regularly look at ways of disrupting your own business model. The smart way to stay ahead in the digital economy is to cannibalise your own value proposition, before others do it to you.

Think of your current success as, at best, a transient advantage.

Many of the changes we are witnessing are driven by new technology. An observer would perhaps note that new technology has steadily permeated both work and life, and looks set to continue in that vein. That would be a linear prediction. The reality is that technology growth is exponential in nature.

The progress we have seen to date is simply a pre-launch sequence before the rocket actually takes off. It is literally impossible to predict how the world will change as a result. But, what will be certain is that the future will be dramatically different from today.

In the digital economy, the goalposts are forever moving. Do not take your eye off the goal.

A word of warning: If the goal posts you are pursuing have not moved in a while, then it is very likely that the phrase 'game over' applies.

Principle #11: Discipline

I have touched on the importance of habits throughout this book. It is fair to say that your life is a reflection of your habits. So it makes sense to develop the discipline of acquiring habits that will help you achieve your career goals. Habit specialists talk about habit stacking, which in essence turns habits into triggers for other habits. This is worth investigating.

Habits by their very nature, do not consume cognitive capacity.

That saved capacity is thus available to do great work, and it enables us to be more alert to what is happening in our environment.

Principle #12: Be the best

I suspect this title will propel me onto a collision course with whichever arena-filling life coach has trade-marked this phrase. By all means affirm, visualise and incant as you see fit. My point is that in the global market, you need to be the best at what you do in the eyes of the market. However only one person can be the best in the world at any given time.

If you choose acting as a career path, consider whether you are likely to be win an Oscar. Maybe one day. But today, to be the best, you will need to niche up.

Perhaps you can reflect a little on your current capability/traits and conclude that you intend to be the best Shakespearean rapper with a natural grasp of ancient Egyptian affairs and Anglo-Egyptian slang.

Keep in mind that this increased specialisation ultimately creates a market of one. Therefore you, by default, become number one in the market. But, always keep in mind that a market is only a market if there are sellers AND buyers. Sellers alone doesn't quite cut it.

A final thought – time versus money

The biggest shift I have noticed in the transition from the industrial to the digital economy is the changing importance of money and time. The industrial economy gave many people their first opportunity to receive a regular wage. For some, it may have enabled them to build up a surplus beyond their survival needs. As the industrial era was economically attractive to workers, the emphasis for the worker was to get paid as much as one could command. Whether you hated the work, or it consumed your life, was a secondary detail.

Perhaps today, some people are sufficiently confident about their economic survival that they are more focused on the acquisition of discretionary time. A low paying fulfilling job with plenty of free time is more attractive than a high paying job with no time to enjoy the spoils.

Perhaps this is why some people, having been forced to work part time during the downturn, are happy to stick with the arrangement in the upturn.

It may also reflect a change in respect of how people are now increasingly valuing experiences over material goods. Does owning an Aston Martin that spends most of its time in the company/airport car park trump seeing your children grow up?

Of course you can decide which path you take. I just want you to be aware that it is a decision you should review regularly to ensure you don't stray away too far from your goal.

The same is true for those of us that have embraced the mastery path approach. So now we are doing meaningful work. It may even be well rewarded, and you may be making a real difference.

But, if we are doing that at the cost of lost discretionary time, then possibly what we have is an addiction, and not a career. As mentioned, Samurai warriors had hobbies that sat outside the realm of damaging others. Their hobbies were often chosen to counterbalance their highly demanding work.

As the saying goes, all work and no play makes Jack a dull boy. But, if Jack was eventually awarded a Nobel Prize, or his career equivalent, he might consider the trade off to have been worth it.

But you are not Jack. That means you, and you alone, must decide what a meaningful career/life means to you.

Finally

Afterword

The world is changing. The rules of work and life have been thrown up in the air. Those of us who grew up in the industrial era may struggle to come to terms with the new realities. That struggle may manifest itself not just in unemployment but in unemployability. This is an issue for individuals, communities and societies.

Those of us who have just embarked, or are about to embark, on a career, face the same challenges. Your career is your responsibility. The career disciplines you put in place will determine your success.

Whether you are young or old, it is wise to treat your career as if it is an award winning garden in the making. Thus, it requires regular attention and experimentation. Like a gardener, patience is required in respect of your career.

I don't watch many gardening shows. But where I have, I have yet to see the experts recommending that tugging the flowers will accelerate their growth. Nature has its own timeline. Life is easier if you work with that in mind.

The more knowledgeable you become about what can grow in your garden, given the environmental conditions (which will change with increasing frequency), the sooner your gardening investment will yield results.

Occasionally you might plant a dud bulb. Again, the sooner you identify the problem and take corrective action, the better.

Good gardeners become good by starting off as bad gardeners (or, more exactly, inexperienced gardeners). They get their hands dirty and learn quickly as to what does and doesn't work.

And of course the best gardeners make the best compost (though some choose to be cremated). This is mastery in action.

On that final contorted analogy...

Take action

- **Happy digging!**

Appendix A - Clarification

If you have just started the book:

There are a couple of concepts I need us to be aligned on in advance of you reading this book.

If, having read the book, you are only now encountering this appendix:

No problem. It is still worth reading.

Once you have done that, go back to the start, and read the book again. Starting with the 'How to use this book' section.

Just joking (sort of).

Career

I use the term 'career' to mean the path taken in respect of your professional life. It does not imply that you will stick with one employer, stay in one sector, or climb a well-trodden path from gofer to captain of industry. But it might, if that is what you choose to do, and the market permits it.

Post-industrial

This book focuses heavily on how the world of work is changing. An important economic reference point is the industrial era, as that has shaped much of our lives today.

There are a variety of terms people use to describe the next economic era. These include:

- **Post-industrial economy** – Where services generate more economic value than products.
- **Digital economy** – Where technology and data facilitate and drive economic outcomes.
- **Social economy** – Where economic activity takes place within (online) social settings, rather than in traditional markets, and where reputation trumps advertising.
- **Trust economy** – Really another name for the social economy, but with a strong emphasis on the importance of having a good reputation.
- **Attention economy** – We live in a world where we are bombarded with stimulating content. This term highlights that those who are skilled at gaining the attention of their target market will thrive economically.

Not everyone agrees that we are seeing a sufficiently large shift to even suggest we are moving on from the industrial economy. Hence terms such as Industry 4.0.

This book, nonetheless, endeavours to make the case that we are undergoing a seismic economic shift, and as a result we need to review our whole approach to living and working.

Just be aware that these are not terms universally agreed by anthropologists, economists, historians, or even palaeontologists. They are terms created to try to capture an economic model that is different to that of the last few centuries.

In that respect, they are all describing in their own way this next post-industrial phase. I am comfortable using all of them, and so they will pop up in the book here and there.

Though in general, I tend to lean towards digital economy, given my tech background. Though as you will read, this next era in our evolution is less about the technology and more about people.

Value proposition

I use the term value proposition in the book. By that, I am referring to the reason why others might be inclined to employ or engage with you in a professional context. For some people, this may be their ability to sing country and western style songs, or their medical qualification coupled with their ability to speak Flemish.

In short, it is what you bring to the table that is of value to others. Throughout the book, I use the term value proposition, or similar terms such as capability and service offering.

Perhaps think of this as the skills and experiences you have acquired:

- Formally.
  - You have acquired a qualification.
- Informally.
  - Through a training course you attended with your previous employer.
  - Via a summer job you had just after you left school.

But it is important to state that your track record in respect of delivery/results/outcomes will increasingly be more important than your acquired credentials.

Your behaviour is increasingly an important part of your value proposition. You may be highly competent on paper, but if the manner in which you engage with colleagues and clients leaves something to be desired, then your behaviour will have a corrosive effect on your value proposition.

Appendix B - References

In the course of the book I have made reference to a number topics. The following list contains a subset of those sources I dropped into my 'cerebral hopper' before or during the production of this book.

Harari. Y,N. 2014. Sapiens: A Brief History of Mankind. Harper.
I tend to absorb a lot of anthropology and post-human content. This book gathers both themes neatly under one cover. So often, we are so caught up in our day to day to do lists that we forget to zoom out and reflect on how we got to where we are today, and what might lie ahead.

Christian, D. 2011. The History of our World in 18 minutes. Available at: <http://www.ted.com>
For those too time-starved, or too shallow (see below), this concise and engaging video takes us on a 13 million year journey in under twenty minutes. David Christian also reminds us of the fragile conditions under which life exists, and encourages us to reflect on the future. Understanding our careers in the context of 'all time' serves to help us to perhaps consider our work choices, particularly if 'putting a ding in the universe' is important to you.

Gladwell, M. 2008. Outliers: The Story of Success. Penguin
Malcolm Gladwell brings important phenomena to the surface and conveys them in a compelling manner. Outliers identifies characteristics that predispose certain people to success. By understanding which of our characteristics give us a natural advantage, we can steer our careers to what nature and our environment has bestowed upon us. He also draws our attention to the 10,000 hours rule of purposeful practice. Whilst the number of hours is up for debate, the idea that practice needs to be purposeful (read uncomfortable/hurts) is a very valuable insight.

I, Robot, 2004 [Film] Directed by Alex Proyas
This film provides a stimulating dystopian view as to what might happen if robotics and artificial intelligence are not carefully managed. Will Smith is excellent as the law enforcing cyborg Luddite.

Coyle,D. 2009. The Talent Code: Greatness isn't born. It's grown. Bantam

Daniel Coyle's advice will, if you take it, get on your nerves. Albeit in a literal and good way. He is a proponent of the school of hard work, which will appeal to those of us who are still in search of our metier. If you are motivated, and prepared to practise, this book will show you the way.

2001: A Space Odyssey, 1968 [Film] Directed by Stanley Kubrick

A classic science fiction film depicting a number of themes, including human evolution. It might be considered as the Interstellar of the 20th Century. Some young people have suggested, given its relatively slow pace, that to get the best from this film some form of dementia is required.

Malone, T et al. July 2011. The Big Idea: The Age of Hyperspecialization. Harvard Business Review

Thomas Malone and colleagues posit that the nature of work is likely to evolve to a point where workers become highly specialised. The arrival of online resource exchanges are evidence of this. My sense is that this is how things will play out, and so our path to career mastery should be plotted with this notion in mind.

Asimov, I. March 1942. Runaround. In Astounding Science Fiction magazine

This short science fiction story introduced us to the three laws of robotics. We appear to be building an industry, and even a society that seems to regard these fictional laws as a foundation, which I find a little disconcerting.

Sandberg, S. 2013. Lean In: Women, Work, and the Will to Lead. WH Allen

Whilst this book is primarily aimed at women, its messages in respect of confidence, juggling work and life, and leaning in, despite your anxieties, is valuable to all genders.

Robinson, K. 2006. How schools kill creativity. Available at: <http://www.ted.com>

This video is one of the most watched Ted talks of all time. Ken Robinson correctly and entertainingly highlights that our schools are churning out individuals stripped of their creativity. Given that this is a key survival skill in the digital economy, his views are important.

Walking Dead. (Premiered 2010). TV Programme

This popular post-apocalyptic drama, apart from setting new societal standards for gore as entertainment, highlights the issues of being a minority amongst those with a very different outlook on 'life'.

Souza, S. D., Renner, D. 2014. Not Knowing. Lid Publishing.

On the face of it, this book might appear to be a clarion call for the 'ignorance is bliss' movement, and is thus a worrying trend for those of us who are consultants. Its real point is that, in an increasingly tempestuous world, there is a lot we don't know (experts included), and so we must be cautious of the certainties overconfident authority figures relay to us.

National Geographic Magazine. Monthly. National Geographic Society

This 'high production values' publication should, in my view, be part of an educational diet for those who want to discover the world, and for those who want to save it. The title is misleading. It's far reaching attention extends right across the universe(s).

Green, R. 1998. The 48 Laws of Power. Penguin Book.

This is a catalogue of amoral wisdom that can be applied to increasing your power. The book is best suited to high stakes power plays. It is particularly useful if you have it in mind to make a bid to lead an empire. I wouldn't necessarily recommend applying these Machiavellian techniques, as they are a little out of keeping with the social economy. Nonetheless, it is worth being aware of them, so that you can sense when you are about to be played.

Green, R. 2012. Mastery. Viking Press.
This is an extensive and practical guide to seeking mastery. There is a lot to take in. But if you are serious about mastery, you will invest the time. The intention of 'Beyond Nine to Five' is to put mastery in the context of the digital age. Thus, 'Mastery' is important background reading.

Duhigg, C. 2012. The Power of Habit: Why we do what we do and how to change. William Heinemann.
Great careers require the acquisition of good habits. Of the many books I have read on the subject, the Power of Habit stands out. It cleanly dissects the nature of habits, and so provides an approach to replacing poor habits with those that are life transforming.

Csikszentmihalyi, M. 1997. Finding Flow: The Psychology of Engagement with Everyday Life. Basic Books.
In my view, a life well lived is one in which one spends considerable time in a state of flow. Think of this as the path that sits between a life of high anxiety and one of boredom. This is the zone where great careers evolve and are enjoyed. Finding Flow is the definitive book on the topic. It is scientifically sound, concise and practical.

Clark, D. March 2011. Reinventing your Personal Brand. Harvard Business Review
This is a very clear approach to taking something as nebulous as your brand and creating a personal reinvention action plan.

Carr, N. 2011. The Shallows: How the Internet is Changing the Way We Think, Read and Remember. Atlantic Books
Former Harvard Business Review editor, Nicholas Carr, is known for his prescience in respect of business and society. This book flags the reality that the Internet is literally rewiring our minds. In turn, we are gravitating towards living a mentally superficial existence. I encourage you to read it, particularly if you are planning a career that in some way requires you to concentrate.

Ries, E. 2011. The Lean Startup: How Today's Entrepreneurs Use Continuous Innovation to Create Radically Successful Businesses. Crown Business

Whether you plan to build an Internet empire or change career, this is the definitive process book on how to move forward in a risk-minimised manner. Whilst I have railed against 'process' work throughout this book, this is one of the few areas where process trumps creativity.

Burrus, D. 2011. Flash Foresight: How to See the Invisible and Do the Impossible. Harper Business.

I spend a lot of my time in the future (at least mentally). Daniel Burrus is worth paying attention to. His book serves to demystify the future and empower the reader to infer what lies ahead. Given the future is starting to blur with the present, it makes sense to develop one's own ability to look ahead. This book will help you.

About the Author

Ade McCormack is an advisor, writer and speaker on the digital economy, particularly in respect of its impact on business, society and humanity. Clients engage Ade when they need a 'zoom out' view of how the world is changing, followed by 'zoom in' guidance on how they can capitalise on these changes.

He is a former technologist with a degree in Physics/Astrophysics.

Ade's perspectives extend from 'bits' to the boardroom. And from the start of time into the near future. Or so he believes.

Ade has written for a number of publications, including the Financial Times. In fairness to journalists, his contributions are purely opinion based. He has written several business books and has also lectured at MIT Sloan on digital leadership.

Ade is married with one son. He enjoys martial arts, dancing and running. Running being his most effective form of self defence, closely followed by dancing.

Website

www.ademccormack.com

Twitter / Blog

@ademccormack   **#beyond925**

The Digital Strategist – www.the-digital-strategist.com